OUR BLOOD, HIS BLOOD

BeyondBelief.Com

Sensitive stomach

OUR BLOOD,

HIS BLOOD

An in depth look at the blood, its physiological nature and its theological significance

PAUL McCAULLEY

Our Blood, His Blood

Published by Aviation Missions, Inc.
PO Box 1485
Bethany, Oklahoma

Unless otherwise indicated, Bible quotations are taken from the *Authorized King James Version.*

First printing 2002

Printed in the United States of America

ISBN 0-9673318-1-1

Other books by the author:

The Dangers of Neo-fundamentalism

CONTENTS

INTRODUCTION

"He who is not aware of his ignorance will only be misled by his knowledge." Bishop Richard Whately

When God speaks, He must do so in terms of reference and from a perspective that man can understand. The concepts and principles of God have His character. They are holy, infinite and eternal. As such, they are beyond the unaided comprehension of man. God must condescend to speak to man. He has done so. God has spoken through His Creation and through His Word, the Bible.

Initially, He must speak in terms understandable by fallen man that man may be presented with his need and God's provision. Subsequent to conversion, God must continue to speak to man in terms understood by man, but the presence of the Holy Spirit of God within regenerate man will lead that man into all truth.

There are two means by which God communicates to man. They are the Word and Creation. Of course, the Word consists of both the Living Word and the Written Word. Absent these, God still speaks through His marvelous work of creation so that what may be known of Him can be found out in creation.

This principle of God speaking is applied to His communicating to man man's need of redemption and atonement by blood. More than just the literal words found in Scripture, but the typology, symbolism, and analogy must be considered as God speaks to man. What God is saying is found beyond the words He chooses. An infinite and eternal truth communicated through the medium of human language will face the limitations of that language. At the point of that limitation, the Holy Spirit will open the eyes of understanding to the seeking soul to understand the truths, principles, and precepts behind those words. This is true of the doctrine of the blood.

As is most often the case, the more a doctrine is studied, the deeper the truths that are revealed to the seeking soul. There is far more significance and meaning to the blood atonement than meets the casual inquiry into the blood. The search for significance of the blood must of necessity start with what blood is and what it is not. That is its physiological nature. This information is found primarily in nature through the study of biology and physiology, among many other disciplines of study. Scripture has much light to shed upon the physiology of blood from God's perspective. Nature and Scripture combine to give us a proper understanding of the nature of the blood of man.

Once the physiological nature of the blood of man is understood, progression is then made into the theological significance of the blood. This portion of the book will lead to an understanding of what God intended by the institution of the sacrificial system of worship in the Old Testament centered around the blood of the sacrifice and what that system of worship was intended not only to do in the interim, but also to teach man about His God. The whole system was and is intended to teach the Holiness of God, the sinfulness of man, and the means initiated by God for reconciliation and restoration of fellowship.

The blood is at once the deepest, the mightiest, the strangest, and the most heavenly of the thoughts of God. Salvation is God's thought. At the heart of it is the blood. The blood lies at the very root of the covenant between God and man. The power of that blood has no lesser measure than the virtue and value of the Son of God, God the Son. The experience of the believer must know no other standard of peace with God, purity from sin, and power over the world than the blood of Christ imparts.

Despite is done to the blood of Christ and to His person when consent is granted to those who accuse Christians of having a bloody religion. The charge is often made that Christianity is a slaughter house religion. To accede to these charges, to agree with them and confirm that Christianity is a slaughter house religion reveals the shallowness of understanding and the depths of ignorance to which the proclamation of the Gospel has descended.

First, Christianity is not a religion. It is a relationship. It is a personal relationship between sinful, fallen man and his creator God. That relationship is established upon the principles, precepts, and terms dictated by God to man.

In that relationship there does not exist a slaughter house. The Jews of the Old Testament offered up thousands of animal sacrifices. Blood did indeed flow every day. To observe these sacrifices in progress would be to see much blood. All of the Old Testament sacrificial system and its related blood pointed forward to the one sacrifice that would take away sin forever. And that blood, the blood of Christ, was only shed once. It is to be shed never again. He is to die never again.

Christianity is a relationship that is based upon that once and for all sacrifice. It is based upon the shed blood of the Son of God. But Christianity is not a slaughter house religion. Oh, that preachers of the Gospel would cease from such silliness and error.

This book is an in depth study of the blood. Chapter One is a brief scientific overview of the physiology of human blood. In this chapter certain medical facts of creation found in human physiology are discussed in order to lay the foundation for the study of the blood of Christ. The answer to the question, "Is the blood of Christ different than your blood or my blood?" begins to become clear in this scientific overview.

A proper study of the blood of Christ must of necessity include His birth, His person, why He came, and what He did when He came. An understanding of the person of Christ is essential before attempting to understand the blood atonement. His person is studied in Chapters Two through Four.

Chapters Five, Six, and Seven examine life and death. What is life? Where did it come from? What is death? When did it first occur? These are some of the questions answered in these chapters.

In Chapter Eight the Blood Atonement is studied. Before understanding the significance of the blood, an understanding of why the atonement was necessary and how God dictated that it should be accomplished is necessary. How God accomplished the atonement to His holy satisfaction is studied in Chapter Nine.

Chapter Ten answers the question, "So what?" After looking at all the theological aspects of the blood, what does that mean to the individual believer in his daily life? What is the practical application of the study of the blood? Is it even important to my Christian life in the twenty-first century? The title of the chapter is a question, "How Should We Then Live?" The simplicity of the answer may surprise you.

At the end of the book are two case studies to illustrate how false doctrine can adversely impact the doctrine of the blood and how confusion can be created in discussing the blood.

This book is intended to interrupt the busy schedule and priorities of so many Christians today. The work of God has become an end in itself rather than the God whose work it is. So many pastors and Christians have become preoccupied with building churches and spreading the Gospel that they never pause to give thought to Christ, who He is, what He has done, and the significance of His blood today in the lives of every one of His children. The seed of the Word of God must be planted from which grows New Testament churches. Christ will build His church. He said He would. He even left instructions for that work in His Word. But the work itself was never intended to displace Him from the affections and focus of His own people. The work must be done. But He must always remain the focus and attention of the heart.

The blood, oh mysteries of mysteries! It is bathed in grace above all grace. It is filled with mercy beyond degree. The blood demonstrates and speaks of the power of Almighty God as it opens the way for sinful man into God's very presence, the Holy of Holies in Heaven; and opens the way for God into the hearts of the truly repentant of men. The prayer of every sincere believer should be to ask God to make us to know what is the power and work of the blood of Christ.

Finally, the true significance of the blood of Christ will be presented and what that significance means to our Christian life. To quote A. W. Pink,

> An orthodox creed, intellectually apprehended, counts for nothing if it fails to mold the life of the one professing it. I may claim to regard the Bible as the inspired and infallible Word of God, yea, and be ready to defend this

> fundamental article of the faith; I may refuse to heed infidelistic utterances of the higher critics, and pride myself on my doctrinal soundness — as did the Pharisees. But of what worth is this if I know not what it means to *tremble* at that Word, and if my walk is not regulated by its precepts?

Of what worth indeed.

CHAPTER ONE

OUR BLOOD

"For the life of the flesh is in the blood..."
Leviticus 17:11

The blood of man is the life fluid of the body. Human life is dependent upon a continuous supply of substances such as oxygen, nutrients, and certain chemicals necessary for life functions, all carried in the blood and circulated throughout the body. The blood also moves carbon dioxide and other waste materials from throughout the body to the appropriate organs and locations for disposal from the body. Internal temperatures of the body are regulated and maintained by the flow of blood increasing and decreasing as necessary to remain within acceptable limits under various external conditions. The white blood cells are transported throughout the body to fight off infection and invasion by foreign microorganisms. If the flow of blood through the body ceases for any reason, death occurs within minutes because of the unfavorable effects upon the body's cells. And death is a very unfavorable and undesirable effect.

Most of us give little to no thought about our blood as we go about our daily lives. That is until we see it. We may see it in a scratch or cut. We may see it running from a major wound or wipe it from a bleeding nose after an encounter considered less than desirable. Something within us sounds an alarm that varies in intensity with the amount of blood. A small scratch signals a low key alarm, and we undertake to treat the area with washing, antiseptic ointment, and a bandage. On the other hand, a large wound from which blood is flowing causes a much higher state of alarm. Suddenly, we become aware of the loss of our blood and realize that if this loss is not stopped, we will die.

What is the blood made of? What does it do? are questions we might ask if we pause for a moment's reflection. These questions are the starting point in this investigation into the blood of Jesus, what its real significance is, and a better understanding of the ongoing arguments in Christianity over the blood of Jesus Christ. This chapter will be a brief scientific overview of the blood.

* * *

The most readily identifiable characteristic of blood is the color. The color of human blood ranges from bright red to almost scarlet as it passes through the arteries and ranges from a darker red to crimson returning through the veins. The hemoglobin in the blood imparts the color that varies according to the oxygen content. Blood comprises approximately one-twelfth to one-thirteenth of the total weight of the human body and in the average person will amount to about twelve pounds in weight and twelve pints in volume. It is 4½ to 5½ times the viscosity of water, flowing more slowly than water under the same conditions, and is slightly heavier than water. Blood has a characteristic odor, is salty to the taste, and has a temperature of about 100.4° F.

In order to do its job, the blood must be circulated throughout the entire body. This is accomplished by the circulatory system consisting of a pipeline made up of blood vessels such as arteries, veins, and capillaries thousands of miles in length. This pipeline must service one hundred trillion cells in the human body. Each cell must be supplied individually with the specific chemical needs of that cell. The blood makes available a continuous supply of oxygen, amino acids, nitrogen, sodium, potassium, calcium, magnesium, sugars, lipids, cholesterols, and hormones to each cell individually.

To accomplish the task of home delivery for every need of each of the one hundred trillion cells, not just once, but on a repetitive basis every day of our lives, requires a system of divine origin. The heart is the central pump responsible for keeping the flow regulated and meeting the needs of the body. With increased activity there is an increase in the blood flow necessary to conduct that activity. Conversely, as activity becomes dormant, such as during sleep, the flow of blood is reduced to meet the needs of that activity. When this is compared to everyday life, the efficiency of the human body is seen to far excel that of human activity. For example, if only the pizza delivery people could get to the right address every time and the pizza still be hot! What a thought!

Yet, with every beat of the heart, a fresh supply of blood containing all of the necessary elements for life makes its rounds supplying each and every cell. And even more amazing is that each cell only withdraws from the blood the specific elements it requires and only in the proper amounts.

The primary function of the blood is to act as a transporting mechanism. As such, many functions of the blood's components can then be accomplished. These functions include:

- Carrying oxygen from the lungs to the tissues and carbon dioxide from those tissues to the lungs;
- Carrying nutrients that are absorbed from the digestive system to the tissues;
- Carrying products formed in one tissue to sites throughout the body where they are needed and used (For example, transporting hormones to the tissues requiring them);
- Carrying metabolic waste materials to the lungs, kidneys, intestines, and skin;
- Helping to maintain body temperature at normal levels;
- Helping to maintain the normal acid-base balance of the tissues;
- Constituting a defense mechanism against the invasion of organisms harmful to the human body;
- Helping to maintain fluid balance between blood and tissues;
- Preventing loss of blood by clotting after damage is sustained to tissue or blood vessels.

All of these functions are required for normal physical life to continue in man. If any of these functions are not performed, or if they are disproportionate to normal human existence, sickness or death is the result. This is true for all humans. There are no exceptions. How does the blood perform these functions? An overview of these functions follows below to establish the sheer necessity of the blood in man, by design of the Creator and to lay the foundation for the theological significance of the blood.

* * *

After delivery of the materials required to fuel the microscopic engine inside the cell occurs, all the waste byproducts of the chemical reactions within the cell are uploaded to the blood and carried away. This process is illustrated in everyday life. The pizza delivery boy delivers the stack of pizzas to the front door of the house. The "fuel" is ingested to sustain life. The refuse (soggy bottom boxes that smell up the house) is removed from the house and carried away by the refuse team (holidays excepted). We should be thankful that the delivery and removal system of the blood and circulatory system are more efficient than the systems designed by man.

How does the blood accomplish this? All the various components of the blood must be up to the task at hand and work in harmony with each other as designed by the Creator. First of all, blood consists of cells, or corpuscles, suspended in a liquid called plasma. Just under half, about 46%, of the volume of blood is composed of the blood cells. These cells are the red cells, the white cells, and platelets. There are three kinds of white cells — lymphocytes, monocytes, and granulocytes. Under the microscope, a drop of blood the size of the letter "o" would contain 5,000,000 red cells, 7,000 white cells and 300,000 platelets.

Blood cells originate in the bone marrow as stem cells, so called because they are the "mother" cells that develop into any of the other three kinds of cells — red cells, white cells, and platelets. In other words, blood cells "stem" from the cells originating in the bone marrow. The body knows how many of which kind of cell is needed and produces the proper number of the right kind.

* * *

Red Blood Cells. Most stem cells become red blood cells, or erythrocytes. The primary function of the red blood cells is to transport oxygen from the lungs to all the tissues of the body. It is in these cells that hemoglobin (which gives blood its distinctive red color) is found. The hemoglobin picks up and stores oxygen as the blood passes through the blood vessels lining the lungs. The red blood cell forms a biconcave disk, a shape that provides a large surface to volume ratio, thus greatly enhancing efficiency. After delivering oxygen to the tissues, the red cells absorb and carry off the carbon dioxide. The red cells pass through the kidneys on their return trip to drop off their load of waste. Much like stopping off at a landfill to dump the garbage before continuing the trip.

The round trip from the heart to the extremities of the body and back lasts a short twenty seconds normally. An average red cell undergoes the process of loading up with the necessary materials, making the journey to the tissue for unloading, and returning to start over again a half million times in a little over four months. The last trip for the red cell is through the spleen where it is stripped of its parts and recycled into new cells. Three hundred billion such red cells die and are replaced every day, and we do not even take notice of the process.

Since oxygen is not stored in the body, it must be continuously supplied through the lungs from the atmosphere. Heavy exercise increases the requirement for oxygen as fuel for the cells. The volume of oxygen may increase from the normal activity level of about four gallons per hour to as much as seventy-five gallons per hour. To meet this demand, the heart rate must increase as much as two or three times its normal rate. Of course, the lungs also increase their activity to pass the needed amount of air through them for the extraction of the oxygen. If the lungs cannot meet the increased demand for oxygen, reinforcements are called into action by the red cells. The red cell count in a sample speck of blood may climb from five million to seven or eight million.

The rarified air at altitude, as in the mountain communities of the Rocky Mountains, will cause newcomers to tire more easily and their lungs to work harder to provide the oxygen needed by the cells. After a few months, however, the body adjusts by increasing the normal level of red cells present in the blood during normal activity. This may result in as many as ten million cells being present in a sample speck of blood. This adaptability is another example of the wonder of creation and the normal processes of the body required to sustain life for all humans.

If cells are deprived of oxygen for only a few minutes, they will die. And if cells start dying, the effect upon the human body is obviously not desirable. Without hemoglobin-containing red blood cells in the blood of man, man dies. This is true, as we shall say over and over again, for all humans.

Exercise, high altitude, and strong emotion require additional oxygen to the tissues and more red cells to do the job. Since the bone marrow cannot keep up with the needed production in these cases, the body stores in the spleen red blood cells that are released when conditions require an increase in oxygen supply to the tissues of the body. Adrenaline is produced within the body that stimulates the spleen to release this surplus of red cells to meet the immediate need.

The term applied to various conditions associated with a deficiency of red blood cells or a deficiency of hemoglobin in the cells is anemia. This deficiency can result from (1) hemorrhage, (2) hemolysis (hemoglobin leaking from the red cells), or (3) an inability to produce new red cells due to a lack of proper diet, diseases of the bone marrow, and various infections. Insufficient iron in the diet may also be a cause of anemia.

* * *

White Blood Cells. Battles rage within our bodies constantly. The white blood cells are poised and ready to launch on a search and destroy mission against any and all invaders. Upon detection of an invader, a chemical alarm is sounded calling the troops to battle. Each group within the army of cells has its own particular mission and tactics. The white blood cells form an initial assault force and travel throughout the body, slipping between cells, to find, attack, and destroy every invader. The initial assault force attempts to overwhelm the invader with numbers. A subsequent attack is comprised of white cells with heavier ammunition. The difference might be compared to the assault force of light infantry followed by a smaller force consisting of main battle tanks. Still other white cells are free floating in the bloodstream acting as snipers as they chance upon an invader. And yet another force of white blood cells conducts battlefield cleanup removing all the debris from the battle.

During times of peace (no foreign invaders coming into the body) the standing army of cells may be comprised of as many as twenty-five billion on patrol throughout the bloodstream. The first cadre of reserve cells consists of about another twenty-five billion on standby on blood vessel walls, ready for immediate call up. After the attack has commenced, billions more are called from within the bone marrow ready to be prepared for specific duty against a specific invader.

The reason for so many white cells is that the individual white cell is designed to attack a specific invader of disease. Thus, when an invader is detected many white cells rush to encompass it, identify the exact make-up of the invading force, and apply the exact remedy of white cells specifically for that invading organism. At this point, specific reserves are called up that are an exact match to thwart the invader.

This happens rather quickly. The average white blood cell only lives for about ten hours. A select cadre of white cells live for sixty or seventy years to preserve the chemical memory of dangerous invaders. Every few minutes, these cells check with headquarters in the lymph glands for additional information or missions. It is these chemical memories within the white cells that safeguard the defense secrets of the body and retain the orders and instructions to be issued to the friendly force upon detection of invasion.

A white cell must somehow find its target before attacking and destroying it. There is a lot of battlefield debris flowing in the blood stream that could cause confusion. An illustration of this would be the smoke of battle between opposing armies diminishing visibility for soldiers hampering their ability to lock on to a target with their weapon system. In order to find the enemy and identify his location for the main battle force, the Army employs scouts to conduct reconnaissance. In our blood, antibodies are the scouts and forward observers for the white cells which are the main force for the attack. Antibodies identify and cling to the enemy marking them for the white cells to see. Meanwhile, the antibodies are softening up the enemy for the white cell attack.

Many antibodies are required in the body since each antibody is designed to identify only one specific invader and mark them. The body can manufacture whatever defense is needed (barring, of course, immune system defects such as AIDS). If a new and unknown invader appears on the scene, free floating antibodies tag it for identification. Lymphocyte cells in the blood stream come in contact with this tagged invader and memorizes its shape. The lymphocyte cells then rush with this battlefield intelligence to the nearest lymph node. Once at the lymph node, the lymphocyte cell transmogrifies into a local chemical factory conveying the information to thousands of other lymphocytes that in turn produce billions of specific antibodies equipped for the new invader. This chemical formula is then stored for future reference.

There are far fewer white blood cells, or leukocytes, than there are red blood cells. The ratio is about one white blood cell for every 700 red blood cells. There are three types of white blood cells: granulocytes, monocytes, and lymphocytes. White blood cells do not have hemoglobin in them or any other pigmentation and so they can only be seen under a microscope if they are stained. Many of the white cells are capable of locomotion; instead of being dependent upon normal blood flow to be carried to a site, these cells can resist blood flow and move through capillary walls into tissue fluids. In addition to their protective function we just discussed, white cells cooperate in promoting tissue repair and regeneration.

Not all of the white blood cells are produced in the bone marrow. Lymphocytes, a part of the immune system that directly resists foreign substances in the body, are produced in the lymph glands. Monocytes are produced in the bone marrow and the liver. Monocytes are capable of surrounding and digesting other cells.

Granulocytes comprise two thirds of the white cells and are larger in size than the red cells. They are called granulocytes due to the granules in their structure, and act as the main force fighting invasion by foreign organisms.

They protect the body from disease by going to the site of the invasion and then swallowing the invaders up.

Monocytes, the largest cells of the blood, make up about seven percent of the white blood cells. They are capable of ingesting infectious agents as well as red cells and other types of large particles. They are considered to be scavengers and may enter inflamed tissues after the granulocytes. They can also be found at sites of chronic infection. These are the battlefield cleanup crews.

About thirty percent of the white cells of the blood are lymphocytes which are only slightly larger than red cells. Lymphocytes are primarily concerned with vital defense mechanisms pertaining to acquired immunity to foreign cells and antigens. They are responsible for immunologic reactions to invading organisms and foreign cells. Another function of the lymphocytes is to permit the body to distinguish between its own tissues and material of foreign origins. It is this function that makes organ transplantation difficult. Rejection of tissue is largely accomplished by immunity mediated by cells; lymphocytes migrate to the location of the graft or foreign organ and cause its rejection and destruction. This is a protective function of the body to prevent continuation of growth of something foreign to the body.

White blood cells accumulate in the region of a wound and act as barriers against infection. When tissues become inflamed as the result of a wound, injury, or infection, there is irritation that is followed by an increase of blood supply to the affected area. This continues until engorgement results. Leukocytes migrate to the affected tissues in large numbers and engage the invaders. When this inflammation is deep and not readily observable, knowledge of the increase in white blood cells in the blood to sustain the attack against foreign substances and invaders is of assistance in determining the severity of the infection and the success the body is having in combating it. This requires counting the white cells present in the blood stream. This number is compared to the number of white blood cells in the blood under normal conditions of health and well being. The differential count is then analyzed to determine the nature of the infection and the resistance of the body to the infection. Without the leukocytes functioning properly, man is susceptible to death from the slightest invasion of foreign organisms.

* * *

Plasma. The liquid portion of the blood is called plasma. Plasma is a solution of enormous complexity and contains a great variety of substances containing more than 90 percent water. It serves as the source of nutrition and as a means of waste removal resulting from metabolism. The water proportion of plasma is kept fairly constant by the intake and expulsion of water in conjunction with the exchange of water that takes place between the blood, intercellular tissue fluid, and the cells. This water is also important in the temperature regulatory function of the blood as it keeps internal temperatures constant, under normal conditions and activity.

* * *

CLOTTING

One of the mechanisms placed by our Creator in the human body that is essential to the survival and continuation of life in man is a process called clotting, or coagulation. The purpose of clotting is not to fight infection or foreign invaders in the body. Rather, its primary purpose is that of a plumber plugging leaks in the system. If the body does not plug leaks in the circulatory system, blood loss will exceed the threshold necessary to sustain life.

The hemostatic mechanism of controlling bleeding by the body has three main components: blood clotting, aggregation (collecting together) of platelets, and contraction of blood vessels. The activation of one or more of these components is dependent on integrated and interdependent reactions within the body. When the body detects a leak or circumstance requiring the attention of the clotting mechanism, a determination is made as to which of the three components to engage and in what proportion. If this mechanism is defective, persistent bleeding from the slightest of injuries will occur or, conversely, a clotting of the blood will block major blood vessels with the possible result of heart attacks, strokes, or even death. The theological implications of this mechanism within man will be addressed later in the section on theological significance.

Although the blood of man is a fluid, when it is removed from a living body it soon becomes viscid, resistant to flow, and, if left undisturbed, forms a soft jelly. If we were to observe the process under a microscope, we would see threadlike fibers beginning to form. These fibers are composed of a substance called fibrin, and are essential parts of the clot. As more and more of these fibers appear, they form an interlacing network that enmeshes red cells and some white cells. This mass is called a blood clot. I am reminded of the wire mesh screens in the faucets at my house. After years of water flowing through these screens, there is a buildup of particles from the water on the screen that restricts the flow of water. Of course, my solution is to remove the screens so we can get the water flowing again. That means, I guess, that we now drink all those particles coming through the pipe from our water treatment plant.

That wire mesh screen in my faucet caught the particles as they flowed by. In the blood, as the fibrin net forms, it captures more and more red cells and white cells restricting flow and forming a clot. It is not wise to then remove the clot since to do so would reestablish the leak.

Clotting occurs when there is an occurrence of circumstances that would endanger life if the body did not have an adequate defensive mechanism. Blood coming in contact with a rupture, or opening of a blood vessel, as in an injury or wound, will clot. Another example is when blood comes in contact with a rough surface in the blood vessel caused by such things as erosive infections that cause the interior surface of the blood vessel to assume a rough shape. In this latter example, the purpose of the clotting is to repair the damaged area and aid in reconstruction and regeneration of the damaged area.

Platelets are the smallest of the blood cells and assist in clotting (under certain circumstances) by sticking together to help plug holes in the walls of blood vessels or line the interior of a damaged blood vessel. Platelets themselves plug very small holes in the blood vessels. If the opening is larger, clotting occurs when clumps of platelets adhere to the intersections of the fibrin mesh and normally will then cause the retraction of the fibrin. During this retraction, the fluid in the clot is squeezed out, leaving a solid mass of fibrin and cells.

Clotting of the blood is of extreme importance in sustaining life by arresting bleeding resulting from injuries or wounds received. The clotting of the blood is vital to check the progress of hemorrhage and to work in conjunction with the hemostatic system when blood vessels are contracted requiring smaller clots.

That shed blood soon clots is a very familiar experience. To not do so would be evidence of abnormal conditions within the body and a defective hemostatic system. People who are on blood thinners because of heart conditions or blood pressure conditions must be very careful not to cut themselves or otherwise poke unnecessary holes in their bodies. Their medicine prevents the blood from clotting and they would bleed to death from what ordinarily would be a minor cut of little to no consequence.

In rare individuals the blood does not clot readily or at all, so that any injury or operation involving hemorrhage is dangerous and life threatening. This condition of abnormality is called hemophilia. Hemophilia is a defect and not present in normally functioning human bodies.

God created man in such a way that man is protected by this process of clotting. It was His design from the beginning. It is a system and process that is still not completely understood by modern medical science. The clotting of the blood is just another example among many of the marvelous features built into man when God formed man from the dust of the earth.

* * *

HEREDITY, REPRODUCTION AND EMBRYOLOGY

Before leaving this overview of the blood, a quick side trip must be taken into the field of heredity as it impacts human reproduction and a study of the blood of a baby in the womb. This is necessary because so much that is being discussed today in Christian circles in reference to the blood of Christ leads to false theological conclusions and consequently to heresy. If Christians are to understand the theological significance of the blood of Christ, we must start with the physiological nature of His blood. We start that particular inquiry here with a brief overview of normal human physiology as designed by God. As seen later, the design of man by God in creation was, from God's perspective, developed after the design of redemption. In the grand design by God, Calvary came before Creation. It all fits together for His manifest glory.

The process of heredity governs the transmission of biological traits from one generation to the next. Behavioral, mental, physical, physiological, and biological traits are inherited from parents. Some of these traits are directly dependent upon the genetics of the parents. At this point, some may wish they could change their children's genes to modify behavior. We are not going there since that is not possible. Nice try though.

The physical key to heredity can be found within the nucleus of the cell in structures known as chromosomes. Carried on the chromosomes are smaller substances called genes, which contain the hereditary coding of an individual. Every normally functioning human has 46 chromosomes carried in pairs within each and every cell of the body. These chromosomes carry thousands of genes that pass on traits to the following generations. Among the common inherited physical traits are straight or curly hair, color blindness, and blood type. When cells divide they produce exact duplicates of each chromosome giving each cell of the body exactly the same genes.

It is amazing to note that people (mostly women) who have inherited curly hair spend hours and much effort to straighten their hair for the next day. Women with straight hair spend comparable time and effort to curl their hair. Expensive colored contacts are bought to change the color of ones eyes. All this notwithstanding, the genes remain in control.

The sex cells are different in that when they divide they divide twice resulting in gametes (sperm cells and ovum cells), that are used in fertilization. Each gamete, the sperm and the ovum, receives only one of each chromosome pair. During fertilization, a single male and female gamete unite to form a fertilized egg, or zygote. Upon completion of the formation of the zygote in fertilization, the genetic material is released from the head of the sperm. These 23 chromosomes are then united with the 23 chromosomes from the ovum and form a complete set of 46 chromosomes containing all the genetic material for the new individual. The infant inherits his parents' genes.

At this point, the moment after conception when the 46 chromosome set is completed, a new individual exists. That individual is unique and will not change genetically for the rest of his or her life. A person has come into existence and that person is known by God. That person has life — human life. And that life must be respected for what it is in the sight of God, precious.

Although the genes for each trait are produced in pairs, the resultant manifestation of certain traits, characteristics, and physiology in the child depends upon how the two genes are combined. Some genes are dominant and some genes are recessive. The presence of one or two dominant genes results in the expression of that dominant trait. An example of a dominant trait over a recessive trait is that of brown eyes over blue eyes. To inherit a recessive trait it is necessary to inherit two recessive genes from the parents.

The process of heredity is conducted by the transmission of the genetic code biochemically through DNA, a complex molecule capable of duplicating itself exactly. DNA is responsible for the replication and transmission of genetic traits at the biochemical level, including blood type in humans.

Blood type is inherited. It is transmitted from parents to children by individual genes, one gene from each parent. In what is known as the ABO blood groups, the genes determining blood type are codominant, one is not recessive and the other dominant. For example, An A from one parent does not take precedence over a B from the other. The gene for the O type creates a protein that is inactive; therefore, if an O from one parent is paired with an A from the other parent, the child's blood type will be

A. The four possible blood types in the ABO system are: A, B, AB, O. This can be seen in the following combinations:

AA or AO results in A

BB or BO results in B

AB results in AB

OO results in O.

As mentioned earlier, the starting point for the human body is the zygote, or the resultant union of a sperm and ovum. The sperm and ovum each carry 23 chromosomes and upon union in fertilization are joined together to produce the proper number of chromosomes, 46. The zygote thus contains all the genetic material for this new and unique individual. At this point, a series of consecutive cell divisions is initiated, called mitosis. From a single cell, the zygote, many cells are formed that will develop into the human body. Each cell will have the exact DNA of the original zygote that was formed by the union of the sperm and ovum. The nature, characteristics, and type of blood are determined in the zygote as a result of the combination of genes on the chromosomes received from both the mother and father.

Both the mother and the father contribute genes necessary for the development of the blood in the baby. The blood type cannot change after this initial point. This is an important point to remember. The blood type of the baby is determined by and dependent upon genes from both the mother and the father. This is the natural process created by God when He created man. And it works quite well. It is a fact of medicine and creation.

In the early weeks of embryonic development, primitive red blood cells are produced in the yolk sac.

During the middle trimester of gestation, the liver is the main organ for the production of red blood cells, as well as some red cells produced by the spleen and lymph nodes.

The placenta is the organ that develops around the embryo from its implantation in the uterus. It is through the placenta that the developing baby receives the necessary nutrients and oxygen from the mother, and at the same time eliminates waste. The structure of the placenta is based on numerous tiny fetal blood vessels called chorionic villi. These vessels are bathed in the blood of the mother within the placenta. The walls of the blood vessels allow osmosis to occur so that an exchange of oxygen, nutrients, waste, and even small molecules such as antibodies between the baby's and mother's circulatory systems can happen freely. Red blood cells, however, are unable to penetrate the walls of the blood vessels. The red cells of the mother and the baby always remain separate. There is no mixing of actual red blood cells within the placenta. There is a mixing of antibodies, nutrients, oxygen, and waste matter between the blood of the mother and the blood of the baby. This mixing process, established by the Creator, is necessary to the life of the developing baby. Without this mixing of certain components of the baby's blood and the mother's blood the baby would die.

* * *

What does all of this have to do with the blood of Christ?

In studying the blood of Christ, a foundation of physiological facts must be laid concerning the blood of man. This is necessary in developing the doctrine of the blood of Christ.

Why?

Because Christ was man.

The physiological aspects tie in directly with the theological aspects and help in understanding who Christ was and is, understanding why He came and what He did, and understanding the significance of the blood of Christ. Not only is the significance made plain, but the importance of the blood of Christ in Christian doctrine. Without the blood of Christ, Christianity crumbles.

Why?

Because Christ is God.

This chapter presented the physiological aspects of the blood, genetics, heredity, and embryology present in Creation. These are medical facts. These truths are God's truths and are not in contradiction with revealed truth found in Scripture. Combining the truths of Creation with the truths of Divine revelation of Scripture helps us to understand the nature of the blood of Christ. These truths do not bring Christ down to man's level nor raise man up to His level.

The source of blood from both parents, the genetics of inherited traits, the care and development of a baby in the womb are all part of God's created order. In looking at Christ and His blood, these facts of Creation must not be ignored nor "suspended" to account for and explain Christ. Rather, these medical facts, these observable facts in Creation, in concert with the facts of Scripture contribute to understanding Him and lifting the fog surrounding the doctrines of the Bible. And the ultimate aim remains to get to know Him better.

CHAPTER TWO

HIS COMING

"Forasmuch then as the children are partakers of flesh and blood, he also himself likewise took part of the same;" Hebrews 2:14

In Chapter 1, the physiological nature of man's blood was discussed in necessary preparation for a discussion of the physiological nature of the blood of Christ. There must be a basic understanding of man's blood before we can attempt to understand His blood not only from the physiological perspective but also from the theological perspective. The question has been answered, "What is man's blood like?", now the question, "What was His blood like?" must be answered.

Ultimately, an understanding of the physiological nature of Christ's blood and the blood of man is requisite to avoiding doctrinal error, heresy, or digression into cultic beliefs and teaching present in Christianity today.

The starting point in looking at the blood of Christ is to identify who He was and is. Very simply and emphatically stated, **Jesus Christ of Nazareth is the Son of God, God the Son**. This fact is fundamental to the study at hand and a proof of His Deity as God the Son is not given here. The fact of His deity is accepted and used as a foundation point for our examination into the physiological nature and theological significance of His blood. If Christ be not God, we are lost in our sin.

Just a few verses of Scripture are given here in support of this fact and as a starting point for the reader to pursue a further study of the deity of Christ.

> *Then they that were in the ship came and worshipped him, saying, Of a truth thou art the Son of God. (Matthew 14:33)*
>
> 15 *He saith unto them, But whom say ye that I am?*
>
> 16 *And Simon Peter answered and said, Thou art the Christ, the Son of the living God.*
>
> 17 *And Jesus answered and said unto him, Blessed art thou, Simon Barjona: for flesh and blood hath not revealed* it *unto thee, but my Father which is in heaven. (Matthew 16:15-17)*
>
> *Who is a liar but he that denieth that Jesus is the Christ? He is antichrist,*

> *that denieth the Father and the Son. (I John 2:22)*

The following quote from A. W. Pink sums up the deity of Christ well,

> Let us settle it firmly in our minds that the Deity of Christ is one of the grand foundational truths of Christianity, and let us be willing to go to the stake rather than deny it. Unless our Lord Jesus is very God of very God, there is an end of His mediation, His atonement, His priesthood, His whole work of redemption. These doctrines are useless blasphemies unless Christ is God.

The question may be asked, "Why did He come to earth?" This shall be addressed later. Knowing that He did come, however, the question at hand is "How did He come?" More accurately, "How did He come when He came?"

Why He came *when* He came determined *how* He came and *what* He did. This is a good rule of thumb to apply to a study of Christ. It may be applied in retrospect as well as prospect. In retrospect, application is made to His appearances in the Old Testament (known as theophanies) and His first coming about 2000 years ago.

As prophecy is studied, the statement is modified to read, *why* He comes *when* He comes determines *how* He comes and *what* He does. For a simple look at the latter statement, consider two future events — the rapture and second coming. A further study of the application of these statements to the appearances of Christ shall not be pursued herein. For the purpose of this study, the first statement, *why* He came *when* He came determined *how* He came and *what* He did is applied to His incarnation.

In this chapter, consideration is given to the *how* of the *when* at Bethlehem. The *why* and *what* of that coming is looked at in greater detail later in the study of the theological significance of His blood.

The proper understanding of the answer to the question, "How did He come?" forms the basis for an understanding of the physiological nature of His blood. The progression in studying how He came must of necessity end up with the virgin birth which is how He came. Prior to looking into the virgin birth, it is vital to understand what is called the kenosis and the hypostatic union, since our understanding of who and what He was after the virgin birth is derived from these doctrines. These terms shall be defined and explained after some basic stubby pencil work to establish some foundational truths.

The point of departure into this examination is Hebrews 2:14, quoted at the beginning of this chapter.

> *Forasmuch then as the children are partakers of flesh and blood, he also himself likewise took part of the same. (Emphasis added)*

The "he" of this verse is the Lord Jesus Christ. This verse speaks of the Incarnation — God become flesh. The word incarnation does not appear in the Bible. It is derived from the Latin *in* and *caro* (flesh), meaning in flesh, clothed in flesh, the act of assuming flesh.

The text and context of this passage is very clear. He (Jesus Christ) "took part of the same." The same what? The same flesh and the same blood as the "children are partakers of." Again, we remind ourselves that sin is excepted when referring to Christ. The text clearly teaches that Christ "took part" and became the same flesh and the same blood as we are. The Bible is here speaking of literal flesh and literal blood. This does not lower Him to the level of man. But as shall be seen later, it does show and explain that He was 100 % human (sin excepted) at the same time that He was 100 % God.

The Incarnation is of such magnitude and nature that it is outside the range of possible complete human natural comprehension. It can only be apprehended and comprehended to the degree possible by the enlightenment of the Scriptures by the Holy Spirit to the soul of regenerate man. The unregenerate man or woman will be at a total loss to attempt to comprehend this great and significant event in the history of creation and the universe. The regenerate man or woman who is not in fellowship with God will also be at a loss to comprehend or apprehend this truth unless and until there is restoration of fellowship and a sincere desire to seek and to know Him. This is clearly seen in the following Scripture verses:

> 9 *But as it is written, Eye hath not seen, nor ear heard, neither have entered into the heart of man, the things which God hath prepared for them that love him.*
>
> 10 *But God hath revealed* them *unto us by his Spirit: for the Spirit searcheth all things, yea, the deep things of God.*
>
> 11 *For what man knoweth the things of a man, save the spirit of man which is in him? even so the things of God knoweth no man, but the Spirit of God.*
>
> 12 *Now we have received, not the spirit of the world, but the spirit which is*

of God; that we might know the things
that are freely given to us of God.
13 *Which things also we speak, not*
in the words which man's wisdom
teacheth, but which the Holy Ghost
teacheth; comparing spiritual things
with spiritual.
14 *But the natural man receiveth*
not the things of the Spirit of God: for
they are foolishness unto him: neither
can he know them, *because they are*
spiritually discerned.
15 *But he that is spiritual judgeth*
all things, yet he himself is judged of no
man.
16 *For who hath known the mind*
of the Lord, that he may instruct him?
But we have the mind of Christ.
(1 Corinthians 2:9-16)
1 *That which was from the*
beginning, which we have heard, which
we have seen with our eyes, which we
have looked upon, and our hands have
handled, of the Word of life;
2 *(For the life was manifested, and*
we have seen it, *and bear witness, and*
shew unto you that eternal life, which
was with the Father, and was manifested
unto us;)
3 *That which we have seen and*
heard declare we unto you, that ye also
may have fellowship with us: and truly
our fellowship is *with the Father, and*
with his Son Jesus Christ.
4 *And these things write we unto*
you, that your joy may be full.

5 This then is the message which we have heard of him, and declare unto you, that God is light, and in him is no darkness at all.
6 If we say that we have fellowship with him, and walk in darkness, we lie, and do not the truth:
7 But if we walk in the light, as he is in the light, we have fellowship one with another, and the blood of Jesus Christ his Son cleanseth us from all sin.
8 If we say that we have no sin, we deceive ourselves, and the truth is not in us.
9 If we confess our sins, he is faithful and just to forgive us our *sins, and to cleanse us from all unrighteousness.*
10 If we say that we have not sinned, we make him a liar, and his word is not in us. (1 John 1:1-10)

The first step in understanding the issues surrounding the blood of Christ is to ensure that one is born again. If not, discernment or understanding of these matters is impossible. For those who are born again and out of fellowship with the Father and the Son there will be difficulty in attempting to understand the blood of Christ until there is true repentance and restoration of fellowship. The Holy Spirit must not be quenched or grieved so that He may lead into all truth.

A dangerous mind-set must be avoided at this point. A person can become so convinced of what he believes that the Holy Ghost of God cannot teach him anything or take him deeper into the truths of Scripture unless and until there is repentance and restoration of fellowship with God.

This is not to say that a person should be easily dissuaded from the truth, but, conversely, led deeper into that truth.

A distinction must be made at the outset between the Incarnation and the virgin birth of our Lord. They are not the same. These two truths are so very often confused the one for the other or are used interchangeably. This should not be so. The Incarnation of the Son of God, God the Son, is the fact of God becoming Man, and this fact involved several aspects. The virgin birth is one of those aspects; and that aspect is the method by which God the Son became man. The subject of the virgin birth and Scriptures supporting it will be examined in a later chapter.

The Incarnation was a voluntary act of our Lord as He was sent by God the Father as seen in Galatians 4:4, 5:

> 4 *But when the fulness of the time was come, God sent forth his Son, made of a woman, made under the law,*
>
> 5 *To redeem them that were under the law, that we might receive the adoption of sons.*

Of course, since He was sent as the Son from the Father, this presupposes that God the Father had a Son. The Lord Jesus Christ is that Son in His eternal relationship with the Father and who was in intimate communion of glory and blessedness with the Father from eternity. This truth is of utmost importance in that it establishes the Divine nature of the Son, sharing the Godhead coequally with the Father and the Holy Ghost in eternity.

The doctrine of the Incarnation is vital to and at the core of Christianity. By this act, God becoming flesh, we understand the true nature of God, the true nature of man, the atonement provided for in Christ, and all the other doctrines that follow. Since we are saved by grace through faith, *(For by grace are ye saved through faith; and that not of yourselves: it is the gift of God: Not of works, lest any man should boast. Eph 2:8-9),* it is important that we understand the object of our faith, i.e., the Lord Jesus Christ Himself. Accuracy is vital to the doctrine of the Incarnation and the method and aspects of God becoming man. The complaint that this is getting too technical is a defense for ignorance, heresy or laziness. The Word of God must be rightly and accurately divided and studied with all due diligence. Inaccuracy, even in the slightest, may result in deviant doctrine, heresy, and eventually apostasy as the truth is compromised upon the table of mortal understanding and convenience. We must get better acquainted with Him.

We understand that which we understand, we comprehend that which we comprehend, we apprehend that which we apprehend, and we accept by faith that which we do not understand, comprehend, or apprehend. On the face of this statement its meaning appears rather obvious. But it is worth reviewing and applying this statement to the doctrines of the Bible in order to press on in our Christian life.

Well, what is the difference between understand, comprehend and apprehend?

What is the big deal?

The big deal is to not get hung up pondering the imponderable until one becomes completely frustrated.

To apprehend is merely to perceive, to become aware of something through one or more of the senses, while to comprehend something is to grasps its meaning in its entirety. To understand, although close in meaning to comprehend, also means to have insight into or sympathy with something. When we are unable to understand something in our limited human understanding, we then understand through faith as we are exhorted in Hebrews chapter 11.

> The subject of the Incarnation is at once initial and fundamental. All the significance of the crises that follow, grows out of this first, and most marvellous mystery. The Lord Jesus Christ is a Person infinitely transcending the possibility of perfect human comprehension. Nevertheless the Scripture declares certain facts concerning Him, which account for His glory and His grace, and without which He remains an unsolved problem, defying every successive age in its attempts to account for Him. It should at once be admitted that no final words of explanation can be written concerning Him. And yet it is of the utmost importance that so much as has been revealed should be recognized, in order to a comprehension of the true meaning of His mission.[1]

Because it involves the Son of God, at the foundation of the Incarnation is the doctrine of the Trinity. That doctrine simply stated is that God is one God existing in three persons subsisting in one divine nature. Three distinct persons comprise the unity of the Godhead — God the Father, God the Son, and God the Holy Ghost. All three persons of the Godhead are co-equal and eternal. The Son of God is one of these persons. God does not have three personalities, He is three persons yet one God. God does not have three natures, He has one divine nature in three persons.

The doctrine of the trinity is one of those doctrines that is beyond human comprehension. Man can understand parts of it, how it works in certain ways, and how it applies to Scripture. But in order to understand the trinity in its entirety would be possible only if man were equal to God. That thought is of course absurd. Illustrations seen in nature have been offered up in the past in an honest attempt to help people understand the nature of the trinity.

No illustration can adequately or accurately portray the trinity. We can only attempt through these poor illustrations to understand a portion of the nature of the trinity in the hopes that, as we get to know Him better and more intimately, we can then understand His Word better and what He is saying to us through that Word.

One of those poor illustrations is that the trinity is like water existing as a liquid, a solid, and a vapor: water, ice, steam. The same substance existing in three different forms. This illustration is woefully lacking and presents a wrong perception of the nature of the trinity. Water cannot exist as a liquid and a solid and a vapor simultaneously. They are separate and distinct, not having anything in unity except the identity of the molecules as H_2O. It is a very poor illustration of the trinity and should not be used in the teaching of children or new Christians.

Another example from nature that comes much closer to illustrating the trinity is three identical candles in a room. There are three separate, distinct and identifiable candles with the flame giving off light. However, as you observe the room, there is only light. You cannot say that the light in the right hand corner of the room comes from candle number one, or that the light is from candle number two, etc. There is only light, one light, the essence and nature of which is identical to each of the candles, yet the light is one. This example does not address many of the attributes of God, such as His omnipresence, present everywhere at all time. The purpose of the picture is to illustrate that the triune God is of one essence, one nature; He is one, yet there are three persons. This admittedly narrow and confined picture is helpful in understanding the essence and nature of God as we study the kenosis and hypostatic union.

A common misconception or false teaching is that the Godhead became incarnate. This is wrong. The Bible is clear and unambiguous that one of the persons of the Godhead became flesh and dwelt among us.

> *And the Word was made flesh, and dwelt among us, (and we beheld his glory, the glory as of the only begotten of the Father,) full of grace and truth. (John 1:14)*

In other words, it was not the Father and the Son and the Holy Spirit who became flesh. The Son of God, who is also called the Word, alone and in distinction from the Father and Holy Spirit became flesh. The divine nature or essence did not incarnate, but a person who has the divine nature and essence in unity with the Father and Holy Spirit, yet distinguished and distinguishable from the other two, became flesh. And that person was the Lord Jesus Christ, the Son of God, God the Son.

This distinction is necessary to the truth not only of the trinity but to the truth of the work of Christ. To not be so distinguished from the Father and Spirit would cause confusion when attempting to reconcile the actions of God. Questions arise.

How could the same person send and be sent?

How could one rule and yet empty himself?

How could one give the law and yet be subject to the law?

How could one pour out wrath and yet endure that wrath?

Such confusion is eliminated by a proper understanding of the Trinity as One God in divine nature and essence existing as three distinct persons. One of those persons, the Son of God, came to this earth and took on him the form of a servant and became flesh — the incarnation.

The first term mentioned previously for consideration is the term kenosis. When one considers that the working vocabulary of the average American is 850 words and the vocabulary of the King James Bible is about 8000 words, a challenge is seen. That challenge is not to bring the King James Bible down to the level of the average church member as is being done with modern versions. Rather, the challenge is for serious Christians to expand their vocabulary as needed to understand the Bible. It is rather exciting. Strange words are not to be avoided nor should they invoke fear and trepidation. Some false teachers like to throw them around impressing people with their so-called theological grasp only to lead people astray. A look at some of these words and the doctrines behind them is necessary in order to better understand our Saviour and His blood.

This word, kenosis, is derived from the Greek word used in Philippians 2:7,

> *But made himself of no reputation, and took upon him the form of a servant, and was made in the likeness of men. (Emphasis added)*

The word is here translated "made himself of no reputation." In other versions of the Bible, it is translated "He emptied himself." This one word and its translation are responsible for a dilemma that has faced earnest Bible students for centuries. A problem is introduced if we state that the Son of God emptied himself.

Of what did He empty himself?

Can Christ empty himself of deity and yet remain God?

This is impossible because one of the attributes of God is His immutability, He cannot change even in the slightest. To do so would make Him less than God and other than God. This is clearly seen in Scripture.

> *For I* am *the LORD, I change not; (Mal 3:6)*
>
> *Every good gift and every perfect gift is from above, and cometh down from the Father of lights, with whom is no variableness, neither shadow of turning. (James 1:17)*

Well, if He did not set aside His deity, did He set aside certain attributes as God? The same problem arises if He set aside attributes. He would then have changed, and He cannot change. If He set aside even one attribute, He would no longer be God, and God He was and is. It is argued by some that He set aside His lesser attributes. This argument is weak and meaningless on its face and has no depth to it. What is there of God that is greater or lesser? How can one say, and who is to judge which if any of God's attributes are greater or lesser? What an absurdity. He is God. That must be understood in its fullest. As God He is immutable, changeless, unchanging, and unchangeable.

The immutability of Christ is also brought into question if it is stated that He only set aside the prerogatives of His attributes. He did not set aside the actual attribute, it is argued, but just set aside the prerogative of some of His attributes. Of course, this is not possible since to do so would be to set aside the attribute itself. He could not have an attribute without the prerogative to exercise it. To do so would have involved change and made Him less than God. He is and was God Eternal.

As God He was not confined to His body as man, as taught by some preachers today. This position that Jesus was confined to His body is a surprising statement to find today in Fundamentalism. This position on the kenosis holds that Jesus Christ was not omnipresent or omnipotent while in the flesh. Somehow, it is alleged and taught, He limited Himself by being contained in and constrained by His body. Although He did limit Himself in the exercise of His power and attributes as God, He did not do so through containment.

A pastor preached recently that by containing Himself in a human body, and thereby restricting His powers, Jesus did something as great if not greater than His death on the cross by humbling Himself so low as to be contained in a body of flesh and blood. This, of course, is patently false. Indeed, He humbled Himself to take on the form of a servant. But this He did toward the end of accomplishing the greatest act ever — that of dying in our place upon the cross to pay the penalty for sin.

This containment theory attacks the immutability of God the Son. He is unchanging and unchangeable. He retained all the power and attributes that are His with the Father when He assumed our humanity. He simply did not exercise them as God as was His right to do so.

How could He be God and be in a human body at the same time?

The answer is very, very simple. He is God.

This pastor that is teaching that Christ lost some of His power upon becoming flesh and blood and being contained therein is going to have a hard time explaining how Christ now has that power back and remains in a body of flesh and bone seated at the right hand of God the Father. This same pastor sits on the board of a Bible college. This ought not so to be.

These arguments surrounding the kenosis of Christ are a subtle and covert attack upon His absolute deity. They can be viewed no other way than a lessening of who and what Jesus Christ was when He came in the flesh. These arguments may stem from heresy and apostasy in an attempt to justify sin and rebellion against God. They may also arise from ignorance due to improper Bible study, wrongly dividing the Word of Truth, or following the teachings of the wrong man whose Biblical scholarship is questionable at best. These arguments introduce difficulties and falsehoods that confound the redemption plan so plainly laid out by God in His clearly written Word.

What then is the kenosis?

Properly understood in the light of who God is, kenosis is a voluntary act by the Son of God of setting aside the *exercise* of those attributes which He fully retained and that were and are His in the full, voluntarily restricting their independent use in obedience to the Father and subjection to the Father's will; all of which was in keeping with His purpose in coming to this earth. The whole immutable divine person of the Son of God with the same divine immutable essence of the Godhead continued to subsist as the eternal person of the Godhead that He is. He now embraced a perfect human nature united with the divine nature.

The question may be asked, "What is the difference between setting aside the prerogatives of the attributes of deity and setting aside the exercise of those prerogatives?"

The place to start is the definition of prerogative. The noun prerogative means an exclusive and unquestionable right belonging to a person. Not only is it a right and characteristic privilege peculiar and inherent to a person, but it is *exclusive* and *unquestionable*. For example, as a parent, a father has the exclusive and unquestionable right and privilege to discipline his children anywhere and anytime. This is granted to Him by God. The father chooses the time, place, method, and extent of chastisement. If his children misbehave in a supermarket in public view, discretion in these days in this country causes him to temporarily set aside the exercise of the prerogative that is his until he gets them home. Of course, the long period of anticipation on the part of the offender adds to the severity of the correction, at least in the mind of the offender. The point is that the father, at his own discretion, set aside for a short time the exercise of a prerogative that is his. The father did not change, nor lose any attributes he possessed before the visit to the supermarket. He remained unchanged. Under control of his will and discretion he simply set aside the exercise of his prerogative for a time and did not act in a specific manner.

To insist that Christ emptied Himself of even one attribute, or the prerogatives of one or more attributes, is to thus rob Him of deity. The conclusion would then be that God is no longer immutable, therefore He is less than God. The attributes of God the Son cannot be categorized into greater and lesser attributes, as some have done in an attempt to defend "empty Himself," with the lesser attributes being set aside during His humiliation. That assumes that one attribute is more essential to deity than another. That, of course, is absurd.

A simple way to state the kenosis is that while Jesus walked this earth He veiled the glory that was His with the Father, hiding His glory from man and making it possible for man to see God without being consumed by the brightness of His holiness. John wrote that no man has seen God at any time, yet the Son declared Him.

> *No man hath seen God at any time; the only begotten Son, which is in the bosom of the Father, he hath declared* him. *(John 1:18)*

Had Jesus behaved as God, exercising all the attributes that were and are His, no man could have seen Him. But though God, He behaved as man was created to behave while veiling the glory of God in human flesh. He voluntarily submitted Himself to behave within the limitations that make man a man as He as God created man to be. That is a man wholly indwelt and occupied by His Creator submitting Himself at all times and in every circumstance to the will of the Father. He thus left us an example to follow. That example is not much what to do as it is what to be. Just as He submitted Himself as man completely to God the Father, we are to submit ourselves completely to Him as Lord. All of this was a voluntary act by the Son of God in not exercising the independent use of His attributes of deity. All that He did He did in the power of the Father and the Holy Spirit.

> *For he whom God hath sent speaketh the words of God: for God giveth not the Spirit by measure* unto him. *(John 3:34)*
>
> *Believest thou not that I am in the Father, and the Father in me? the words that I speak unto you I speak not of myself: but the Father that dwelleth in me, he doeth the works. (John 14:10)*

If the Apostle Paul had thought that Christ could have or would have set aside any attribute of deity, thus reducing Him to less than God, he would not have written of Him as he did throughout his epistles as the Divine Son of God, God the Son. Paul's comment, made under the inspiration of the Holy Spirit, in Colossians 2:9 makes that very clear.

> *For in him dwelleth all the fulness of the Godhead bodily.*

The three letter word "all" means all.
"All."
How much clearer can it be?

“All the fulness” means “all the fulness. Not most. Not some. Not even all but a few lesser. It is simply amazing how much light a direct reading of God’s Word sheds on the ignorant teachings of men.

If Christ is not at one and the same time both fully God and fully man in the same person, He could not have died, or His death would have not availed for man. If Christ is not fully man, we worship a myth; if He be not fully God, we are in idolatry. Yet we are told that to not worship Him is to disobey the Father.

> *That all* men *should honour the Son, even as they honour the Father. He that honoureth not the Son honoureth not the Father which hath sent him. (John 5:23)*

The doctrine of the kenosis is not just a purely academic area for theologians to debate. It involves the very heart and center of the Christian faith. If there is to be an understanding of the significance of His blood, and His atonement, there must be a proper understanding of this underlying doctrine of God becoming a man. The charismatics today have developed some very weird and heretical teaching concerning the kenosis and combined it with some new-age philosophy to produce the so-called faith movement. Their teaching is that Jesus left His powers and attributes behind and lived as nothing more than a mere man. One of the leading proponents of this movement, Kenneth Copeland, would have us believe that born-again believers are just as much an incarnation of God as Jesus was. This of course is heresy and flies in the face of what the Bible teaches concerning man and Christ. If Jesus Christ was not the God-Man, fully God and fully man, when He died upon the cross of Calvary in our place, then the integrity of the atonement is destroyed and we are not redeemed.

The false kenotic teachings derive from an improper understanding of Philippians 2:7. This verse must be interpreted in the context of the entire passage. A text out of context is pretext. In the second chapter of Philippians, Paul uses the Incarnation of Christ as an example to the Philippians as to how they should live their lives. He was stressing self-sacrifice and avoiding personal glory in their Christian life as they served one another. The phrase "made Himself of no reputation" also translated "emptied Himself" is talking of outward expression, manifestation. This is seen in the earlier verse where the word morphe, or form, is used concerning Christ in the form of God.

The plain sense of Scripture here is that Christ's kenosis was regarding the outward glory, majesty and manifestation of Godhood accomplished by taking on the form of a servant. And this is exactly what the subject is that Paul is addressing to the Philippians. Context is vital here. The Apostle is not telling them to lay aside anything — natural abilities, talents, powers, attributes — he is telling them to submit themselves to God and His will and to each other for the good of the whole church. There is nothing in this passage that teaches that the Eternal Word of God, Jesus Christ, emptied Himself of anything or laid anything aside to assume humanity. He only veiled the outward manifestation of the glory that was His from eternity with the Father, the glory of the Godhead; and voluntarily submitted Himself to the Father's will and the Father's glory..

There are no grounds for teaching or believing that Christ emptied Himself of any part of His Deity. Simply stated, He set aside one form of manifestation for another. The first form of manifestation that Christ held with the Father revealed that He was equal with God and was God possessing all the attributes of God. The second form of manifestation was one in which it was necessary for a season of time to veil the holiness and glory of God in the form of a servant, submissive to the Father and the Father's will, for the express purpose of declaring the Father to man. He simply changed His form of manifestation for the mission on which He was sent.

---

[1] G. Campbell Morgan, The Crises of the Christ (New Jersey: Revell company, 1936), p. 67.

CHAPTER THREE

HIS PERSON

"Jesus of Nazareth, a man approved of God." Acts 2:22
"But unto the Son he saith, Thy throne, O God, is for ever and ever." Hebrews 1:8

At this point, the temptation is to ask many questions because the doctrine of the hypostatic union, the relationship of the divine and human natures in Christ, is a doctrine difficult to understand. These questions may be asked. These questions should be asked. Many cannot be answered to man's satisfaction or understanding because it involves the study of an infinite and holy God. Faith must be exercised in the statements of fact contained in Scripture about the mystery of the Incarnation and all that surrounds it. This mystery and revelation of God by God through the means of God becoming a man is the center of Christianity, without parallel, equal, or possibility of complete understanding.

What is possible, however, is to study to understand what God has said about this mystery in the Bible and look as deeply as allowed by the Holy Spirit into this truth. The use of Scripture may appear to be over done in this section of the book. Rather than demote the many verses that speak to this issue to the status of footnote or endnote, they are included here in the body of the text for the reader to read exactly what God is saying through His Word. The intention is that this book will be read with a Bible at hand. By including the verses in the body of the text, it is hoped that the reader will be saved some time in looking them up.

The next term in consideration of the blood of Christ is the hypostatic union. This is a theological term used in reference to the Incarnation to express the revealed truth that in the Lord Jesus Christ one person subsists in two natures, the Divine and the human. The phrase "hypostatic union" is not a phrase used commonly in conversation. It is not even used by most when discussing such doctrines as the first coming of Christ.

The word hypostasis refers to that which lies beneath as a basis or foundation. This term was in common usage by Greek philosophers to denote reality as distinguished from appearances. Whatever the appearance of Christ to the human eye or human understanding, the hypostatic union is the reality. That reality is that Jesus Christ is God in the flesh. This is clearly stated.

> *In the beginning was the Word, and the Word was with God, and the Word was God. (John 1:1)*

> *And the Word was made flesh, and dwelt among us, (and we beheld his glory, the glory as of the only begotten of the Father,) full of grace and truth. (John 1:14)*
>
> *Jesus said unto them, Verily, verily, I say unto you, Before Abraham was, I am. (John 8:58)*
>
> *For in him dwelleth all the fulness of the Godhead bodily. (Colossians 2:9)*
>
> *But unto the Son* he saith, *Thy throne, O God,* is *for ever and ever: a sceptre of righteousness* is *the sceptre of thy kingdom. (Hebrews 1:8)*

He is fully God and fully man. Therefore, He has two natures: the Divine nature of God and the human nature of man, sin excepted. He is not half God and half man. He is 100% God at one and the same time that He is 100% man: man as He as God created man to be. At no time since His birth can it be said that Christ lost His divinity or any part or attribute of His deity.

> 5 *Let this mind be in you, which was also in Christ Jesus:*
>
> 6 *Who, being in the form of God, thought it not robbery to be equal with God:*
>
> 7 *But made himself of no reputation, and took upon him the form of a servant, and was made in the likeness of men:*
>
> 8 *And being found in fashion as a man, he humbled himself, and became obedient unto death, even the death of the cross.*

> [9] *Wherefore God also hath highly exalted him, and given him a name which is above every name:*
>
> [10] *That at the name of Jesus every knee should bow, of* things *in heaven, and* things *in earth, and* things *under the earth;*
>
> [11] *And* that *every tongue should confess that Jesus Christ* is *Lord, to the glory of God the Father. (Philippians 2:5-11)*

The Lord Jesus Christ was always and will always be God in the fullest. Some very wrong teaching is present today in Christianity, even among so-called Fundamental Christians, that after Jesus died physically on the cross He somehow lost or gave up His divinity and suffered in Hell at the hands of Satan and his demons for three days and three nights for our sins. This is absolutely and unequivocally wrong and is patent heresy. Our redemption was paid in full when He cried out from the cross, "It is finished."

> *When Jesus therefore had received the vinegar, he said, It is finished: and he bowed his head, and gave up the ghost. (John 19:30)*
>
> *Christ hath redeemed us from the curse of the law, being made a curse for us: for it is written, Cursed* is *every one that hangeth on a tree: (Galatians 3:13)*
>
> [5] *Wherefore when he cometh into the world, he saith, Sacrifice and offering thou wouldest not, but a body hast thou prepared me:*

6 *In burnt offerings and* sacrifices *for sin thou hast had no pleasure.*
7 *Then said I, Lo, I come (in the volume of the book it is written of me,) to do thy will, O God.*
8 *Above when he said, Sacrifice and offering and burnt offerings and* offering *for sin thou wouldest not, neither hadst pleasure* therein; *which are offered by the law;*
9 *Then said he, Lo, I come to do thy will, O God. He taketh away the first, that he may establish the second.*
10 *By the which will we are sanctified through the offering of the body of Jesus Christ once* for all. *(Hebrews 10:5-10)*

The wages of sin is death — always has been, always will be. God so announced in the beginning and Paul enumerated it again in his Epistle to the Romans.

But of the tree of the knowledge of good and evil, thou shalt not eat of it: for in the day that thou eatest thereof thou shalt surely die. (Genesis 2:17)

For the wages of sin is death; but the gift of God is eternal life through Jesus Christ our Lord. (Romans 6:23)

He paid the price for our sin upon the cross, that price was death, and He then declared that it (the purpose for which He came, our redemption) was finished. There is not one passage of Scripture that teaches that Christ suffered in Hell. There is not one passage of Scripture that even allows a loose or liberal interpretation that Christ went to Hell and suffered at the hands of Satan and his demons who are defeated foes. There was no reason in the plan of God for Him to do so. It makes absolutely no doctrinal or theological sense. Like the arguments about the kenosis, these arguments lead only to confusion and error.

An example of this error can be seen by the response of the academic dean of a small independent Fundamental Baptist Bible college in Oklahoma. When confronted with this false teaching that Christ was only man and He suffered in Hell for our sin, this dean defended that position and would not correct the teaching of this heresy by a faculty member in the school. The presence of this error should be a matter of grave concern. It should be of concern to the board of that school. It should be of concern to the deacons of that church. It should be of concern to parents who send their children there supposedly to receive a Bible education. They must decide either to stand for the truth of Scripture or follow a man. An improper understanding at his point in the Incarnation understandably leads to incorrect teaching on the blood of Christ and can result in a form of idolatry. At the least, heresy was being taught and tolerated in a Fundamental Baptist Bible College.

In order to properly approach the study of such a complex topic as the hypostatic union, around which there is much confusion and false teaching in addition to the scope of a most difficult doctrine, the concept of a Biblical mystery must be understood and admitted. The admonition of the Apostle in Hebrews 11 that "Through faith we understand" must be heeded. There are some things that the natural mind can comprehend through reason and observation. However,

> *the natural man receiveth not the things of the Spirit of God: for they are foolishness unto him: neither can he*

know them, because they are spiritually discerned. (1 Corinthians 2:14)

In matters of the spirit, the presence and teaching of the Holy Spirit are required for illumination. Even with the teaching of the Holy Spirit, man will not be able to understand all things until he is present with our Lord in Heaven. Until then, man must accept and understand by faith those things so clearly presented in Scripture.

The first point to consider in attempting to understand the doctrine of the hypostatic union, that is the union of the Divine nature and human nature in one person, as a mystery in Scripture is that God is unsearchable. The sovereign unsearchable God has condescended to communicate to man certain truths. Some of these truths are expressed in Scripture as a "mystery." Christ Himself, the Incarnate Deity, is a Biblical mystery.

How that by revelation he made known unto me the mystery; (as I wrote afore in few words, Whereby, when ye read, ye may understand my knowledge in the mystery of Christ) (Ephesians 3:3-4)

That their hearts might be comforted, being knit together in love, and unto all riches of the full assurance of understanding, to the acknowledgement of the mystery of God, and of the Father, and of Christ; (Colossians 2:2)

For in him dwelleth all the fulness of the Godhead bodily. (Colossians 2:9)

7 *But we speak the wisdom of God in a mystery,* even *the hidden* wisdom,

which God ordained before the world
unto our glory:
8 *Which none of the princes of this*
world knew: for had they known it, *they*
would not have crucified the Lord of
glory.
9 *But as it is written, Eye hath not*
seen, nor ear heard, neither have
entered into the heart of man, the things
which God hath prepared for them that
love him.
10 *But God hath revealed* them
unto us by his Spirit: for the Spirit
searcheth all things, yea, the deep things
of God.
11 *For what man knoweth the*
things of a man, save the spirit of man
which is in him? even so the things of
God knoweth no man, but the Spirit of
God.
12 *Now we have received, not the*
spirit of the world, but the spirit which is
of God; that we might know the things
that are freely given to us of God.
13 *Which things also we speak, not*
in the words which man's wisdom
teacheth, but which the Holy Ghost
teacheth; comparing spiritual things
with spiritual.
14 *But the natural man receiveth*
not the things of the Spirit of God: for
they are foolishness unto him: neither
can he know them, *because they are*
spiritually discerned.

15 But he that is spiritual judgeth all things, yet he himself is judged of no man.

16 For who hath known the mind of the Lord, that he may instruct him? But we have the mind of Christ. (1 Corinthians 2:7-16)

Schofield defines a mystery in Scripture as "a previously hidden truth, now divinely revealed, but in which a supernatural element still remains despite the revelation."[1] The mystery of Christ, although kept secret from the beginning of the world, has been revealed in the Incarnation and Scripture. We understand this mystery more fully than the prophets but must still understand by faith the greater truths surrounding His Incarnation. This need not present difficulties to the ardent student of the Bible. Faith takes over where intellect falls short.

Those difficulties that do present themselves in understanding the doctrine of the hypostatic union, however, become less severe and fade into proper comprehension when the central issues are addressed and clarified. In other words, the larger doctrine is broken down into smaller parts for ease of understanding when they are all put back together — one step at a time. This can be compared to learning calculus. You do not start in the middle of the text book or go directly to the last chapter to do the problems. There must be prerequisite courses finished, such as algebra and trigonometry, and then as you study each problem, you break it down into its individual components solving as you go. Eventually, after solving each step of the problem, the whole problem is solved. Complex concepts are understood in this way. Such is the case also with certain doctrines of the Bible.

Basically, this doctrine concerns the union of two natures and NOT the union of two persons. This must be clear and explicit. Jesus Christ was not two persons in one body. He was one person bodily with two natures subsisting in that body. These two natures are the divine and the human — substantially united in one person, the God-Man. A distinction must of necessity be made between nature and person. These are not interchangeable terms for the same entity.

Nature is defined as: the inherent essential character or basic constitution of a person or thing; the qualities that make a person or thing what it or he is; essence. In writing about nature, Walvoord states it is "the real essence, the inward properties which underlie all outward manifestation."[2] Nature refers to the totality of all the essential qualities of a person that make that person what or who that person is. Nature could also mean that intrinsic composition of being without which being would cease to exist.

In other words, the human nature of Christ is referring to His intrinsic human nature, His humanity, without which the incarnate person of the Godhead could not have existed as man. The divine nature of Christ refers to His intrinsic deity without which Christ could not have existed either before Bethlehem or after — i.e., He could not be God.

The word person can be distinguished from nature in that person is a complete substance; a nature with something added, namely, independent subsistence and individuality.[3] The term person is inclusive of intellect, emotion, will, self-awareness, and produces a moral identity larger than personality but inclusive of it. The one person of Christ has two distinct natures in perfect union.

Christ has two natures, but He is one person. The importance of this cannot be overemphasized. There was a union of the two natures in one person, the God-Man Jesus Christ, and not a commingling in some moral union. The two natures were substantially united. We are forbidden from dividing the person or confounding the natures. The divine was so conjoined and united with the humanity that the entire properties of each nature remain in their entirety, and yet the union of the two natures constitutes only one Christ.[4]

The closest thing analogous to this found in nature would be man himself. Man is spirit, soul and body.

> *And the very God of peace sanctify you wholly; and* I pray God *your whole spirit and soul and body be preserved blameless unto the coming of our Lord Jesus Christ. (1 Thessalonians 5:23)*

Essentially, man is a dichotomy (comprised of two parts) — the **visible**, tangible part of man, the body; and the **invisible**, intangible part of man, the soul. The soul is not the body, nor is the body the soul. The two retain their own distinctive properties yet are united vitally in one man.

At this point, it is necessary to dispel a misconception about the constitution of man that has been preached by a well known Fundamental Baptist preacher in Oklahoma City. This misconception borders on a cultic belief concerning man that is becoming more prevalent today through the Word of Faith movement. By preaching this error, this particular Baptist preacher has ill equipped those of his congregation and those who follow his preaching to ward off the temptations of the cults. Far too many Christians have been drawn away from doctrinal soundness into the cults of one form or another because of irresponsible and ignorant preaching.

The error seems harmless at first flush. He states that "you are not a body with a soul, you are a soul with a body." This is exactly what the Word of Faith cult uses as its basis for their position on the nature of man. They teach that man as a species is in the same class of being as God.

By this they mean that man and God both possess a common nature: both are spirit beings. Kenneth Hagin, a leader in this false religion, says that man is not a physical being, but man is a spirit. The only difference in nature between God and man is of degree, not of kind. A definition used throughout the Word of Faith cult is that man is a spirit, who possesses a soul, and who lives in a body. In other words, man's spirit is the real man. Hagin insists that we live in a body, but we are spirit beings. These teachings are also found in the writings of Mary Baker Eddy. She wrote that man is not material, he is spiritual; spirit is real, matter is unreal. This spiritualized view of the nature of man is not the Judeo-Christian viewed revealed by God in the Bible.

For a preacher to say that man is not a body with a soul, but a soul that has a body, is to play right into the hands of the cults and endanger those who hear the teaching. First, the statement is not Biblically accurate. Second, combined with other weak positions on doctrine, this places church members in the precarious position of being easy prey for the cults. "They say what my preacher says, so it must be true."

The underlying error is a faulty understanding of the nature of man. Man is not a spirit being (soul) who just happens to have a body. Man is an integrated being of spirit, soul, body.

> *And the very God of peace sanctify you wholly; and* I pray God *your whole spirit and soul and body be preserved blameless unto the coming of our Lord Jesus Christ. (1 Thessalonians 5:23)*

The Hebrew understanding of man is wholistic: man is an organic whole rather than the sum of his parts. The body is every bit as important to one's personal identity as the spirit. When God created man, He formed his body from the dust of the ground, breathed into his nostrils the breath of life, and man became a living soul — this final phrase refers to the whole man as an animated being.

> *And the LORD God formed man* of *the dust of the ground, and breathed into his nostrils the breath of life; and man became a living soul. (Genesis 2:7)*

The real you is all of you: dust and breath, body and spirit, as one integral whole. To preach otherwise is dangerous heresy deriving from either ignorance or outright apostasy. It is a matter that should be considered seriously.

Getting back to our analogy, there is that which can only be said of the soul which cannot apply to the body and conversely. To do so would be absurd. However, that which is said of the whole man cannot be said of the body or soul separately. Two substances consisting as one. This requires much reflection and thought to discern. Likewise, we cannot think of Christ as two persons but as one in unity.

In studying the union of these two natures, consideration must be given to a closer examination of each. First, the human nature is examined, followed by the divine and then considered in their union.

* * *

Jesus Christ was a man.

> *And I will put enmity between thee and the woman, and between thy seed and her seed; it shall bruise thy head, and thou shalt bruise his heel. (Genesis 3:15)*

15 *The LORD thy God will raise up unto thee a Prophet from the midst of thee, of thy brethren, like unto me; unto him ye shall hearken;*

16 *According to all that thou desiredst of the LORD thy God in Horeb in the day of the assembly, saying, Let me not hear again the voice of the LORD my God, neither let me see this great fire any more, that I die not.*

17 *And the LORD said unto me, They have well* spoken that *which they have spoken.*

18 *I will raise them up a Prophet from among their brethren, like unto thee, and will put my words in his mouth; and he shall speak unto them all that I shall command him.*

19 *And it shall come to pass,* that *whosoever will not hearken unto my words which he shall speak in my name, I will require* it *of him. (Deuteronomy 18:15-19)*

For unto us a child is born, unto us a son is given: and the government shall be upon his shoulder: and his name shall be called Wonderful, Counsellor, The mighty God, The everlasting Father, The Prince of Peace. (Isaiah 9:6)

The book of the generation of Jesus Christ, the son of David, the son of Abraham. (Matthew 1:1)

But when the fulness of the time was come, God sent forth his Son, made

> *of a woman, made under the law, (Galatians 4:4)*
>
> *And being found in fashion as a man, he humbled himself, and became obedient unto death, even the death of the cross. (Philippians 2:8)*
>
> *For* there is *one God, and one mediator between God and men, the man Christ Jesus; (1 Timothy 2:5)*

Peter so declared in his sermon on the day of Pentecost when he said, "Ye men of Israel, hear these words; Jesus of Nazareth, **a man** approved of God among you by miracles and wonders and signs, which God did by him in the midst of you, as ye yourselves also know:" Acts 2.22 (Emphasis added)

The Apostle Paul called Christ a man in Romans 5:15, *"But not as the offence, so also is the free gift. For if through the offence of one many be dead, much more the grace of God, and the gift by grace, which is by one* ***man****, Jesus Christ, hath abounded unto many."* (Emphasis added))

The Lord Jesus Christ Himself testified that He was a man in John 8:40, *"But now ye seek to kill me,* ***a man*** *that hath told you the truth, which I have heard of God: this did not Abraham."* (Emphasis added)

Jesus Christ is a man. This is indisputable. Those who argue on the contrary deny the truth.

This is made clear by the statement of Paul in 1 Timothy 2:5 where he says, *"For there is one God, and one mediator between God and men,* ***the man*** *Christ Jesus;"* (Emphasis added)

The testimony of the inspired Word of God on this point is very clear, explicit, and unambiguous. Whatever else Jesus Christ may have been or is, he most certainly was and is a man.

Jesus Christ had a human body.

He was not some phantom like figure that appeared to the eyes as human, or some shadowy form of humanity. It was a literal, physical and visible human body like unto our body that bore the weight of the cross up that long path to Calvary and was then nailed to that cross in our place. It was a literal, physical and visible human body like unto our body that was pierced by a spear in the side from which wound flowed blood and water. It was a literal, physical and visible human body like unto our body that was prepared and laid in a borrowed tomb. It was a literal, physical and visible human body that rose from the dead on the third day to be seen by more than five hundred witnesses. It was a literal, physical and visible human body bearing the scars of the crucifixion that Thomas was exhorted to place his hand in the wound and to be not faithless. It was a literal, physical and visible human body bearing the scars of the crucifixion that walked with the disciples from Emmaus and they knew not that it was Christ until He illumined their understanding. His resurrected human body was flesh and bones.

> *Behold my hands and my feet, that it is I myself: handle me, and see; for a spirit hath not flesh and bones, as ye see me have. (Luke 24:39)*

The literal, physical and visible human body of our Lord Jesus Christ had the appearance, organs, systems, and characteristics common to human bodies. This is clearly seen in many facets. He was born through normal human birth, although conceived supernaturally. The conception and birth are separate and distinct.

> *And Jacob begat Joseph the husband of Mary, of whom was born*

Jesus, who is called Christ. (Matthew 1:16)

And knew her not till she had brought forth her firstborn son: and he called his name JESUS. (Matthew 1:25)

And she brought forth her firstborn son, and wrapped him in swaddling clothes, and laid him in a manger; because there was no room for them in the inn. (Luke 2:7)

For unto you is born this day in the city of David a Saviour, which is Christ the Lord. (Luke 2:11)

The physical birth of Jesus Christ in the stable of Bethlehem was not miraculous in and of itself. It was the normal birth of a baby as is common to man since Eve. The miracle occurred nine months earlier in that the conception in the womb of Mary was supernatural and miraculous, being conceived of the Holy Ghost.

And the angel answered and said unto her, The Holy Ghost shall come upon thee, and the power of the Highest shall overshadow thee: therefore also that holy thing which shall be born of thee shall be called the Son of God. (Luke 1:35)

The conception was miraculous and supernatural; the birth was normal and human. He who was born of Mary, conceived of the Holy Ghost, was the Son of God.

He had a normal human development, in stature and wisdom.

And the child grew, and waxed strong in spirit, filled with wisdom: and the grace of God was upon him. (Luke 2:40)

And Jesus increased in wisdom and stature, and in favour with God and man. (Luke 2:52)

He had normal human physical needs such as food, water, sleep.

And when he had fasted forty days and forty nights, he was afterward an hungred. (Matthew 4:2)

Now in the morning as he returned into the city, he hungered. (Matthew 21:18)

6 *Now Jacob's well was there. Jesus therefore, being wearied with* his *journey, sat thus on the well:* and *it was about the sixth hour.*

7 *There cometh a woman of Samaria to draw water: Jesus saith unto her, Give me to drink. (John 4:6-7)*

After this, Jesus knowing that all things were now accomplished, that the scripture might be fulfilled, saith, I thirst. (John 19:28)

And, behold, there arose a great tempest in the sea, insomuch that the ship was covered with the waves: but he was asleep. (Matthew 8:24)

And he was in the hinder part of the ship, asleep on a pillow: and they awake him, and say unto him, Master, carest thou not that we perish? (Mark 4:38)

He became weary and fatigued.

Now Jacob's well was there. Jesus therefore, being wearied with his *journey, sat thus on the well:* and *it was about the sixth hour. (John 4:6)*

He had normal human emotions.

And when he was come near, he beheld the city, and wept over it, (Luke 19:41)

And being in an agony he prayed more earnestly: and his sweat was as it were great drops of blood falling down to the ground. (Luke 22:44)

When Jesus therefore saw her weeping, and the Jews also weeping which came with her, he groaned in the spirit, and was troubled, (John 11:33)

Jesus wept. (John 11:35)

Then said the Jews, Behold how he loved him! (John 11:36)

Now is my soul troubled; and what shall I say? Father, save me from this hour: but for this cause came I unto this hour. (John 12:27)

He had normal human features in common with man. The various parts of His body are mentioned — His hands, His feet, His side, His head, His brow, His cheek, His breast upon which the beloved disciple leaned, His beard. The entire representation by Scripture of the Son of God,

Jesus Christ, presents Him possessed of such outward form, influenced by normal human bodily feelings, and engaged in normal human bodily acts as to assure us of the reality and humanness of His body. No other theory or explanation is possible than that Jesus Christ was a man. This fact, therefore, that Christ in His incarnation possessed a literal, physical and visible human body is put beyond all question or doubt.

Jesus Christ had a human soul.

The evidence of this has been regarded as conclusive as that for His human body. A difficulty arises when some suppose that if He had a human soul, He must have been two persons and not one person only with two natures. That He is one person with two natures we have shown previously. It has been taught that He had no human soul, but that His divine nature took its place. This theory has been soundly rejected each time it is proposed when the true doctrine has been set forth.

If the divine nature had simply dwelt in His body as a mere tabernacle of flesh, and hence supplied a substitute for the human soul, it could not be said that Jesus Christ increased in wisdom.

> *And Jesus increased in wisdom and stature, and in favour with God and man. (Luke 2:52)*

The mere material fabric of flesh and bone and blood in which He was supposed to have tabernacled as God, that tabernacle having no soul, could not have had wisdom. If that were the case, the wisdom in which He increased was divine wisdom susceptible to increase and change. This is not so and could not be so. God is immutable. He is unchanging and unchangeable.

He was made in all things like His brethren.

> *Wherefore in all things it behoved him to be made like unto* his *brethren, that he might be a merciful and faithful high priest in things* pertaining *to God, to make reconciliation for the sins of the people. (Hebrews 2:17)*

He would not have been a brother, a member of the human family, a man, made like the rest, if there were no human soul dwelling in His human flesh. Without a human soul, Jesus Christ would not have been a man. He may have looked like a man in appearance and form, but would not have been a man.

Of course, if He did not have a human soul, He could not have said in Mark 14:34, *"My soul is exceeding sorrowful."* Nor could it have been said by the prophet Isaiah, *"When thou shalt make his soul an offering for sin."(53:10)* If His soul had not been human, He would not have been an acceptable substitute for the sin of man. Accordingly, He took upon Him not the nature of angels, but the seed of Abraham.

> *For verily he took not on* him the nature of *angels; but he took on* him *the seed of Abraham. (Hebrews 2:16)*

Man is more than body, he is body and soul. The soul that sinneth, it shall surely die.

> *Behold, all souls are mine; as the soul of the father, so also the soul of the son is mine: the soul that sinneth, it shall die. (Ezekiel 18:4)*

The soul that sinneth, it shall die. (Ezekiel 18:20)

Since redemption of man must of necessity include the soul, Christ must have had a human soul to be a suitable substitute for sinners. This shall be addressed later in the theological applications.

One fact must always be foremost in discussing the human soul of Jesus Christ — He was without sin.

For we have not an high priest which cannot be touched with the feeling of our infirmities; but was in all points tempted like as we are, yet *without sin. (Hebrews 4:15)*

Were He not to have a human soul, but rather to have the divine nature fill that capacity and function in the human body, the statement of Hebrews 4:15 is superfluous and meaningless. It was of course possible for Christ to be a man without being depraved; Adam was without sin in the garden before the fall. In this light and respect as to public heads, Adam is called the first man, and Christ is called the Second Man.

The first man is *of the earth, earthy: the second man* is *the Lord from heaven. (1 Corinthians 15:47)*

Christ's humanity, including both body and soul, was as real as Adam's. It was as real as ours, sin excepted.

Extreme caution and vigilance is required when the humanity of Christ — His incarnation, His human body and human soul — is questioned or denied. To deny the humanity of Christ come in the flesh is the spirit of antichrist.

And every spirit that confesseth not that Jesus Christ is come in the flesh is not of God: and this is that spirit *of antichrist, whereof ye have heard that it should come; and even now already is it in the world. (1 John 4:3)*

For many deceivers are entered into the world, who confess not that Jesus Christ is come in the flesh. This is a deceiver and an antichrist. (2 John 1:7)

To deny that Christ is fully God and fully man, possessing a human body like ours and a human soul like ours, sin excepted, is of the spirit of antichrist. To go further and state that Christ was man before the incarnation at Bethlehem is also the spirit of antichrist denying that He came as He did. The teaching of the eternal humanity of Christ, that He was man before the virgin birth, is not only heresy but it is apostasy. Those who teach such should be marked, reproved, and removed from any position of responsibility in Christianity. The slightest deviation on the doctrine of Christ, and His blood, results in heresy and apostasy of this ilk.

* * *

Jesus Christ was God.

For unto us a child is born, unto us a son is given: and the government shall be upon his shoulder: and his name shall be called Wonderful, Counsellor, The mighty God, The everlasting Father, The Prince of Peace. (Isaiah 9:6)

But thou, Bethlehem Ephratah, though *thou be little among the thousands of Judah,* yet *out of thee shall he come forth unto me* that is *to be ruler in Israel; whose goings forth* have been *from of old, from everlasting. (Micah 5:2)*

And Simon Peter answered and said, Thou art the Christ, the Son of the living God. (Matthew 16:16)

1 *In the beginning was the Word, and the Word was with God, and the Word was God.*

2 *The same was in the beginning with God. (John 1:1-2)*

And declared to be *the Son of God with power, according to the spirit of holiness, by the resurrection from the dead: (Romans 1:4)*

Whose are *the fathers, and of whom as concerning the flesh Christ* came, *who is over all, God blessed for ever. Amen. (Romans 9:5)*

15 *Who is the image of the invisible God, the firstborn of every creature:*

16 *For by him were all things created, that are in heaven, and that are in earth, visible and invisible, whether* they be *thrones, or dominions, or principalities, or powers: all things were created by him, and for him:*

17 *And he is before all things, and by him all things consist. (Colossians 1:15-17)*

For in him dwelleth all the fulness of the Godhead bodily. (Colossians 2:9)

And without controversy great is the mystery of godliness: God was manifest in the flesh, justified in the Spirit, seen of angels, preached unto the Gentiles, believed on in the world, received up into glory. (1 Timothy 3:16)

14 *That thou keep* this *commandment without spot, unrebukeable, until the appearing of our Lord Jesus Christ:*

15 *Which in his times he shall shew,* who is *the blessed and only Potentate, the King of kings, and Lord of lords;*

(1 Tim 6:14-15)

3 *Who being the brightness of* his *glory, and the express image of his person, and upholding all things by the word of his power, when he had by himself purged our sins, sat down on the right hand of the Majesty on high;*

8 *But unto the Son* he saith, *Thy throne, O God,* is *for ever and ever: a sceptre of righteousness* is *the sceptre of thy kingdom.*

10 *And, Thou, Lord, in the beginning hast laid the foundation of the earth; and the heavens are the works of thine hands:*

11 *They shall perish; but thou remainest; and they all shall wax old as doth a garment;*

12 *And as a vesture shalt thou fold them up, and they shall be changed: but thou art the same, and thy years shall not fail. (Hebrews 1:3, 8, 10-12)*

And he hath on his *vesture and on his thigh a name written, KING OF KINGS, AND LORD OF LORDS. (Revelation 19:16)*

Jesus said unto them, Verily, verily, I say unto you, Before Abraham was, I am. (John 8:58)

And now, O Father, glorify thou me with thine own self with the glory which I had with thee before the world was. (John 17:5)

Father, I will that they also, whom thou hast given me, be with me where I am; that they may behold my glory, which thou hast given me: for thou lovedst me before the foundation of the world. (John 17:24)

Without father, without mother, without descent, having neither beginning of days, nor end of life; but made like unto the Son of God; abideth a priest continually. (Hebrews 7:3)

I am Alpha and Omega, the beginning and the end, the first and the last. (Revelation 22:13)

6 *Who, being in the form of God, thought it not robbery to be equal with God:*

> 9 *Wherefore God also hath highly exalted him, and given him a name which is above every name:*
> 10 *That at the name of Jesus every knee should bow, of* things *in heaven, and* things *in earth, and* things *under the earth;*
> 11 *And that every tongue should confess that Jesus Christ is Lord, to the glory of God the Father. (Philippians 2:6, 9-11)*
>
> *But to us* there is but *one God, the Father, of whom* are *all things, and we in him; and one Lord Jesus Christ, by whom* are *all things, and we by him. (1 Corinthians 8:6)*
>
> *And to make all* men *see what* is *the fellowship of the mystery, which from the beginning of the world hath been hid in God, who created all things by Jesus Christ: (Ephesians 3:9)*

Jesus Christ was not a god. Jesus Christ was and is God. Just as the humanity of Jesus Christ, conceived by the Holy Ghost in the womb of the virgin Mary, could not be known or proven but from Scriptures, so too His deity could not be known without the truthful testimony of the inspired Word of God. The conception by the Holy Ghost in the womb of the virgin Mary is alone sufficient to indicate that he who was so conceived and born was not to be an ordinary man. Quite the contrary is true, He was declared to be the Son of God. As such, it follows that He was to be a partaker of that divine nature inherent in deity. He was God. He was not part God and part man. He was not something between God and man, as the ancient heathen demigods were and as some today would have Him to be. It has been shown that He was properly a man, sin excepted, and now can be shown that He was properly God in the fullest.

Proofs on this point are abundant and so only a few will be chosen for sake of brevity.

The names of God are ascribed to Jesus Christ.

This is most clearly seen in John 1:1, "*The Word was God.*" It is John's design in writing the gospel, and later his epistles, to introduce us to the One in whom we have placed our faith. He gets very specific. The Word became flesh.

> *And the Word was made flesh, and dwelt among us, (and we beheld his glory, the glory as of the only begotten of the Father,) full of grace and truth. (John 1:14)*

The Word dwelt among us and His name was Jesus Christ. The name of the Word was used by John in writing the book of Revelation when referring to Christ.

> *And he* was *clothed with a vesture dipped in blood: and his name is called The Word of God. (Revelation 19:13)*

What a hoax John would have perpetrated upon all of Christianity if he started out his gospel account with a lie and misled the followers of Jesus if Jesus were only man.

The Apostle Paul explicitly states the humanity and Godhood of Jesus Christ in Romans 9:5, "*Whose are the fathers, and of whom as concerning the flesh Christ came, who is over all, God blessed for ever. Amen.*" In addition to His humanity, His divinity is clearly brought out. He was more than man; above that, He was over all, God blessed for ever.

Jesus Christ did not correct or rebuke Thomas when he said, *"My Lord and my God."*

> *And Thomas answered and said unto him, My Lord and my God. (John 20:28)*

A very brief exclamation, but to the point. Had this statement not been true, Jesus would have been encouraging His disciples in idolatry.

Paul was not confused when he wrote in Hebrews 1:8, *"Thy throne, O God, is for ever."* He was simply telling us who Jesus was and is — God.

The attributes of God are ascribed to Jesus Christ. The first attribute to consider is eternity. The prophet Isaiah, when prophesying the first advent of Christ, said, *"His name shall be called...the Everlasting Father." (Isaiah 9:6)* The name, or term, Everlasting Father has specific reference to God's eternal existence, without beginning and without ending. Since Isaiah wrote under the inspiration of the Holy Ghost, we must accept that this name was not inappropriate for Jesus Christ.

Another prophet, Micah, in writing of the coming of Christ said, *"whose goings forth have been from of old, from everlasting." (Micah 5:2)* Just to make sure that the application of this prophecy was not misunderstood, the Holy Ghost inspired Matthew to apply it to Jesus Christ.

> *And thou Bethlehem,* in *the land of Juda, art not the least among the princes of Juda: for out of thee shall come a Governor, that shall rule my people Israel. (Matthew 2:6)*

The book of Proverbs introduces wisdom as an adumbration (foreshadowing, symbol, prefiguring) of Christ in the eighth chapter. John 1:1-3, 1 Corinthians 1:24, 30 clearly make New Testament application of wisdom as Christ who is eternal.

Of course, the testimony of Christ Himself is that He is eternal.

> *Jesus said unto them, Verily, verily, I say unto you, Before Abraham was, I am. (John 8:58)*

When He claimed to be pre-existent to Abraham, He was not speaking of His human nature. His divine nature, the person of the Son of God, the eternal "I AM" spoke. That was the precise language of the Old Testament and the Pharisees understood exactly what Christ was saying. He wasn't claiming to be older than Abraham physically, He was exclaiming His deity and equality with the Father. That is why they wanted to stone Him. He was actually claiming to be God. And God He was, in the flesh, standing before them. Jesus Christ is eternal.

The next attribute to consider is the immutability of God. Two verses ascribe this attribute to Jesus Christ.

> *Jesus Christ the same yesterday, and to day, and for ever. (Hebrews 13:8)*
>
> *They shall perish; but thou remainest; and they all shall wax old as doth a garment; And as a vesture shalt thou fold them up, and they shall be changed: but thou art the same, and thy years shall not fail. (Hebrews 1:11, 12)*

Jesus Christ has not and cannot change.

Christ claimed the attribute of omnipresence when He promised His disciples that He would be with them always, even until the end of the world.

> *Teaching them to observe all things whatsoever I have commanded you: and, lo, I am with you alway,* even *unto the end of the world. Amen. (Matthew 28:20)*

He also stated that where two or three are gathered together in His name, He would be in the midst.

> *For where two or three are gathered together in my name, there am I in the midst of them. (Matthew 18:20)*

In order to do these, He would of necessity have to be omnipresent, present everywhere always.

He claimed to be both on earth and in Heaven at the same time.

> *And no man hath ascended up to heaven, but he that came down from heaven,* even *the Son of man which is in heaven. (John 3:13)*

This also would require the attribute of omnipresence since He was standing on earth when He said it. This requires the exercise of His divine nature, not His body. As God, Jesus Christ was and is omnipresent. As man, He stood before them.

Jesus Christ was omniscient. This means that He was all-knowing. He knew the thoughts of man.

> *And needed not that any should testify of man: for he knew what was in man. (John 2:25)*

In Jeremiah, God says,

> *I the LORD search the heart,* I *try the reins, even to give every man according to his ways,* and *according to the fruit of his doings. (Jeremiah 17:10)*

This very attribute is expressly claimed by Jesus Christ as He addresses the Church at Thyatira in Revelation 2:23, *"...and all the churches shall know that I am he which searcheth the reins and hearts."* Peter appealed to the omniscience of Christ in defense when Christ questioned his love for Him.

> *He saith unto him the third time, Simon,* son *of Jonas, lovest thou me? Peter was grieved because he said unto him the third time, Lovest thou me? And he said unto him, Lord, thou knowest all things; thou knowest that I love thee. Jesus saith unto him, Feed my sheep. (John 21:17)*

Jesus Christ is omniscient.

Jesus Christ is omnipotent. This is seen in the works of His hands which shall shortly be discussed. The Apostle Paul appealed to His power when he said he could do all things through Christ.

> *I can do all things through Christ which strengtheneth me. (Philippians 4:13)*

Christ was claiming omnipotence with the Father in describing the work of the Son with the Father.

> 17 *But Jesus answered them, My Father worketh hitherto, and I work.*
> 18 *Therefore the Jews sought the more to kill him, because he not only had broken the sabbath, but said also that God was his Father, making himself equal with God.*
> 19 *Then answered Jesus and said unto them, Verily, verily, I say unto you, The Son can do nothing of himself, but what he seeth the Father do: for what things soever he doeth, these also doeth the Son likewise. (John 5:17-19)*

John, under inspiration of the Holy Ghost, calls Christ the Almighty.

> *I am Alpha and Omega, the beginning and the ending, saith the Lord, which is, and which was, and which is to come, the Almighty. (Revelation 1:8)*

Jesus Christ is omnipotent.

The works of Christ are described as divine. The foremost of these works is creation.

> *All things were made by him; and without him was not any thing made that was made. (John 1:3)*
> *And to make all* men *see what* is *the fellowship of the mystery, which*

from the beginning of the world hath been hid in God, who created all things by Jesus Christ: (Ephesians 3:9)

For by him were all things created, that are in heaven, and that are in earth, visible and invisible, whether they be *thrones, or dominions, or principalities, or powers: all things were created by him, and for him: (Colossians 1:16)*

For it became him, for whom are *all things, and by whom* are *all things, in bringing many sons unto glory, to make the captain of their salvation perfect through sufferings. (Hebrews 2:10)*

Thou art worthy, O Lord, to receive glory and honour and power: for thou hast created all things, and for thy pleasure they are and were created. (Revelation 4:11)

Jesus Christ is the Creator. The Son of God cooperated with the Father in the work of creation, and did so as supreme and sovereign God. He sustains the world and all creation by the word of His power.

Who being the brightness of his *glory, and the express image of his person, and upholding all things by the word of his power, when he had by himself purged our sins, sat down on the right hand of the Majesty on high; (Hebrews 1:3)*

15 *Who is the image of the invisible God, the firstborn of every creature:*

16 *For by him were all things created, that are in heaven, and that are in earth, visible and invisible, whether* they be *thrones, or dominions, or principalities, or powers: all things were created by him, and for him:*

17 *And he is before all things, and by him all things consist. (Colossians 1:15-17)*

When the disciples performed miracles, they did so in the name of Jesus Christ and with His power and authority.

And when Peter saw it, *he answered unto the people, Ye men of Israel, why marvel ye at this? or why look ye so earnestly on us, as though by our own power or holiness we had made this man to walk? (Acts 3:12)*

Be it known unto you all, and to all the people of Israel, that by the name of Jesus Christ of Nazareth, whom ye crucified, whom God raised from the dead, even *by him doth this man stand here before you whole. (Acts 4:10)*

But when Christ raised the dead and performed miracles, He claimed the power He exercised when performing the miracles.

For as the Father raiseth up the dead, and quickeneth them; *even so the Son quickeneth whom he will. (John 5:21)*

Of course, all was done in subjection to the Father's will. Jesus Christ forgave sins, a prerogative only of God to do.

> 1 *And he entered into a ship, and passed over, and came into his own city.*
> 2 *And, behold, they brought to him a man sick of the palsy, lying on a bed: and Jesus seeing their faith said unto the sick of the palsy; Son, be of good cheer; thy sins be forgiven thee. (Matthew 9:1-2)*

A yet future work of Christ is when He shall sit in final judgement as God.

> *For the Father judgeth no man, but hath committed all judgment unto the Son: (John 5:22)*
> *And he commanded us to preach unto the people, and to testify that it is he which was ordained of God* to be *the Judge of quick and dead. (Acts 10:42)*
> *But why dost thou judge thy brother? or why dost thou set at nought thy brother? for we shall all stand before the judgment seat of Christ. (Romans 14:10)*

The works of Jesus Christ are the works of God.

Jesus Christ is equated with Jehovah, God, of the Old Testament.

> *The voice of him that crieth in the wilderness, Prepare ye the way of the*

LORD, make straight in the desert a highway for our God. (Isaiah 40:3)

In those days came John the Baptist, preaching in the wilderness of Judaea,

2 *And saying, Repent ye: for the kingdom of heaven is at hand.*

3 *For this is he that was spoken of by the prophet Esaias, saying, The voice of one crying in the wilderness, Prepare ye the way of the Lord, make his paths straight.*

(Matthew 3:1-3)

21 *Tell ye, and bring* them *near; yea, let them take counsel together: who hath declared this from ancient time?* who *hath told it from that time?* have *not I the LORD? and* there is *no God else beside me; a just God and a Saviour;* there is *none beside me.*

22 *Look unto me, and be ye saved, all the ends of the earth: for I* am *God, and* there is *none else.*

23 *I have sworn by myself, the word is gone out of my mouth* in *righteousness, and shall not return, That unto me every knee shall bow, every tongue shall swear.*

(Isaiah 45:21-23)

9 *Wherefore God also hath highly exalted him, and given him a name which is above every name:*

10 *That at the name of Jesus every knee should bow, of* things *in heaven, and* things *in earth, and* things *under the earth;*

11 *And* that *every tongue should confess that Jesus Christ* is *Lord, to the glory of God the Father. (Philippians 2:9-11)*

And I will pour upon the house of David, and upon the inhabitants of Jerusalem, the spirit of grace and of supplications: and they shall look upon me whom they have pierced, and they shall mourn for him, as one mourneth for his *only* son, *and shall be in bitterness for him, as one that is in bitterness for* his *firstborn. (Zechariah 12:10)*

And again another scripture saith, They shall look on him whom they pierced. (John 19:37)

Jesus Christ claimed to be God.

Therefore the Jews sought the more to kill him, because he not only had broken the sabbath, but said also that God was his Father, making himself equal with God.

(John 5:18)

69 *Hereafter shall the Son of man sit on the right hand of the power of God.*

70 *Then said they all, Art thou then the Son of God? And he said unto them, Ye say that I am.*

71 *And they said, What need we any further witness? for we ourselves have heard of his own mouth. (Luke 22:69-71)*

Jesus said unto them, Verily, verily, I say unto you, Before Abraham was, I am. (John 8:58)

I and my *Father are one. (John 10:30)*

But if I do, though ye believe not me, believe the works: that ye may know, and believe, that the Father is *in me, and I in him. (John 10:38)*

He receives worship both of angels and men, this worship being commanded.

And as they went to tell his disciples, behold, Jesus met them, saying, All hail. And they came and held him by the feet, and worshipped him. (Matthew 28:9)

And again, when he bringeth in the firstbegotten into the world, he saith, And let all the angels of God worship him. (Hebrews 1:6)

12 *Saying with a loud voice, Worthy is the Lamb that was slain to receive power, and riches, and wisdom, and strength, and honour, and glory, and blessing.*

13 *And every creature which is in heaven, and on the earth, and under the earth, and such as are in the sea, and all that are in them, heard I saying, Blessing, and honour, and glory, and power,* be *unto him that sitteth upon the throne, and unto the Lamb for ever and ever. (Revelation 5:12-13)*

And he said, Lord, I believe. And he worshipped him.
(John 9:38)
And Thomas answered and said unto him, My Lord and my God. (John 20:28)
And they worshipped him, and returned to Jerusalem with great joy: (Luke 24:52)

If Jesus Christ was not God, then He was a liar, a fake, and justly condemned to death by the Jewish authorities. He got what was coming to Him, if He were not God. This argument is not made with any irreverence or appearance of such, but is an argument from facts in the Word of God. For, if Jesus were rightly judged to die for claiming to be God, then He is another Jesus from the Gospel of God, simply a man like any other, subject to the judgement of the Sanhedrin.

When asked by the High Priest in Luke 22:67, "Art thou the Christ?" He could answer in the affirmative without possibility of blasphemy and condemnation. But when asked a few verses later in 22:70, "Art thou the Son of God?" His answer became the grounds of their judging Him worthy of death. If His claim were a false one, He was correctly judged and condemned. However, although condemned by the council, God justified Him and His claim by raising Him from the dead after three days.

And declared to be *the Son of God with power, according to the spirit of holiness, by the resurrection from the dead: (Romans 1:4)*

Jesus Christ was fully man and fully God. He was man as He as God created man to be and was God as God is from eternity. This involved the union of two natures, human and divine, in one person, Jesus Christ of Nazareth. Understanding the union of the two natures is a prerequisite to understanding how He came, who He was, and consequently the nature and significance of His blood.

Jesus Christ referred to Himself often by one of two names: the Son of God and the Son of Man. Both names were used by Him and the writers of Scripture to denote one and the same person — Jesus Christ of Nazareth. In John 5:25-27, Jesus calls Himself both the Son of God and the Son of Man in the passage.

The attributes of one nature are ascribed to His person, and referenced by the name deriving from His other nature. For example, in John 3:13 Jesus said, "*And no man hath ascended up to heaven, but he that came down from heaven, even the Son of man which is in heaven.*" He here attributes omnipresence, a divine nature attribute, to His person referred to as the Son of man, His name deriving from His human nature. Another example is in Mark 2:28 where Jesus Christ claims that "the Son of man is Lord of the sabbath." His sovereignty over the sabbath belongs to His divine nature, but He refers to Himself by His human nature, the Son of man. Divine attributes are ascribed to the person of Christ in His humanity because of the indissoluble union of the two natures. He is one person having two natures in perfect union. Examples of the converse can be found where human attributes are ascribed to the person referred to by His divine name.

The perfect union of the two natures in no way or manner affects the characteristics peculiar to each. They remain distinct and identifiable, without commingling. His divinity is not humanized nor His humanity deified by actions or attributes originating from one of the two natures. How this perfect union of two natures so vastly different could be so, man cannot fully comprehend. But observation and study of the revelation of God by God reveals much to be learned about the person Jesus Christ and the nature of the perfect union of the two natures.

The first observation is that the perfect union of the divine and human natures resulted in one person. That person was Jesus Christ of Nazareth, the Son of God, God the Son, and called the Son of Man. This one person had one mind, one will, one set of emotions. He was not confused at any point concerning which nature to employ, He was one person and acted accordingly. There was complete coherence in His personality and actions.

The second observation is that the perfect union of the divine and human natures was complete and all encompassing. Jesus Christ did not act as God on some occasions and as man on other occasions as the circumstances might have dictated. He could not have behaved as God while walking the earth as man for no man hath seen God at any time.

> *No man hath seen God at any time; the only begotten Son, which is in the bosom of the Father, he hath declared* him. *(John 1:18)*

That is, no man can see God behaving as God, in the fullness of glory, majesty and power. But men and women, boys and girls, saw Jesus Christ who said in John 14:9, *"He that hath seen me hath seen the Father."*

It cannot be said that Christ performed miracles as God and suffered as man upon the cross. This would be to divide the person and confound the two natures. He was and is at all times and in all ways the God-Man. And He acted as such. He never had a conversation between His two natures. He is constantly and universally referred to in the singular. Conversely, God who is Triune, a unity in plurality, could discuss creation between the persons of the

Trinity, and could discuss the situation in Israel in the presence of Isaiah.

> *And God said, Let us make man in our image, after our likeness: and let them have dominion over the fish of the sea, and over the fowl of the air, and over the cattle, and over all the earth, and over every creeping thing that creepeth upon the earth. (Genesis 1:26)*
>
> *Also I heard the voice of the Lord, saying, Whom shall I send, and who will go for us? Then said I, Here* am *I; send me. (Isaiah 6:8)*

The third observation is that the perfect union of the divine and human natures was constant. This has been seen in the previous paragraphs. Some have tried to explain the hypostatic union and the nature of the God-Man by attributing some of His works and words as God and some as man. Both the divine and human natures were constantly present, active and in full capacity; guaranteed to be so by the divinely designed hypostatic union of the two natures in one person.

The fourth observation is that the perfect union of the divine and human natures is eternal and indissoluble. Christ did not discard His human flesh when He rose from the dead. When He appeared to His disciples just prior to His ascension He told them to handle Him because He was not a spirit; He had the same body that was crucified, blood excepted; He had flesh and bones.

> *Behold my hands and my feet, that it is I myself: handle me, and see; for a spirit hath not flesh and bones, as ye see me have. (Luke 24:39)*

> *And when he had so said, he shewed unto them* his *hands and his side. Then were the disciples glad, when they saw the Lord. (John 20:20)*

The Lord "*Jesus Christ the same yesterday, and to day, and for ever" (Hebrews 13:8)* will forever be the God-Man, the Lamb in the midst of the throne, appearing in His glorified humanity and who alone is worthy of worship and praise.

> *For the Lamb which is in the midst of the throne shall feed them, and shall lead them unto living fountains of waters: and God shall wipe away all tears from their eyes.*
> *(Revelation 7:17)*
>
> *Thou art worthy, O Lord, to receive glory and honour and power: for thou hast created all things, and for thy pleasure they are and were created. (Revelation 4:11)*
>
> *Saying with a loud voice, Worthy is the Lamb that was slain to receive power, and riches, and wisdom, and strength, and honour, and glory, and blessing. (Revelation 5:12)*

The Son of God we worship today, and will worship throughout eternity is both God and man, the God-Man. The human body and nature that was perfectly united with the divine nature in the womb of the virgin Mary; was born in Bethlehem; grew in stature; walked among men; was crucified on Golgotha; this same body is now seated at the right hand of the throne of God.[5]

Who being the brightness of his *glory, and the express image of his person, and upholding all things by the word of his power, when he had by himself purged our sins, sat down on the right hand of the Majesty on high; (Hebrews 1:3)*

24 *But this* man, *because he continueth ever, hath an unchangeable priesthood.*

25 *Wherefore he is able also to save them to the uttermost that come unto God by him, seeing he ever liveth to make intercession for them. (Hebrews 7:24-25)*

For there is *one God, and one mediator between God and men, the man Christ Jesus; (1 Timothy 2:5)*

---

[1] Footnote to Matthew 13:11

[2] Walvoord, John, Jesus Christ our Lord, (Chicago: Moody Press, 1969)

[3] Louis Berkhof, Systematic Theology, (Grand Rapids, MI; Eerdmans Publishing Co., 1941), p. 321

[4] Calvin's Institutes, Book Second: Chapter 14.

[5] Hebrews 1:3; 7:24, 25; 1 Timothy 2:5

CHAPTER FOUR

HIS BIRTH AND HIS BLOOD

"Behold, a virgin shall conceive, and bear a son"
Isaiah 7:14

Jesus Christ became flesh and walked upon this earth as man.

> *And the Word was made flesh, and dwelt among us, (and we beheld his glory, the glory as of the only begotten*

of the Father,) full of grace and truth. (John 1:14)

Forasmuch then as the children are partakers of flesh and blood, he also himself likewise took part of the same; that through death he might destroy him that had the power of death, that is, the devil; (Hebrews 2:14)

And looking upon Jesus as he walked, he saith, Behold the Lamb of God! (John 1:36)

After these things Jesus walked in Galilee: for he would not walk in Jewry, because the Jews sought to kill him. (John 7:1)

And Jesus walked in the temple in Solomon's porch. (John 10:23)

This involved the doctrines of the kenosis and hypostatic union that have been discussed. These concepts describe the nature of Christ as man and as God. That He came is evident and who He was while on earth in His humiliation is seen in the study of the union of His two natures.

The difference between the Incarnation and the virgin birth of our Lord was pointed out earlier. The Incarnation is the fact that He became flesh and the virgin birth is the method by which He chose to take upon Him the form of a servant, of the seed of Abraham.

For verily he took not on him the nature of *angels; but he took on* him *the seed of Abraham. (Hebrews 2:16)*

Of course, this was not the only method He could have chosen to come as a man. He is not limited in the methods from which to choose. He is the infinite and sovereign God. The theophanies (a physical presentation or personal manifestation of the presence of God to man[1]) in the Old Testament illustrate that He could have just appeared on the scene as a man as He did when He appeared to Joshua.

> 13 *And it came to pass, when Joshua was by Jericho, that he lifted up his eyes and looked, and, behold, there stood a man over against him with his sword drawn in his hand: and Joshua went unto him, and said unto him,* Art *thou for us, or for our adversaries?*
> 14 *And he said, Nay; but* as *captain of the host of the LORD am I now come. And Joshua fell on his face to the earth, and did worship, and said unto him, What saith my lord unto his servant?*
> 15 *And the captain of the LORD'S host said unto Joshua, Loose thy shoe from off thy foot; for the place whereon thou standest* is *holy. And Joshua did so. (Joshua 5:13-15)*

As such, He would appear to the human eye as a man and be easily mistaken as just like any other man. Joshua thought He was a man when He appeared to Joshua outside Jericho.

Then Jesus spoke. When Joshua recognized who He was, he worshipped Him and was not rebuked for doing so because He was worthy of worship. What caused Joshua to recognize this man as the Lord of Heaven? It is true that God illumines our understanding and opens our spiritual eyes to perceive and behold His truth; but, could it be that

Joshua recognized the voice of the One whom he had heard before? Did Joshua instantly become aware that he was hearing and seeing the One who spoke with Moses in the tabernacle and on the Mount?

Joshua was Moses' minister and went where Moses went or was not far off. Maybe Joshua heard God speak on the mount and maybe he did not. As Moses met with God in the tabernacle and Joshua waited outside, could Joshua have overheard the conversation? Maybe Moses told Joshua so much about the Lord in their many discussions that Joshua was very familiar with Him. The Bible does not tell us what caused Joshua to recognize Him as the Lord. It is evident that the Lord's statement combined with Joshua's familiarity with the voice of Him whom he served caused him to instantly be aware of the presence of God.

Are we that familiar with God's voice that we recognize when He is speaking? Do we spend enough time in close communion with Him to instantly recognize His voice and His presence that causes in us immediate worship and obedience?

This was not the appearance of an angel or any other created being, but a preincarnate appearance of the Son of God in human form. Likewise, He could have simply appeared full grown as a man, in the form of a servant, 2000 years ago to the Jews. That was an option open to Him before the foundation of the world. But He did not choose that method to come as the Messiah and Redeemer.

The method of incarnation chosen by God for His Son to accomplish the purpose of God's counsel from before the foundation of the earth was the virgin birth. The doctrine of the virgin birth of Christ is not a take it or leave it proposition in Scripture. It is not up for debate. It is not open to interpretation. The virgin birth of Christ is one of the foundation doctrines of Christianity and it is to be rejected at man's peril. Rejection of the virgin birth causes Christianity to crumble. If the virgin birth is not a fact, all other doctrines concerning Christ and the Word of God are destroyed. If the virgin birth is not a fact, then thirty (30) books of the Bible are unreliable because they are written by men who taught the virgin birth.[2] Next to the verbal plenary inspiration and inerrancy of Scripture, the virgin birth of Jesus Christ is a test for true Christianity.

The virgin birth can be studied from four perspectives: prophetic, historic, physiological, theological. The first three will be discussed here and the theological significance of the virgin birth will be discussed later.

The first perspective of the virgin birth is prophetic. Three Old Testament writers wrote of the birth of Christ: Moses, Isaiah, and Jeremiah. Moses wrote of the virgin birth under the inspiration of the Holy Ghost in Genesis 3:15,

> *"And I will put enmity between thee and the woman, and between thy seed and **her seed**; it shall bruise thy head, and thou shalt bruise his heel."(Emphasis added).*

In Biblical hermeneutics (the study of the general principles of Biblical interpretation), there is a principle called the First Mention Principle. This is the principle by which God, who wrote the Word of God using human authors, indicates in the first mention of a subject the truth with which that subject stands connected in the mind of God. The first time a subject or topic is mentioned in the Bible determines the meaning it will carry with it throughout the rest of Scripture. This is not surprising given that there is only one Author of Scripture and many human instruments. The immutability of God is transferred to His Word. In other words, God will not say and mean one thing in the Old Testament then say and mean something else in the New Testament when referring to a subject or topic.

In Genesis 3:15, God is revealing for the first time that there is salvation available for man and in so doing implies the virgin birth when speaking of the "seed" of the woman. The Saviour was not to have a human father or descend from the seed of man, but of the woman, thereby not inheriting the sinful Adamic nature of fallen man. God would be the Father of His only begotten Son and the woman, a virgin, would give birth to "her seed."

Isaiah is where the most well known verse is found proclaiming the virgin birth.

> *Therefore the Lord himself shall give you a sign; Behold, a virgin shall conceive, and bear a son, and shall call his name Immanuel. (Isaiah 7:14)*

Some have argued that Isaiah did not mean a "virgin" but rather a "young maid" when he wrote this prophecy. This is not a new argument. It has been around a long time. But, please keep in mind that longevity does not equate to correctness or validity. Although the Hebrew word "*almah*' may be translated either way, it has been shown conclusively in Hebrew studies that in the other passages where it occurs that it is impossible to prove in any of these occurrences that the word means anything else other than "virgin."

The context in which Isaiah is speaking demands the use of "virgin." It would not have been a sign for anyone or anything for a maid to have a child. That would not have been very extraordinary. On the contrary, it is normality and generally not noteworthy as regards prophecy. For Isaiah to have declared that a maid was going to have a child and that this birth was a sign to the Jews would have gotten him laughed out of town and ignored. That kind of birth would not have fit in any way into prophecy or been of any significance to the Jewish nation.

Another principle of hermeneutics is applicable here, and that is the Progressive Mention Principle. That is the principle by which God makes the revelation of any given truth increasingly more clear as the Word of God proceeds to its consummation. As the Word of God is read further from beginning to end in chronological order, a progression of details brings into clearer focus the truths God wants to teach the sincere searcher.

In Isaiah, the use of the Hebrew word "*almah*" was not by mistake although a different word, "*bethulah*" could have been used to indicate a virgin. The difference is significant. *Bethulah* suggests the state of a maiden who is living with her parents, and whose marriage is not yet impending. On the other hand, *almah* indicates a maid who has been withheld from intimacy with a man, but who is approaching readiness to engage in marriage. The choice of words becomes evidently clear and mandatory when considered in connection with the Gospel accounts of the birth of Christ by Mary. Citing Isaiah in relation to the birth of Christ, Matthew points out the fulfillment of prophecy to the Jews.

> 22 *Now all this was done, that it might be fulfilled which was spoken of the Lord by the prophet, saying,*
>
> 23 *Behold, a virgin shall be with child, and shall bring forth a son, and they shall call his name Emmanuel, which being interpreted is, God with us. (Matthew 1:22-23)*

The third Old Testament writer of prophesy of the virgin birth is Jeremiah.

> *"How long wilt thou go about, O thou backsliding daughter? for the*

LORD hath created a new thing in the earth, A woman shall compass a man." (Jeremiah 31:22)

This verse clearly presents and teaches not only the virgin birth but the direct involvement of God in the process. Although women have been giving birth to men since Eve's firstborn, Cain, the emphasis in this passage of Scripture is not on the latter portion, *"A woman shall compass a man,"* but rather on the middle phrase, *"for the LORD hath created a new thing in the earth."* The two taken together describe the virgin birth.

The key to the passage is the Hebrew word *bara*, translated "created" in English. The new thing that the LORD created is that a woman shall compass a man. This requires an event or thing that is unique in history and experience, not just another birth of a baby boy. The word *bara* is always used with God as the subject and is of profound theological significance. The consequent theological significance of this event, the LORD creating a new thing, a woman compassing a man, produces a physiologically significant event — a conception and birth like no other. To the Jews, this was to be a sign as well as an encouragement that their Creator-God will provide.

The verb *bara* expresses creation out of nothing and emphasizes the initiation of the object by divine action. The object here is the baby boy to be born of woman. A careful study of the passages where this term occurs will show that the writer uses precise language to declare that God was the initiator and creator of the object, bringing it into being from previously non-existent material. The use of this word in Old Testament writings is limited to divine activity exclusive of any effort or part by man and completely outside of human ability. As shall be seen in a later discussion of the nature of the virgin birth, this act of God in bringing into existence a new thing from previously non-existent material does not necessarily preclude the use of previously existent material in combination with the new.

A good example of this is the creation of Adam. Adam was formed by God his Creator of the dust of the ground, a previously existing material. After God formed man from the dust of the ground, He breathed into his nostrils the breath of life. A "new thing" had been created: man. Herein is obtained a correct understanding and perspective of the nature of the virgin birth. The primary emphasis seen in the use of this word is on the newness and uniqueness of the created object as a direct result of Divine activity.

The object in this passage in Jeremiah is more specific than the man child. Given that Jesus Christ, the Son of God, is eternally pre-existent, it was impossible for Him to be created or brought into existence by the virgin birth. More specifically, it is the human body, flesh and blood, the form of the servant, prepared by God for the Son.

> *Wherefore when he cometh into the world, he saith, Sacrifice and offering thou wouldest not, but a body hast thou prepared me: (Hebrews 10:5)*

This body, as seen in the study of the union of two natures, was more than just a tabernacle for Deity to dwell in, but was a fully human body, with a human nature (sin excepted) in which the divine nature dwelt in complete harmony with the human nature. This was a "new thing" created by God and possible only through the virgin birth — the God-Man.

This verse is misused by over-zealous defenders of the blood of Christ. Defense of anything, including the blood of Christ, taken to the extreme often leads to erroneous conclusions and erroneous teaching. That is the case with the misinterpretation of this verse.

As we saw in the chapter on the kenosis, everything about the body of our Lord was and is human, sin excepted. To state, as some do today, that "Christ's blood is divine, not human, because it was prepared by God," using Hebrews 10:5 as a proof text, is to miss the mark. First, His blood was and is human, sin excepted, as this study shall bear out. If His blood was not human He could not be and was not the kinsman redeemer. Second, this verse is misinterpreted and taken out of context to prove that His blood was not human. Finally, to assert that His blood was divine and not human misses the central truth of the hypostatic union. These people who hold such a position do not understand or accept that His blood could be both divine and human at the very same time. It was and is both divine and human.

Of course, the question arises at this point that if this verse teaches that His blood was not human because God prepared it, then His body was not human because God prepared it also according to this verse. If His body were not human, then what was it? If His body were not human what was He? He could not have been the God-Man. By asking these questions we are not denying the divinity of Jesus Christ. We affirm His deity. But at the same time we must affirm His humanity as the God-Man.

Another question that arises from the flawed logic that states His blood was not human because it was prepared by God as evidenced by Hebrews 10:5 is, Was Adam's body (blood) divine and not human because it too was prepared (formed) by God? This sort of flawed logic in the extreme defense of truth leads to error and confusion. We are best served by simply sticking with the clear teaching of Scripture from Genesis to the Revelation. The clear teaching of Scripture in Hebrews 10:5 does not support the argument that Christ's blood was not human because it was prepared by God.

There are some old and often repeated Hermeneutical rules of Biblical interpretation that must be looked at. One of these rules quoted so frequently is that the words of Scripture should be understood in their literal sense, unless such literal interpretation involves a manifest contradiction or absurdity. In practice, this manner of interpretation is merely an appeal to every man's rational judgement. What seems absurd or improbable to one person, may be regarded as perfectly simple and straightforward by another.

Another rule heard so often is when the plain sense of Scripture makes common sense, seek no other sense, but take every word in its primary, literal meaning unless the facts of the immediate context clearly indicate otherwise. As with the previous rule, this one seems to make man's common sense the judge of Scripture. This cannot be the basis for interpreting the Bible. Quite often, when God speaks His truth it does not measure down to our common sense; but it is God's Word none the less. Just because we do not understand something is no criterion for interpretation. One man's common sense is nonsense to another man. Absent from this process is the teaching of the Holy Spirit who will lead us into all truth.

After stating that the words should be taken literally, this latter rule adds a caveat concerning immediate context. As mentioned earlier, text out of context is pretext. However, missing from the equation is remote context. These rules should be abandoned for proper Biblical interpretation principles that have held to the truth down through the millennia. The Bible must be interpreted by the literal, grammatical, historical, and theological principles of hermeneutics. The Context Principle of Biblical interpretation is that principle by which God gives light upon a subject through either near or remote passages bearing upon the same theme. Every sentence or verse in the Bible has something that precedes it and something that follows it — except Genesis 1:1 and Revelation 22:21.

The near context will throw light on Scripture and explain passages that are dark and difficult to understand. Sometimes the context is not only near but remote, especially in the study of types and anti-types. Everything must be studied in light of the entire Bible which is one organic whole. If an interpretation fits one place but not in another in context, the interpretation must be rethought. Properly interpreted, the passage will fit in context both near and remote.

In looking at this passage in Hebrews, we must first consider to whom it was originally written. That does not mean it has no application to or for us today. We must simply put the book of Hebrews in its historical setting. The book of Hebrews can be considered the doctrinal primer for Jewish believers as the book of Romans can be considered the doctrinal primer for Gentile believers. The Apostle Paul wrote both books. (There is some minor debate concerning his authorship of Hebrews, but is not substantial enough to discount his authorship.)

This in mind we observe that death is very prominent in the Epistle to the Romans with blood mentioned only three times. Conversely, in Hebrews blood is the prominent of the two, death and blood. The reason for this is the cultural and religious background of the saints to whom Paul was writing. Furthermore, Hebrews provides an excellent commentary for both the Jews of his day and believers of our day on the book of Leviticus. Hebrews was written primarily with Jews in mind who were familiar with the Old Testament sacrifices and the typology for which they stood.

The focus of the book of Hebrews is a person. That person is our Lord Jesus Christ. It presents Him as not only better than all the former things, but a fulfillment and antitype of them. By the time the reader gets to Chapter ten he is reminded of the utter insufficiency of the sacrifices under the law to do what was needed to take away sin or perfect the worshipper. The contrast is then presented in Christ whose sacrifice was of an infinite virtue and worth and efficacy to take away sin forever. Again, the focus is on Christ and His sacrifice. But it was a peculiar and particular type of sacrifice of which the Jews were intimately aware. A sacrifice of death through the shedding of blood, that blood containing the life poured out in death as an acceptable substitute for the worshipper.

That is the context, both near and remote, in Hebrews 10. The context is sacrifice for the taking away of sin. The direct connection between the blood of bulls and goats on the one hand and the body of Christ on the other is not focused on the blood but on sacrifice. In both instances blood was required and necessary. In the former, the blood was inferior. In the latter, the blood was more than superior, it was the blood of the Son of God. But the focus is past the blood to the sacrifice.

Verse five begins with *wherefore*, introducing the proof of the argument by Paul of the invalidity of the former sacrifices and the efficacy of the one sacrifice of Christ. He does this by quoting from the Psalms a passage that could only have its full meaning and completion in the Messiah. That passage is Psalm 40:6-8. Paul emphasizes two very significant phrases from the Psalm: a body hast thou prepared for me, and lo, I come to do thy will, O God.

Having just written of the sacrifices under the law, he shows that they never were what God really willed: they were but shadows pointing to something better, to a spiritual reality, a life in the body given up to the will of God. This was divine prophecy revealing Christ in His humiliation and humanity. God the Son, eternally preexistent with the Father and the Spirit before His incarnation, when He was coming into this world through the virgin birth, to become part of this world by uniting a holy human nature to the divine nature, reminds the Father that the sacrifices and offerings under the law were not what He really desired. They could not take away sin.

"But a body hast thou prepared me." This is a key phrase. Abandoning sound principles of interpretation at this point leave us stranded on uncertain ground. To examine only the word *prepared* from the original language and make application based upon that to the body and blood of Christ is unsound. Since God the Father "prepared" the body for the Son is not the reason He was divine. He was divine because He was God the Son incarnate. If He was divine because God prepared His body, Adam was divine because God there literally formed and prepared Adam's body from the dust of the earth. That is false logic. Jesus Christ was divine simply and only because He was God the Son.

To further carry the false thinking to the blood, it is asserted that since His body was divine, having been prepared by the Father, His blood was divine because His entire body with all its components were divine. This reduces the focus from that intended by God through the Apostle Paul to simply a matter of physiological components.

Indeed, the body prepared by the Father was prepared differently than ours because that which was united with the egg of Mary was done so in the power of the Holy Ghost, as discussed previously. But focus must be maintained upon that which is of importance in this passage. Preparation of the body is not the subject nor the focus, with the requisite quality of the blood. Rather, the focus is on sacrifice. Again, this is not at the expense of the preciousness of the blood of Christ; it is to remain true to Scripture to learn what Scripture has to tell us.

"But a body hast thou prepared me." This expression does not appear in Psalm 40:6-8:

> 6 *Sacrifice and offering thou didst not desire;* ***mine ears hast thou opened****: burnt offering and sin offering hast thou not required.*
>
> 7 *Then said I, Lo, I come: in the volume of the book* it is *written of me,*
>
> 8 *I delight to do thy will, O my God: yea, thy law* is *within my heart. (Emphasis added.)*

The expression appearing in the Psalm is *"mine ears hast thou opened."* Paul, in quoting the Psalm, does so from the Septuagint, which is the Greek translation of the Old Testament. In the Septuagint the phrase was changed from *"mine ears hast thou opened"* to *"a body hast thou prepared me."* How this change arose we do not know, but since the change is included in the canon of Scripture through apostolic authority we accept it as no mistake by the writer and a reading equally inspired. In any case, this passage speaks of the Son of God as coming into the world at His incarnation equipped for service; and that service in a real and material body, by actual life and death, setting aside all the types and shadows of the law that went before.

"Mine ears hast thou opened." This speaks of the Messiah's instant and unqualified obedience to do His Father's will. The prompt obedience of our Lord is the main thought and focus of this phrase. This phrase comes from the practice of boring the ear of a servant who refused, out of love for his master, to take his liberty and be free to do as he pleases. His perforated ear was a token of perpetual service. It is spoken of in the singular, the ear. Here we have *ears*. This is a true picture of our Lord's absolute fidelity to the Father and the Father's will. Jesus gave Himself irrevocably up to be the servant of servants for our sake and for His Father's glory. Thus were His

"ears bored" which could not have been had He not assumed and been clothed with a human body.

Christ's assuming a human body in order to die the death of a slave was a voluntary submission to the Father's service. The preparation of a body for Him is not with a view to His incarnation merely, but to His expiatory sacrifice in contrast to the sacrifices and offerings under the law.

The focus in this passage is not on the preparation but on the body and the blood; especially, in this case, the body. Instead of the sacrifices that went before, God prepared a body for Christ which He so offered up or sacrificed that we have now been sanctified by the offering of the body of Jesus Christ once for all. Andrew Murray puts it this way:

> Christ's body was to Him just what any man's is to him — the dwelling and organ of the soul; the channel for intercourse with the outer world, susceptible of impressions of pleasure and of pain, and therefore one of the first occasions of temptation. His body was a part of His human personality and life. He was in danger, just as we are, of using the body for His own service or pleasure, a means of gratifying self. But He never did this. He was filled with one thought — God prepared Me this body; I have it for His disposal, for His service and glory; I hold it ready every moment to be a sacrifice to Him. The body comes from God; it belongs to Him; it has no object of existence but to please Him. The one

value my body has is, that I can give it a sacrifice to God.

That is the main thrust of the phrase. As Christ obediently and without question assumed the body prepared for Him by the Father in which to make His self-sacrifice, so ought we present our bodies to the Father a living sacrifice; it is only reasonable. (Romans 12:1)

The focus of Hebrews 10:5 has been contorted by those who would look only at the individual words and derive from them a meaning beyond their intent that the Father prepared a body for Christ that was somehow not human, but looked human. The true meaning has been shown to be far more than that. The true meaning includes His divinity, not based upon the source of His body, but based upon who He is — the Son of God, God the Son.

The second perspective of the virgin birth is historical. Four writers of the New Testament were inspired by God to write about the virgin birth of Jesus Christ. These writers are Matthew, Luke, John, and Paul.

Matthew very clearly understood the prophecy concerning the birth of Jesus Christ and made it clear in his writings that Mary was a virgin until the birth of Christ. He plainly states that this birth was the fulfillment of the prophecy given in Isaiah 7:14.

> *Therefore the Lord himself shall give you a sign; Behold, a virgin shall conceive, and bear a son, and shall call his name Immanuel. (Isaiah 7:14)*
>
> 22 *Now all this was done, that it might be fulfilled which was spoken of the Lord by the prophet, saying,*
>
> 23 *Behold, a virgin shall be with child, and shall bring forth a son, and*

they shall call his name Emmanuel, which being interpreted is, God with us. (Matthew 1:22-23)

Twice in the account of the birth of Christ in the first chapter of his gospel, Matthew states that the Holy Spirit was the source of Mary's son.

> 18 *Now the birth of Jesus Christ was on this wise: When as his mother Mary was espoused to Joseph, before they came together, she was found with child of the Holy Ghost.*
>
> 20 *But while he thought on these things, behold, the angel of the Lord appeared unto him in a dream, saying, Joseph, thou son of David, fear not to take unto thee Mary thy wife: for that which is conceived in her is of the Holy Ghost. (Matthew 1:18, 20)*

Matthew was very careful to list Joseph as the husband of Mary and not to list him as the father of Jesus. This is not by accident. No other genealogy contains such wording. The marriage by Joseph to Mary was with his full and complete understanding of her condition and the source of that condition. Joseph did not have physical relations with Mary until after the birth of Christ.

> *And knew her not till she had brought forth her firstborn son: and he called his name JESUS. (Matthew 1:25)*

Also notice in verse twenty-five of the first chapter of Matthew's gospel that the baby is referred to as "her firstborn son" and not as "Joseph's son" or "his son" or even as "their son."

Luke was a medical doctor as well as an historian and writer. He was concerned with detail and accuracy. He referred to Mary as a virgin two times in the first chapter of the Gospel that bears his name.

> *To a virgin espoused to a man whose name was Joseph, of the house of David; and the virgin's name* was *Mary. (Luke 1:27)*

He recorded her conversation with the angel and the question she had concerning the angel's message. She asked the angel how it was possible for this thing to be "seeing I know not a man."

> *Then said Mary unto the angel, How shall this be, seeing I know not a man? (Luke 1:34)*

Luke presents the virgin birth through carefully selected phrases and names when referring to Jesus Christ. He calls Him "the Son of the Highest" and "the Son of God."

> 32 *He shall be great, and shall be called the Son of the Highest: and the Lord God shall give unto him the throne of his father David:*
>
> 35 *And the angel answered and said unto her, The Holy Ghost shall come upon thee, and the power of the Highest shall overshadow thee: therefore also that holy thing which*

shall be born of thee shall be called the Son of God. (Luke 1:32, 35)

Nowhere does Luke refer to Christ as the son of Joseph or to Joseph as His father. Luke, as a medical doctor and historian, would have investigated this account thoroughly before setting out to write it down so that we might "know the certainty of those things."

That thou mightest know the certainty of those things, wherein thou hast been instructed. (Luke 1:4)

John presents the historical aspect of the virgin birth through the most unusual of sources, the Pharisees. Jesus plainly told them that He came from His Father in Heaven. The Jewish leaders responded by saying that Abraham was their father. Then they made the accusation that Jesus was born out of wedlock. It is apparent from this statement by the Jewish leaders, who would have been well informed on all the latest rumors and gossip, that Mary's condition before the marriage to Joseph was well known by all. This so-called knowledge gives historical credibility to the virgin birth and that Joseph was not the father of Christ because the Jews would have been very careful to have their facts straight and supportable. So far as the Jewish leaders were concerned, Joseph was not the father and the father was unknown to them. Sadly, this was truly the case. The Jews did not really know the Father whom Jesus came to manifest so clearly to the house of Israel.

The virgin birth of Christ is clearly taught in Scripture from the prophetic and historic perspectives. This fact is acknowledged and accepted. The third perspective by which to approach the virgin birth is physiological.

Before proceeding to discuss the physiology of the virgin birth of Jesus Christ, an admonition given by Milne is valuable to consider.

> On the other hand there is a danger of building too much on the virgin birth. All it implies is that Jesus' human nature was not derived as is ours from a human father. The Scriptures, however, nowhere cast God the Father in the role of the male progenitor supplying the male chromosomes for the developing foetus. A moment's reflection shows the questionableness of this position, for a being so produced would certainly not be a true God-Man, but a half-human hybrid. A similar view of Jesus arose in the 5th century and was declared heretical.[3]

We might add that this position is still heresy today. For an independent, fundamental Baptist, or any preacher for that matter, to teach that God the Father has a corporeal body is heretical and falls into the category of cult teaching. Those preachers are to be marked and avoided.

There is more to be implied from the virgin birth than simply the source of the human nature of Christ. The point to be taken from Milne's quote is that excesses have arisen in defense and declaration of the virgin birth that have severe adverse and heretical implications. Great care should be exercised in this matter. As we shall see, statements made and positions taken ostensibly in support of the virgin birth when taken to their normal and logical conclusion may produce heresy at worst and confused and ill informed Christians at best. This admonition must be kept in mind as we pursue the physiological perspective of the virgin birth.

Two sources of information are consulted when studying the physiology of the virgin birth of Christ. They are Scripture, which is primary, and nature. All truth is God's truth. This premise is true whether that truth be found in Scripture or in creation for both have the same author. Since both have the same author, they must and do agree in unity. They cannot be contradictory. This is not to suggest that God cannot operate outside of His creation and outside the physical laws He has established for its conduct. He is sovereign and does as He pleases. But it does suggest that in search of the truth it can be found in both creation and the Scriptures. God's revelation consists of His written Word and His creation.

> *Whatsoever the LORD pleased,* that *did he in heaven, and in earth, in the seas, and all deep places. (Psalms 135:6)*
>
> 19 *Because that which may be known of God is manifest in them; for God hath shewed* it *unto them.*
>
> 20 *For the invisible things of him from the creation of the world are clearly seen, being understood by the things that are made,* even *his eternal power and Godhead; so that they are without excuse: (Romans 1:19-20)*

Care must be exercised in searching for truth. Three approaches can be used: from the point of view of revelation only, from revelation plus reason, and from reason alone.[4] Reason alone as an approach is rejected because that ends up with rationalism and humanism, rejecting God's truth, making man the measure of all things. Revelation alone involves the danger of not employing the reasoning capacity given to man by God to be used under the control and influence of the Spirit of God. Thus, revelation plus reason, reason guided by the Spirit of Truth, will lead to apprehending and discovering new aspects of the truth revealed by God in His Word and His creation.

Revelation is found in only two places — the Bible and Creation. There is no new revelation from God today as is preached by many televangelists. Confusion results from such so-called revelation which is contradictory to the already revealed Word of God. Those who say they have a new revelation from God lie.

Where there appears to be disagreement between Scripture and scientific observation, several considerations must be made. First, the disagreement may be perceptual and not actual. This would be the result of our limited knowledge in either of the two realms of revelation, Scripture and creation. Second, the basis of the disagreement may be incorrect measurements and incorrect conclusions within nature. This has been seen repeatedly in the creation-evolution debate as so-called facts of science have been disproved and the Bible found to be true. Third, we must accept that there are things in both Scripture and creation that cannot be understood by the mind of man and must be accepted, apprehended and appropriated by faith. The integration of faith and learning in these areas does not compromise the validity of God's truth but allows us to grow in the knowledge of God and His creation while we "see through a glass darkly."[5] The ultimate criterion of truth, however, remains God's written Word which sheds much light on His creation.

Scriptures and nature reveal all we can know about the virgin birth of Christ. Where Scriptures and physiology contradict or appear in disagreement, the Scriptures are the final authority.

What do we know?

He was born of a woman. In the birth of human beings there are mysteries that go beyond the understanding or mere speculation of man and enter realms best left unexplored because neither science nor reason can enter there. At that point we must heed the admonition, "We ought not to be wise above that which is written." One of these mysteries is that at conception an immaterial intangible principle or substance, the human soul, is joined in unity of life with the tangible material substance, the physical visible body, and from that point the integrated whole develops into the person that is born. This union happens conjointly with the union of the 23 chromosomes from the mother and the 23 chromosomes from the father. The resultant cell, or zygote, contains all the genetic material for the development of the individual person conceived as well as the intangible substance, that which is known as the soul.

Contained in this united cell is the human nature of that distinct person known by God. In the case of our Lord, the union of the Logos, the Son of God, deity, the divine nature, coincided with the supernatural conception wrought by the Holy Ghost resulting in Christ having not only a human nature (received from His mother) but the divine nature which is eternally pre-existent and one with the Father. Thus, He who was born of Mary could be called in all truth and exclusive sense the Son of God.

This understanding of the conception and birth of our Lord stands in opposition to the Anabaptists who believed that the Lord brought His human nature with Him from heaven, and that Mary was merely and simply a channel or conduit through which He passed with His nature. If the Anabaptist position is believed, this presents a problem with His nature. It would mean that His nature was really a new creation, similar to ours, but not exactly like ours nor organically connected to ours. The doctrinal importance of this is readily apparent in its shortcomings and error. If the human nature of Christ was not derived from his mother Mary, it was then not derived from the same stock as ours, that is human, but only resembled it. Were this true, the necessary relationship that must exist between us and Christ for Him to be the Kinsman Redeemer and Mediator of and for mankind does not exist and He could not and did not save man for He was not an acceptable substitute.

Our Lord's human nature was conceived in the womb of Mary by the power of the Holy Ghost and without the means or assistance of a man. This sets the conception of Christ apart from all other conceptions in its supernaturalness and allows Him to be properly called the Son of God. The work of the Holy Ghost in connection with the conception of Jesus Christ was twofold: (1) He was the efficient cause of what was conceived in the womb of Mary, and thus the activity of a man was excluded in its entirety. This allows for the fact that the person born of Mary was not a fallen man, but the person of the Son of God, who as such was fully human and fully divine, thereby free from guilt and outside of the covenant of works under which man was then born. (2) The Holy Ghost sanctified the human nature of Christ in and from its very conception and inception, thus keeping the human nature of Christ completely free from sin. How the fallen nature of man is passed on to his offspring is still a mystery. But we do know that it must of necessity involve a fallen father. The birth of our Lord could not then, and in fact did not, involve a human father.

The divine nature and the human nature were united within the single cell formed at conception in the womb of the virgin Mary. From this we understand that the second person of the Trinity was present at conception and was present throughout the pregnancy, birth, childhood, and adult ministry of our Lord.

39 *And Mary arose in those days,*
and went into the hill country with haste,
into a city of Juda;

40 *And entered into the house of Zacharias, and saluted Elisabeth.*

41 *And it came to pass, that, when Elisabeth heard the salutation of Mary, the babe leaped in her womb; and Elisabeth was filled with the Holy Ghost:*

42 *And she spake out with a loud voice, and said, Blessed* art *thou among women, and blessed* is *the fruit of thy womb.*

43 *And whence* is *this to me, that the mother of my Lord should come to me?*

44 *For, lo, as soon as the voice of thy salutation sounded in mine ears, the babe leaped in my womb for joy. (Luke 1:39-44)*

He came at conception and stayed until His ascension. That which was conceived in Mary, that single cell of 46 chromosomes, the zygote, the result of the overpowering of the Holy Ghost, was divine, deity, the Son of God, the Son of Man, had two natures in perfect union, and was the God-Man.

Concerning that which occurred at conception from the physiological standpoint, we approach from the perspective of before and after. Simply put, what was there before the overpowering of the Holy Ghost and what was there after the overpowering of the Holy Ghost? At this point, reason under the guidance and influence of the Holy Ghost in conjunction with revealed Scripture and science must direct our thinking.

Prior to the overshadowing of Mary by the Holy Ghost, Mary was a virgin. Of course, she remained a virgin until after the birth of Christ. But at the occasion of the overshadowing, she was a normal virgin woman. Approximately nine months later, Jesus was born. Moving backward from the birth to the conception would reveal the normal development of a human, albeit in this case that being was divine. Physically, the baby developed normally from a single cell with 46 chromosomes and was born a natural human birth. The baby, if truly human, and truly human He was, originated from the union of 23 chromosomes from the mother, Mary, and 23 chromosomes from the father, in this case, not a human father. The 23 chromosomes from the mother were necessary to provide His humanity which is required for the purpose for which He came. These 23 chromosomes were present in an egg in the womb of Mary.

The additional 23 chromosomes necessary for the development of a human baby must of necessity come from one of two sources — a human father, or supernaturally from God. There are no other alternatives. They did not come from a human father. Also of importance is the fact that they did not come physically from God the Father. God the Father was not the male progenitor supplying a "divine sperm" to fertilize the egg in Mary. This process would have produced a demi-god, a semi-divine being (as the offspring of a deity and a mortal) thought to possess less power than a god.[6] To take this position would be to teach that God the Father has a corporeal body. That is heresy. "God is a spirit."

> *God* is *a Spirit: and they that worship him must worship* him *in spirit and in truth. (John 4:24)*

Another misconception about the birth of Christ is that the embryo, an already fertilized egg of divine origin, was implanted in the womb of Mary. This could not be the case and our Lord Jesus Christ still be qualified for what

He came to do and be. More on this later in the theological section. Further, He would not have been human as we in the truest sense, but only man-like in appearance.

Whence the 23 chromosomes from the father?

Was it even necessary for there to be these 23 chromosomes to unite with those of the mother?

Could God produce a man in the womb of a virgin without them?

Of course the answer to this last question is the same any time the question is asked, "Could (can) God ...?" With God, nothing is impossible.

> *For with God nothing shall be impossible. (Luke 1:37)*

However, common sense and reason guided by an understanding of the Scriptures lead to a conclusion that a normal human must have 46 chromosomes to be human. Otherwise, they are not human.

Returning to the question, "Whence the 23 chromosomes?", there is only one possible answer — God. God, through the "power of the Highest," and through the person of the Holy Ghost, placed the necessary 23 chromosomes in the selected egg of Mary to unite with the 23 chromosomes of the mother in order to produce the divine zygote, a single human cell, from which would develop a normal human body and individual. Whether that was in the form of a sperm or just the uniting of the chromosomes is not deducible at this time or even relevant.

> *And the angel answered and said unto her, The Holy Ghost shall come upon thee, and the power of the Highest shall overshadow thee: therefore also that holy thing which shall be born of*

thee shall be called the Son of God. (Luke 1:35)

How could God do that? Again, the answer is clear — because He is God! The creator God who spoke the universe and all its elements into existence, who formed man from the dust of the ground and breathed into his nostrils the breath of life, this creator God could very easily place 23 chromosomes, 23 human chromosomes with the DNA of a man as God created man to be, into the egg of a woman, a virgin, and have conceived therein a man-child. These 23 chromosomes, in whatever form — sperm or separate — were from previously non-existent material as revealed by Isaiah.

Nonetheless, they are not less than nor more than human. That bears repeating for emphasis — the union of 23 chromosomes with the 23 chromosomes in the egg of the virgin Mary resulted in a single cell that was neither less than nor more than human, sin excepted. Of course, that conception resulted in the Son of God with the attendant presence of His divine nature uniting in perfect harmony with the human nature at the moment of conception. The result was the Son of God, a person fully man and fully God.

Such conception would produce a person fully man in all respects, sin excepted, physiologically. Everything about Him would be exactly like His brethren. Also, by the introduction of the divine nature at conception, He is fully God. Everything about Him would be divine, though veiled in flesh. Christ was just as divine as if He were not human, and just as human (sin excepted) as if He were not divine. The Son manifested the Father.[7]

No man hath seen God at any time; the only begotten Son, which is in

> *the bosom of the Father, he hath declared* him. *(John 1:18)*

Physiologically, the conception included the normal egg in the womb of a virgin being united with the necessary 23 human chromosomes implanted by God Himself, from previously non-existent material. The product of such conception was that Jesus Christ was 100% fully man in all respects — everything about Him physiologically: skin, hair, eyes, fingernails, internal organs, cardio-vascular system, bodily processes, even His blood, everything was human only possessed by the divine nature in union with the human nature. This is a mystery; but a mystery that is comprehendible with prayerful reflection.

This method of the virgin birth of Christ fulfilled the prophetic requirement for a sign to the nation of Israel and allowed for the incarnation of the Son of God in a manner requisite for His redemptive purpose. Two thousand years ago, a virgin birth, a baby born to a woman that had never known a man, was a physiological impossibility to man. Thus, when Christ was born in such a way, it was truly a sign to Israel. Today, however, a woman can give birth to a baby, without knowing a man in a physical relationship, through the processes of artificial insemination. This leads to the possibility of a "virgin" giving birth. Today, such a birth would not be a sign. Of course, any baby born in such a fashion today would still be the fallen progeny of a fallen man. Such could not be the case for the true Messiah.

The virgin birth of Christ is a matter of great theological importance. As mentioned earlier, if Christ was not man (sin excepted) we are still in our sin. The logic of God's plan of salvation and redemption of man excludes any possibility of a concept that man evolved from animals, even if many "creative interferences" are allowed for. The creation of Adam by direct act of God was an absolutely unique and intentional event showing us what the nature and constitution of Adam's body must have been in order to satisfy God's requirement for a truly substitutionary sacrifice in the death of Christ.

Redemption is the great thought of God. Only He could have formulated the Plan of Redemption as it is found in the Bible. And this Plan is founded upon not only His grace and mercy, but also originates primarily with His love which is a manifestative love. He first loved then He created. The Plan of Redemption preceded the Plan of Creation from God's perspective. The Plan of Redemption as conceived by God drove the train, so to speak, for the way He created man. This shall become increasingly clearer as this study progresses.

Man was created in such a form that the Fall of man into sin was possible but not inevitable. He need not have sinned. Man chose disobedience over obedience by an act of his free will. All of this was an essential step in revealing God's redemptive love. The whole story of Eden was preparatory to Calvary. Calvary was therefore conceived before Eden. The manifestation of God's love and who God is and what God is centers around and focuses upon the Cross of Calvary. From that point, creation was formulated.

The manifestation of His love at Calvary was even the reason He created man. He did not need fellowship because He is self sufficient and self existent. He needs no one or nothing. He is God. But He desired to manifest His love. It pleased God to manifest His love and He does whatever pleases Him. And when He created man in the form that He did, it pleased Him because He saw it as preparatory and necessary for Calvary.

The Crucifixion was not an emergency measure implemented by God to correct something that had gone wrong. The Crucifixion was the focal point from before the beginning. What happened to the First Adam has everything to do with what not only happened to the

Second Adam but what was achieved by the Second Adam. Tampering with the Fall of man in Eden and what happened to Adam renders Calvary meaningless.

The transition from Eden to Calvary must of necessity go through the Virgin Birth and Incarnation. Although there is a miraculous aspect to these and they are beyond scientific analysis, they are not completely out of reach of understanding as the Holy Ghost leads us into all truth. Scientific knowledge and analysis that has only recently come to light serves to increase our wonder without diminishing in the least the miracle of it all. If there is knowledge and light now available upon a subject, we should not reject it for fear of reducing faith. On the contrary, faith remains the basis of understanding and is only strengthened and enhanced as we progress in knowledge. In fact, the further we investigate the more assured we become that our faith is not random or arbitrary. Just the opposite. Our faith becomes vindicated as the Word of God continues to prove true over and over again.

This is exciting. The perfection of God's plan from the beginning is in complete harmony with what is now known in science or better stated is that what we now know in science is coming into harmony with God's plan as revealed in Scripture. The eyes of our understanding slowly become opened. No born again believer should ever apologize for exercising faith. Faith has placed them in a position far ahead of current scientific knowledge.

Let us be very clear concerning the miraculous. Just because we understand some aspects better as the result of modern research does not mean there is a lessening or even removal of the miraculous. The fact of the supernatural aspects of the Virgin Birth and Incarnation remain despite advances in scientific knowledge. We simply understand better what has happened from a scientific perspective. That which we are unable to understand from a scientific perspective, we understand by faith. The two do not conflict. There is nothing wrong with that.

The object in understanding various aspects of the Virgin Birth is not to make it easier for skeptics to believe or accept. That is ridiculous and unbiblical. Saving faith is never generated by intellectual persuasion of observable facts. Saving faith is a gift from God and must be exercised by each individual as they are convicted by the Holy Ghost of their sinful condition and their need of salvation. Rather, the object in mind as we explore scientific aspects of the creation of man and the Virgin Birth is to enlarge our sense of wonder that an infinitely Holy and wise God should have designed the processes of conception and birth in such a way that He could use them without doing violence to His own created order that He might enter into our world of space and time in the likeness of ourselves.

Oh, the wonder of that thought in itself! The Psalmist declares that God humbles Himself to even behold His creation, much less enter into His creation as man.

One more thing must be cleared up at this point. Some may feel that it is inappropriate to discuss or look into such areas. They may even consider it irreverent to do so. This is not the case. Far from it. It is with utmost reverence and awe that we approach a study of this nature totally dependent upon God's Holy Spirit for illumination and careful to insure that He is well pleased and all glory and honor are unto the Father. As we mentioned in the introduction, we simply must get better acquainted with Him.

Before returning to the Virgin Birth, the concept of immortality must be briefly introduced. In this context, immortality does not mean that man cannot be put death or die; it means that he need not die. It was not impossible for Adam to die, but it was possible for him not to die. There is clear distinction.

God is not immortal. Yes it is true that God cannot die. But God is not immortal, God is the self-sufficient, self-existent One. He inhabits eternity. He is separate and distinct, outside of His creation which includes immortality. So God is not immortal, but is God who inhabits eternity. This shall be more applicable as we discuss Jesus Christ as God and Man.

Adam was created immortal. It was possible for him to die; but it was not inevitable or even desirable. Adam was free to eat of the Tree of Life in the Garden. Until, of course, he sinned. Then Adam was driven by God from the Garden and an angel posted at the entrance to the Garden to prevent Adam from partaking of the Tree of Life. Had he partaken of the Tree of Life after falling into sin, immortality would once more have been restored consigning man to a fate of unending life as a sinful creature. A fate too terrible to comprehend. Had Adam not fallen into sin, Adam and Eve would have begotten immortal children who also had access to the Tree of Life.

But Adam fell into sin and died. The gift of immortality imparted to Adam by his Creator was lost. Adam died. Romans 5:12 tells us that not only did Adam die, but all men die because death was passed unto all men.

> 12 *Wherefore, as by one man sin entered into the world, and death by sin; and so death passed upon all men, for that all have sinned: (Romans 5:12)*

Strictly speaking, death, or the loss of immortality, a condition of mortality that was acquired by Adam is transmitted to all his descendents. It is a rare case indeed in the life sciences when an acquired characteristic is inherited. The rule is that an acquired characteristic is not transmitted to following generations. This rule destroys much of evolutionary theory.

A good example would be the loss of a limb. If for some reason, during the course of survival in the jungle, a monkey loses its arm and recovers to live and reproduce, it does not produce one-armed monkeys. Whatever characteristic is acquired by the parents is never passed on to following generations.

Except death.

This will be clearer and its application to the Virgin Birth seen after looking at some life sciences facts of how the seed is formed and reproduce.

As we saw earlier, life (and as we shall see, death also) is passed on to succeeding generations by the union of two seeds, one contributed by the father and one by the mother. This union results in the formation of the zygote which then divides into two cells, then four cells, then eight cells, then sixteen, then thirty-two cells. These thirty-two cells are known as the morula stage.

At this point a change takes place. A process of differentiation begins and a new type of cell arises by further division building around the original 32-cell morula a structure which is concerned primarily with providing a vehicle or carrier for the original germ cells. Prior to this process of differentiation, all the cells were duplicates of the original fertilized ovum. The new differentiated cells lack the total capacity of the germ cells. There is a distinction. The differentiated cells are known as the somatic cells or body cells. These somatic cells originate from the germ cells; but the germ cells never originate from the somatic cells.

The end result of the process is the completion of the body that is born nine months later and grows into adulthood. This body, by way of oversimplification, will release from itself ova, which when fertilized will initiate the next generation. And the process happens all over again. The germ cells do not only reproduce themselves, they ensure that a body is constructed around them as a carrier. The body of each generation dies, but the germ cells do not. The germ cells are potentially immortal. This point is fundamental. A closer look at the theory of the continuity of the germ cells (also called germ plasm) is needed.

This look at the theory of the continuity of the germ plasm, although somewhat drudgery, will be enlightening to our understanding of not only the Virgin Birth but also immortality to some degree. This theory submitted that a special hereditary substance known as the germ cells or germ plasm exists in all animal life forms, including man. Unlike the physical body (the somatoplasm) that degenerates and returns to dust, the germ plasm is transmitted from generation to generation essentially without modification. This germ plasm is derived solely from the reproductive cell of the parent. None of the characteristics of the germ plasm depend upon the somatoplasm or body of the parent. This theory has stood the test of time with minor qualifications. In fact, the theory has been substantiated in large part and to a surprising degree by genetic research.

A look at this theory in graphic form would be something like the following:

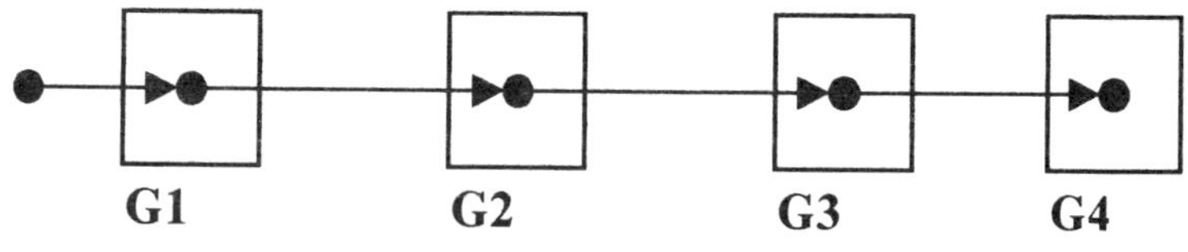

The black dot represents the fertilized seed, ovum, or germ plasm. The square represents the body, or somatoplasm, which carries it. The theory of continuity proposed that the germ plasm of succeeding generations derive solely and completely from the germ plasm of the preceding generation. This germ plasm then builds a body (soma) around itself without losing its own unique identity or integrity as germ plasm separate from somatoplasm. This is seen in the labels in the figure above. Generation four (G4) germ plasm derives from generation three (G3) and builds a body around itself. The same happens from two to three and one to two. The body built around the germ plasm is in no way responsible for the germ plasm carried therein.

Another graphical portrait of this process is seen below.

In this diagram, the germ plasm, or seed produces a body around itself and also reproduces itself, seed giving rise to seed in self perpetuation. The body is almost incidental to the seed but necessary to the seed. This view is held by virtually all present-day biologists as a result of genetic research and advances.

Foremost in our consideration is the fact that the body (soma) does not produce or generate the seed, but the seed generates itself and happens to also generate a body with which it is conveyed. From this fact we understand that nothing which happens to the body during its lifetime in any way influences or changes the seed or its characteristics except under very exceptional and well-recognized circumstances. Strictly speaking, the body is disposable but the seed is immortal. The body comes and goes; the seed perpetuates itself from generation to generation. And at this point we insert the observable Biblical fact that such perpetuation is "after its own kind (species)."

The seed is in fact not subject to natural death nor is it subject to modification of its character and integrity through happenings imposed upon the body that carries it. (A dog who tragically loses a leg in an accident does not give birth to three legged puppies; etc.) The very limited circumstance under which the seed is modified is an unnatural one and not inherent in the mechanism.

Adam was created an immortal being. He was not incapable of dying; but it was possible for him not to die. As a result of Adam's disobedience and fatal choice in the Garden, he acquired the characteristic of mortality through the judgment of God. Sentence was pronounced that "dying thou shalt die." Adam acquired the characteristic of mortality. Contrary to the normal process of hereditary transmission, this acquired characteristic of mortality was passed on to the offspring and seed of Adam. It becomes apparent, then, that not only was the body affected, but also the seed of man (germ plasm).

De Beer, a man strongly opposed to Christianity, observed that the doctrine of original sin involves the inheritance of an acquired character, for only genes can be inherited, and, by the nature of the case, neither Adam nor Eve when they first appeared on the scene possessed the character they are alleged to have transmitted to all their descendents.

The Bible speaks very plainly,

> *Wherefore, as by one man sin entered into the world, and death by sin; and so death passed upon all men, for that all have sinned: (Romans 5:12)*

Death entered into the world and mankind through one man, Adam. Not only that, death is then passed to all men because all men are sinners.

Since the body of an organism is derived from the germ plasm, and not the other way around, the body can only inherit what is part of the germ plasm or seed. The words germ plasm and seed will be used interchangeably for they are so in all practicality. Since the seed is not derived from the body (soma), it does not normally reflect in its character what has happened to the body in immediately preceding or even remote generations. A good example of this would be an experiment where the tails of rats were cut off and did not lead to any change resulting in tailless rats. It is only when a modification is so extreme and of such an unnatural character that the seed is also modified with the next and following generations inheriting the modification.

The acquired characteristic of mortality, therefore, must occur in such a way as to affect not only the body but the seed. Since the mortal condition acquired by Adam and Eve as the result of their disobedience was inherited by all following generations, death passing upon all men, it is necessary to understand that something happened to cause a permanent and inheritable change in the seed. This change must have happened to either the male seed or female seed, or to both. This is readily apparent and of physiological and theological significance.

Our knowledge, as a result of long and extensive research, of the seed of the woman, the ovum, leads us to the conclusion that its original potentially immortal endowment has by and large not been given up or affected. Normally, if not fertilized by the sperm, the ovum is rejected from the body and to all intents and purpose "killed" in the process. However, it is possible to induce a process of division entirely on its own. The result is a series of stages of development that are extremely similar to what would happen if fertilized by the spermatozoon. This process of division without the fertilization is known as parthenogenesis. In numerous cases of animals below man, this process has led to the birth of normal offspring. In mammals, it must be noted, parthenogenesis always leads to the birth of a female. Parthenogenesis cannot nor could not lead to the birth of a male child.

The male seed does not have this characteristic or potential for reasons beyond the scope of this study. Consequently, in the case of Adam and Eve who were both created as immortal, the result of the judgment of God upon them for their disobedience, from a biological and genetic perspective, seems to have had a more profound effect upon Adam's seed than upon Eve's seed. This is not inconsistent with Scripture.

> *And Adam called his wife's name Eve; because she was the mother of all living. (Genesis 3:20)*

This naming of Eve by Adam follows the pronouncement of the curse by God and imposition of the judgment of God. Eve quite literally became the mother of all living and Adam became the father of all dying as seen in Romans 5:12.

God created Adam from the dust of the ground. When He created Eve, He took Eve out of Adam. The "seed" prior to the creation of Eve was all contained in Adam. After Eve was taken out of Adam, the seed was now the seed of the man and the seed of the woman. In this way, it was possible for the curse to affect Adam and his seed in a different manner than the woman and her seed yet at the same time passing on to all succeeding generations the acquired characteristic of sinful mortality. This fashion of creation and judgment also made possible that the birth of the Immortal One who would redeem sinful man could be both the offspring of the seed of the woman and truly a Second Adam, all in accordance with Scripture and in fulfillment of God's plan of Redemption established before the foundation of the world.

Even though every child born of woman through natural generation since Adam fell has been mortal and sinful, facing certain death, the potential remained for the Immortal One to be born of woman and bring "life and immortality to light." We see, then, that the seed of the woman (not the woman herself) has been preserved by God intact from the very day that Eve was taken out of immortal Adam, and only needed to be vitalized by some other means than the seed of the man in order to bring forth "life and immortality" in the literal person of the God-Man, Jesus Christ, the promised One.

As seen elsewhere in this study, only one possessing immortality has the right and the ability to freely and voluntarily surrender his life as an act of self-sacrifice. All other so-called acts of self-sacrifice resulting in death are only a choice made by the person to change the time of inevitable death, for it is appointed to men to die. These acts are nothing more than premature deaths by an act of his will and a shortening of his life. But he does not surrender anything more than a few years. Compared to surrendering immortality, unending life, this is nothing. Only an immortal can surrender life itself and accept death by choice rather than by judgment. Our Lord Jesus Christ did not simply choose when to die, He was in a position of authority to choose whether to die or not to die at all.

That makes the person of the Goel (looked at in chapter 10) of utmost importance. The substitute for man must be man but with a choice of whether to die or not. He could not be under the death penalty under which all mankind exists.

Calvary preceded Eden in God's plan and purpose. It can be no other way. To put creation first and then Calvary is to reduce Calvary to an emergency measure on God's part to correct something that has gone wrong in creation.

God, who is love, and to manifest that love as only God can, started with Calvary where His love was manifest and then moved on to Eden in such a manner as to provide for Calvary. In other words, salvation is God's thought as well as creation. However, creation was dependent upon salvation for its design. Creation, especially that of man, was to be a means to an end, that end being Calvary, the manifestation of the love of God. Calvary dictated the design of creation to accommodate the capability in man to choose, and therefore to obey and love God or disobey and sin against God. But that capability in man could not interrupt or preclude the ability for God to come into the world as a man, as the God-Man, for the purpose of redeeming man from sin and restoring him to fellowship with God. That was to be through the seed of the woman.

Adam was created; then Eve was created by separating out of Adam the rib from which she was made. The seed that accompanied each was distinct yet originally of Adam, therefore human. The curse and judgment resulting from the Fall must affect man and woman alike, but not necessarily the seed. There is nothing arbitrary here nor extra-Biblical. Light has been and continues to be shed upon this through the truth of genetic science; and all truth is God's truth.

The Virgin Birth was not absent the miraculous nor was it absent the natural. Faith and understanding work together as we observe how complementary are the supernatural acts of God and the natural acts. Study of the Virgin Birth in this respect does not remove grounds for faith, but, rather, enlarges our faith as we see a little bit more clearly and are led into deeper and deeper truths of our salvation and how God accomplished it at so great a price. Nothing in this study brings Christ lower nor elevates man. It should produce within the heart and soul of the earnest seeker a joy and wonder at God's great love toward us. It should produce a change in attitude and conduct. Only sin and pride gets in the way.

The question arises concerning the blood of Christ, which remains the central point of this investigation, given that He was fully man as well as fully God, "Was His blood different than our blood?" This question has caused much controversy, misunderstanding, and division within Christianity today. Much of that controversy is unnecessary due to the lack of understanding what someone is saying or the position that they hold regarding the blood of Christ. Differences have arisen between brethren simply over semantics. Arguments concerning the blood quite often arise over both sides saying the same thing in a different way using different words. Other differences arise when both sides are wrong and demonstrate a lack of understanding of the Scriptures and the nature of the birth, body, and blood of our Lord Jesus Christ.

Was His blood different than our blood? The answer to that question is twofold — Yes and No. That answer sounds like the kind of answer a Washington lawyer or politician would give. The twofold answer is not, however, intended to elude the issue. On the contrary, the answer to that specific question must be, as we shall soon see, both yes and no.

The question itself is vague in nature and akin to the question "Have you stopped beating your wife?" If you answer in the affirmative you are guilty and if you answer in the negative you are guilty. To this point in our investigation of the birth, body and blood of Christ, the answer to that question is "No." But we must proceed in our investigation.

The question "Was His blood different than our blood?" does not establish parameters or perspective for a concise answer. As mentioned in the previous paragraph, at this point in our investigation of the blood of Christ, the answer must be an emphatic "No" from the perspective of human physiology. He is the God-Man, fully God and *fully* human. We must emphasize that our Lord Jesus Christ was fully human (sin excepted) as He as God created man to be. Therefore, His blood was physiologically no different than our blood. It could not be otherwise. His blood that flowed through His arteries and veins, that was poured out in sacrifice upon Golgotha, and was presented to the Father in the Heavenly Holy of Holies consisted of the same components as our blood; it performed the same physiological functions as our blood; it was indistinguishable from our blood under the scrutiny of a microscope. He was man as we are man, sin excepted. His blood could be none other than the blood of a man, as He as God created man to be. An investigation of His DNA would reveal that it is the DNA of a man. Yet He is the God-Man. And THAT must be the focal point and departure point for any and all discussions regarding not only His humanity, but His blood.

His blood contained red blood cells that carried oxygen and nutrients throughout the body to maintain His human life. They were the normal red cells of a man. His blood contained white blood cells, plasma, fibrin, platelets and amino acids. His blood contained all the same components as our blood and functioned exactly as our blood in sustaining life while circulating throughout His body. This is, of course, of great encouragement. The sheer humanity of Christ encourages the soul as we understand that He identified with us and was touched with the feeling of our infirmities. Of course, He is God. We worship Him. But the fact of His humanity for 33 years provides us with not only encouragement but hope because He came as we are to deliver us from where we are and demonstrate an example of complete submission to the Father's will. As man, He submitted completely to the will of the Father. As man, we should submit completely to His will. He expects no less. We can have no more.

With apologies to Calvin,

> This observation, if the readers apply it properly, will be of no small use in solving a vast number of difficulties. For it is strange how the ignorant, nay, some who are not altogether without learning, are perplexed by [this] expression applied to Christ, without being properly adapted either to his divinity or his humanity, not considering their accordance with the character in which he was manifested as God and man. It is very easy to see how beautifully [this statement] (concerning His blood) accords with [his human as well as his divine nature], provided it is examined by a sober interpreter, one who examines this great mystery with the reverence which is meet. But there is nothing which furious and frantic spirits cannot throw into confusion. They fasten on the attributes of humanity to destroy his divinity; and, on the other hand, on those of his divinity to destroy his humanity. ...he is our Lord and the true Son of God, even according to his humanity, though not by means of his humanity.

One of those furious and frantic spirits of our day preaches that His blood "didn't rot and it didn't clot." Although not completely without learning, this demonstrates the horrors of unskilled labor in the study and proclamation of the Word. While this statement, "didn't rot and it didn't clot," has some truth in it, it also contains some very dangerous error. The man declaring this doctrine proclaims that the blood of Christ was different than our blood because it was the very blood of God, it was God's blood. He goes on to say that the clotting factor in human blood is the sin factor in the fallen nature. In other words, our blood clots because of sin present in the blood. This, of course, is in total disagreement with the teaching of the Bible concerning our sin nature and the seat of sin; not to mention in complete ignorance of human physiology.

This position would be laughable from its baseless foundation if it were not so dangerous in its implications and ramifications. As seen in the first section on the physiology of the blood of man, clotting is a function performed by the blood to preserve life through the arresting of blood loss through leaks in the circulatory system caused by disease or trauma. This function of clotting, a marvelous process not yet completely understood by modern medicine, is an intentional design by our Creator as part of the normal functioning and preservation of the body. It is normal and human for blood to clot. If the blood does not clot properly, a condition known as hemophilia, it is considered abnormal and a defect in that person who suffers from the abnormality. The clotting of blood, a purely physiological normal response by design of the Creator, is independent of the intangible presence of sin in the nature of man. There is absolutely no basis in Scripture or nature, our only two valid sources of revelation from God, for linking the clotting of human blood to the sin nature. It is beyond preposterous.

If the proposition is true that His blood did not clot, Jesus Christ would have been a hemophiliac. If He was a hemophiliac, He would have been in danger every day He worked in His earthly “father's” carpenter shop. He would have been susceptible to many and varied diseases. Most importantly, Jesus Christ would not have survived the beating by the Roman soldiers or the scourging before He was taken to Golgotha for crucifixion. He would have bled to death in Pilate's judgement hall. Any rational examination of the nature and results of a Roman beating and scourging would conclude that He would have bled to death as a man under such treatment. Even many not suffering from hemophilia died under the scourging of the Romans.

Jesus Christ was not a hemophiliac. His blood clotted, just like our blood clots. He did not lose all His blood on the floor of Pilate's judgment hall. He offered it upon the cross. Blood and water came forth from His side when pierced by the Roman soldier.

Another statement popular today in preaching about the blood is that the blood of Christ was the very blood of God. Simply stated, the blood of Christ was not "the very blood of God." This statement is similar to the question about the difference of the blood. It leaves out perspective and parameters. Jesus Christ is God, it is true. Hence, it is deduced that since He is God, His blood is the blood of God. So far so good; but the implications are dangerous in this regard.

The statement that the blood of Christ was the "very blood of God" implies that God has blood. God does not have blood. God is a Spirit. As spirit, He does not have blood. For God to have blood implies that God has a corporeal body of physicality and this is pure heresy and the doctrine of cults. Any one who teaches that God has a physical body is teaching a heresy that has been rejected for almost 2000 years by the true church. This teaching is cultic and must be exposed and avoided. Very simply, do not sit under the teaching or preaching of a person who teaches that God has a physical body with blood. Either he must be removed from his position or a Christian must depart that assembly.

God does not possess a physical body with blood nor is He the male progenitor physically of Christ in the womb of Mary. Jesus Christ, the Son of God, God the Son, has a glorified physical body present in Heaven today. He is the God-Man, second person of the Trinity. God the Father is spirit. The two must be kept distinct when discussing a body and blood.

The statement should be more accurately posited, "The blood of Christ is the very blood of the God-Man." This insures accuracy and removes room for cultic heretical errors concerning God the Father. This is not academic hairsplitting. The cults have made far too many inroads in drawing away earnest Christians by teaching partial truth mixed with heresy and apostasy. They are able to do so only because of the anemic preaching and teaching coming across the pulpits today. In the words of an old philosopher, "To lead an untrained people into war is to throw them away." In the spiritual warfare in which we find ourselves engaged, many pastors are ill equipping their congregations for the war and consequently they are easily drawn into popular cults and thrown away. A most detestable situation.

Some of the confusion surrounding this wrong teaching comes from statements concerning the source of a baby's blood. Some preaching and teaching today is medically errant, especially in the area of the blood of Christ. Sermons have been preached and books written stating that the baby's blood comes from the father and never mixes with the mother's blood. This is then presented as evidence that Christ was able to maintain sinlessness when in the womb and not contaminated with the sin nature of Adam, supposing in error that the blood contains the sin nature. Of course, these statements are medically incorrect and doctrinally in error.

The first section on the physiology of human blood described how the blood type is inherited from **both** biological parents. One gene from each parent is required to determine the blood type of the baby and the baby receives his blood type from this combination of genes. A baby derives his blood from both parents — not just from the father. This is a physiological fact and one that holds true in the case of our Lord.

An erroneous interpretation of Acts 20:28 leads to a misunderstanding concerning Christ's blood and its origin. Acts 20:28 states,

> *Take heed therefore unto yourselves, and to all the flock, over the which the Holy Ghost hath made you overseers, to feed the church of God, which he hath purchased with his own blood.*

This has been used by some to prove that God has blood and that He gave that blood to Christ with which He purchased the Church. Again, if God the Father has blood, we can only assume He has a corporeal body in which that blood resides. This is cultic belief. A proper exegesis of Acts 20:28 clarifies that which frantic spirits confuse and complicate.

The first mistake made by those frantic and confused spirits is that the verse is referring to God the Father. It is not. The Apostle is here affirming the deity of Jesus Christ by calling Him God. This position is held by such men as Matthew Poole, Matthew Henry, and Charles Spurgeon. I could not find a conservative Bible scholar who held that this refers to God the Father purchasing the Church with His (the Father's) blood. The whole context of the near and remote passages refers to Christ as God. He is called God in John 1. The apostles affirm in all their writings that Christ is God. And He is said to purchase His Church with His own blood.

That blood with which He purchased His Church was His as Man, yet subject to the union of the divine and human natures. In that regard it can be called the blood of the God-Man, Jesus Christ, the Lord from Heaven. This is so because it is the blood of Him who is God incarnate; and as such, placed eternal virtue and value in that blood that enabled Him to redeem us and pay the ransom due for our sin. If Christ had not been man, He could have no blood to shed: had He not been God, the blood which He shed could not have been a sufficient price of redemption.

In this verse the transcendent sacredness of the Church of Christ is made to rest upon the dignity of its Lord and the preciousness of that blood which He shed for it. Oh, the depths of the riches of the wisdom and knowledge of God who determined such a plan from the foundation of the world that manifested the breadth, depth, length, and height of the love of Christ for us that He paid such a ransom as this. To God only be the Glory; great things He has done!

Also pointed out in the opening section on the physiology of the blood is that within the placenta there is a mixing of elements from the baby's blood and the mother's blood. Only the red blood cells do not pass from one to the other through the wall of the placenta. All the necessary elements for sustaining life pass through the wall of the placenta. Nutrients, waste materials, antibodies, all pass from the mother to the baby and conversely. All the components of the blood are involved, except the red blood cells. There is mixing of the blood of the baby and the mother. Without this mixing the baby dies.

M. R. DeHaan in his book, *The Chemistry of the Blood*, confuses the issue with unclear statements and statements that are misunderstood and taken out of context..

On page 30 of the book he states,

> It is now definitely known that the blood which flows in an unborn babe's arteries and veins is not derived from the mother but is produced within the body of the foetus.[8]

This has been misinterpreted to mean that "a baby gets his blood from his father." This then is the basis for the argument that the blood of Christ was God's blood since God was the Father of Jesus Christ; hence, the blood of Christ was the very blood of God. The error in this is easily seen and explained.

A closer look at DeHaan's statement reveals that he is talking about the development of the blood within the fetus. Bones develop, muscle tissue develops, and all the organs develop. Fetal blood is developed and formed completely within the fetus and the mother does not produce blood which is then introduced into the fetus. The title of the subsection in his book begins the confusion. The title for that section is, "Origin of the Blood." DeHaan correctly states that the blood develops and forms solely within the fetus without direct contribution on the part of the mother with her blood. This is also true of the muscles, brain cells, bones, etc. Confusion enters with the word "derived" used by DeHaan when he states, "...not derived from the mother."

As seen above, no blood will develop without one gene from the father and one gene from the mother at conception. In this sense, the blood of the baby is derived from both mother and father.

He states on page 31,

> From the time of conception to the time of birth of the infant not One Single Drop of Blood ever passes from mother to child.[9]

This statement, insofar as it goes, is correct. DeHaan then quotes a medical handbook on page 32,

> As has been said, this interchange is effected by the process of osmosis, and there is no **direct** mingling of the two blood **currents**. In other words, no maternal blood actually flows to the foetus, nor is there any direct foetal blood flow to the mother.[10] (Emphasis added.)

To allow for and say that there is an exchange of virtually every substance and component of the blood except the red blood cells excludes the statement that "no actual interchange of a single drop of blood ever occurs normally."[11] This is misleading. It appears that DeHaan, and those who espouse this position, are referring only to the red blood cells as the blood. All other substances and components of the blood are interchanged through the placenta out of necessity to maintain life and development of the fetus.

Confusion results when semantically inaccurate references are made to the blood as not intermingling in the placenta. It is true that the red blood cells do not pass through the wall of the placenta. But it is not true that the blood of the baby and the blood of the mother never intermingle. All the components constitute the blood. Only the red cells are blocked from passing between mother and child.

This process within the placenta is a physiological guard against mixing of blood types and RH factors that could cause death for mother and or the infant. It is a wonderful design by the Creator for the protection and propagation of mankind. It has nothing to do with the sin nature. It is purely physiological.

Christ could not have had a human father because He would then have had a fallen nature inherited from Adam. Thus the necessity of the virgin birth to produce the God-Man. The virgin birth was not necessitated to avoid the blood of man, it was necessary for the human nature of Christ to be sinlessly perfect.

DeHaan states on page 17,

> The breath of God put something in man that made him Alive. That something was blood.[12]

There is no Scriptural basis for this statement. The words used in Scripture clearly indicate breath not blood. When God breathed, He did not spurt blood from His mouth into the nostrils of Adam. Man was created complete with body and blood and man lay on the ground absent only life that made man a man as God intended man to be. The LORD God "breathed into his nostrils the breath of life; and man became a living soul."

> *And the LORD God formed man* of *the dust of the ground, and breathed into his nostrils the breath of life; and man became a living soul. (Genesis 2:7)*

The Bible refers to man being formed out of the dust of the ground. When God created man, man was not alive yet. Not until God breathed into man the breath of life did man become alive — physically and spiritually. The Hebrew word for breath is never translated blood. There is no reason from Scripture or nature to assume that what God breathed into Adam's nostrils was blood. It was the breath of God.

Was the blood of Christ different than our blood? Physically speaking it was not different. The answer, no.

Was the blood of Christ different than our blood? Theologically speaking it definitely was different. The answer, yes. This shall be seen in the theological section later.

When the question is asked about the blood of Christ being different than ours, proper perspective must be maintained and correct parameters set. Specifics must be employed to determine in what regard the question is framed. We should avoid sloppy language and grammar to avoid misunderstanding the truths of Scripture.

---

[1] The New Westminster Dictionary of the Bible. Philadelphia. The Westminster Press, 1970.

[2] The authors of the books of the Bible that teach the virgin birth are: Moses, Isaiah, Jeremiah, Matthew, Luke, John and Paul. Together they wrote 30 books of the Bible.

[3] Milne, Bruce. Know the Truth. Illinois. InterVarsity Press, 1982.

[4] Gaebelein, Frank. The Patterns of God's Truth. Chicago. Moody Press, 1954.

[5] Ibid.

[6] Webster's Third New International Dictionary of the English Language Unabridged. Chicago. Encyclopaedia Britannica, Inc., 1976.

[7] John 1:18.

[8] DeHaan, M. R. The Chemistry of the Blood. Grand Rapids, MI. 1943.

[9] Ibid.

[10] Ibid.

[11] Ibid.

[12] Ibid.

CHAPTER FIVE

DEAD MEN WALKING

"For the wages of sin is death;" (Romans 6:23)

Before proceeding any further in directly addressing the subject of the blood of Christ, it is necessary to pause to establish some principles of the Word of God that may or may not be clearly understood. As mentioned before (and not a thought original with this author) one must get technical before one can get practical. Getting technical begins, quite often, with nothing more than a definition of words or terms. Of course, this is necessary to effective communication between people — the necessity to understand the language. Understanding the language is a leading challenge today.

Take for example vocabulary. The working vocabulary of the average American is estimated at approximately 850 words not including proper names. Compare that to the vocabulary of the King James Bible which contains approximately 8000 words. Exposing the average American to Biblical language today presents an overwhelming challenge that faces every preacher of the Gospel as he stands to proclaim the eternal truths contained therein. The world's approach (and that approach adopted by liberal, ecumenical evangelical Christianity) is to "dumb down" the Bible by rewriting it into many different versions rather than bring people up to the level of the Bible with regards to vocabulary.

Early in our history as a country, the average American read at the level of the King James Bible because it was the primary reader in elementary schools. The Bible has not changed and become harder to read. The education system of our country has failed miserably to educate people sufficiently to read and understand at the level once enjoyed by our forefathers.

As a result, much over-dependence has been placed upon preachers to tell people what to believe and believe it only because the preacher says so. This is dangerous ground. When people cannot read and study the Bible for themselves due to literary ignorance or spiritual shortcomings and from God's Word allow the Holy Spirit to lead them into all truth, ignorant or ill-mannered men posing as preachers can easily lead them astray. Consequently, by and large, there exists a shallow understanding of the doctrines of the Bible or an inability or lack of desire to compare Scripture with Scripture and bring the doctrines of the Bible together into an understandable whole from which and upon which to base our lives. After first getting technical, application of that understanding to practical day to day life is possible.

This chapter is an interlude in the study of the blood to introduce some principles in the Word of God that are of paramount importance in understanding the blood of Christ and what was accomplished upon the cross when He died. This interlude must start with a panoramic view of God's eternal purpose and plan. If there is to be an understanding of what God was doing on the cross, and of what Jesus spoke on His way to the cross, there must first be an understanding of what went wrong that God was making right; and, now that God has made things right, how Christians are to live as a result of what He did.

Later in this study consideration will be given to the life that is in the blood. But before looking at what life is, a look at what death is and what it is not is necessary. Death is not to be feared. It is to be understood. So with that in mind, the diligent searcher for truth must undertake (pardon the pun) a little stubby pencil work and do his homework diligently.

By way of illustration, the story is told of a man who thought he was dead. He was firmly convinced that he was dead and made sure that everyone knew that he knew he was dead. Nothing or no one could persuade him otherwise. His family pleaded with him; his friends and co-workers pleaded with him. He was taken to doctors and psychiatrists; he was counseled by pastors. All of these efforts were to no avail. As far as he was concerned, he was dead and that was all there was to it.

Finally, he was being interviewed by a particularly clever doctor who asked the man, "Do you believe that a dead man can bleed?" Well, the man thought this over for a little while with no little gravity and then replied, "No, a dead man cannot bleed." The doctor took the man quite by surprise when he held his hand and pricked the end of one of the man's fingers with a sharp instrument. At the tip of his finger appeared a tiny red drop of blood. The man looked at it in utter astonishment and shock. After contemplating this drop of blood on the end of his finger, the man said, "Would you believe it? That is absolutely amazing! Dead men CAN bleed!"

Aside from being a somewhat humorous story, one would agree that it is rather tragic when a man or woman who is alive actually thinks that he or she is dead. But that is not as pathetic as a man or woman who is dead and thinks that he or she is alive. More on that subject later. Something far more pathetic than that is someone who is alive and does not really enjoy being alive and lives as though he were dead.

This will all become clearer as progress is made through this chapter — someone who is alive and thinks he is dead and someone who is dead and thinks he is alive.

The best place to start is in the beginning and that place, oddly enough, is in the end of the Bible. In Revelation 4:11, we read the first principle to establish,

> *Thou art worthy, O Lord, to receive glory and honour and power: for thou hast created all things, and* ***for thy pleasure*** *they are and were created. (Emphasis added)*

In other words, God created man to please Him. That is basic and that is fundamental. Now we know WHY we are here — to please Him. Very simple.

How do we please God? This second principle is found in Hebrews 11:6,

> *But without faith* it is *impossible to please* him:

If God created man to please Him (and He did) and without faith it is impossible to please God (and it is), there is only one alternative to faith. That alternative is sin. This we find in Romans 14:23,

> *for whatsoever* is *not of faith is sin.*

It is really that simple. God created us to please Him. He can do that; He is God. And the Bible says that without faith Christians cannot fulfill that purpose for which they were created and put on this earth — to please God. And then very unambiguously the Bible goes on to say that whatever is not of faith, does not have its origin, motivation, and sustenance in faith, whether that be an act, an attitude, or a word, whatever it is, if it is not of faith, it is sin. That includes good works as well as evil works. It might include teaching a Sunday School class, preaching a sermon, visiting the sick and afflicted, or even giving a lot of money to missions. If any of these are not of faith, in the very act of trying to do good, we sin.

And sin deifies self. Sin is an attitude, whether it is acknowledged or not understood, that indicates that a person is adequate apart from God. It is an attitude that says, "I have what it takes." That is the nature of sin. Sin will and does manifest itself in every area of our lives.

It is for this very reason that much of what is happening in churches across America is sin. Even the very act of so-called worship. The reason for this is that an immense amount of Church activity is patterned and programmed by the latest fad or fashion in this church marketing society rather than deriving from the Divine dynamic of the Holy Ghost in accord with the written Word of God. In the act of trying to make churches user friendly (an idea NOT derived from Scripture) people are committing sin. That is the nature of sin. Any activity in which people may engage, no matter what the character by our estimation, no matter how commendable by men, if it does not derive from God Himself it is illegitimate. It does not have its origin in God. It is carnality. It is sin.

The energy of the flesh is perfectly competent to simulate and imitate every form of religious activity. But in the end, that form of activity always produces self-righteousness. It will always advertise itself. It will always put self to the front, always demanding and getting the spotlight. It deifies ego. And this is the nature of any activity that derives from any other origin than God Himself let loose in action in terms of man's humanity through that attitude of faith that in utter dependence upon Him is totally obedient to Him. With this the case, God Himself is going to get into action.

Now, whatever is not of faith is sin. And the wages of sin is death — always has been, always will be. Death. It is of paramount importance to understand the nature of death if there is to be an understanding of what God was doing when He sent His Son, the Lord Jesus Christ, into the world to redeem man.

It is also of paramount importance that Christians understand all of this if they are to present an intelligent Gospel to people that will introduce them to a relationship with the Lord Jesus which will not only make them fit for Heaven but also make them fit to live their lives here and now on earth.

By and large, our churches are full of people who have probably made a genuine decision for Christ, repenting of their sin and having faith in Christ Jesus, and who are genuinely redeemed. Their names are written in the Lamb's Book of Life, but they have not begun to be what they have become nor have they begun to enjoy the life that they have received at that moment of genuine conversion. And these people are weary. True, they are dedicated and earnest in their zeal to serve God out of genuine gratitude, but they are tired. And it is the fault of the preachers in the pulpit who have preached a pathetically inadequate Gospel: a "come to Jesus" gospel which is designed to enable people to escape the punitive consequences of their sin (Hell) without a thought as to the true implications of discipleship and what are His rights in us now as those whom He has redeemed. We are guilty because we have cheated the Lord Jesus out of that for which His blood was shed and we are doing violence to the grace of God and to the blood of Christ.

Now, a person will understand the need for a spiritual new birth on the basis of the redemptive transaction enacted by the Lord Jesus in His vicarious sacrifice upon the cross only to the extent that he understands what happened when man fell. When the Bible says that the wages of sin is death, for the most part, that statement is not fully understood. Preachers sort of hold it, in a sense, as a threat over the head of the lost. One day you will die for your sins unless you repent and receive Christ as your redeemer. Of course, such a statement is on an entirely false Biblical premise.

Much of what is read appears complicated simply because it is unfamiliar. It may be new territory never explored before. But it is good to allow God to stretch our minds and allow the Holy Spirit to lead us into all truth so that we may have a truly intelligent basis for the faith that we proclaim. And what is so exciting is the sheer logic of God's redemptive purpose as seen throughout all of Scripture. It is simply magnificent.

As we study God's Word, principles emerge. But we all too often major upon the periphery, or go off on a tangent. We focus on the consequences of the principle instead of the principle from which the consequences must derive. It is for this very reason that so many Christians turn to the Bible and it really does not make any sense. Maybe a few verses here and there relate to some experience they may have had. But they do not go to the Bible and discover that there are basic principles that are enunciated clearly. These are principles to which you can turn again and again and again and always find them to be true.

The object of every pastor's preaching should be to preach a boy, girl, man, or woman into an appropriation of the principles that govern a man's relationship to God. And having done so, the preacher will not have to always be pumping them up, giving them a shot in the arm to keep them on the move. Introduce them to the basic relationship that must exist between a man and God to let God be the God God is in that man and you can relax. They are in good hands. And if they are not in good hands, then the pastor never knew God in a right relationship. Or, he does not have a God that he is preaching.

If you cannot trust those whom you have committed to God to the God to whom you have committed them, you ought to find another God. That sentence should probably be read again a little slower to grasp its full impact. If you cannot trust those whom you have committed to God to the God to whom you have committed them, you ought to find another God. And, if I am not prepared to commit utterly to the Lord Jesus those I've introduced to the Lord Jesus in an overwhelming unshatterable confidence that He is totally competent for the task at hand, then I need to get better acquainted with Him.

There is a plot that unfolds in the Bible. Once that plot is known and understood, the Bible will make sense anywhere you open it. And, not surprisingly, found at the center of that plot is a person. That person is none other than Jesus Christ our Lord. Therefore, the reader may anticipate that no matter where he turns in the Bible he will find Christ. And everything else derives from Him. This may not be clear now, but will become so as this study progresses.

In Romans 5:12, we read:

> *Wherefore, as by one man sin entered into the world, and death by sin; and so death passed upon all men, for that all have sinned.*

The subject of this verse is death and speaks of two things concerning death. First, it speaks of the occurrence of death. Second, it speaks of the state of death that was precipitated by the occurrence of death. These two must not be confused. They are different.

The first part of the verse says, "Wherefore, as by one man sin entered into the world, **and death by sin**." That was the occurrence of death. Death occurred right there for the first time.

Now, death cannot occur except in the presence of life. The first prerequisite for death to occur is that there must be life present. And that life is pre-existent to the occurrence of death. In other words, life was there first, and then death occurred. In cannot happen any other way. That may be making the obvious obvious. Death occurs when the pre-existent life is suddenly forfeited. That is the nature of death occurring.

Death does not destroy life. It cannot. Death and life cannot be mutually coexistent. They cannot be present at the same place at the same time. Where there is life, there cannot be death. That is why death can never destroy life. Something else may destroy life. But death cannot destroy life.

You may be shot by a .357 magnum. You may step off of the curb in front of a big truck speeding down the street. You could swallow a bottle of poison or die of cancer. These things may destroy life — but death cannot. Whatever it may be that destroys life, a pistol, poison, truck, or disease, there is only one thing left after life has been destroyed. And that is death. Death is what is left after there is no life. That is the nature of death. And death occurs at the moment when pre-existent life is forfeited. That is the occurrence of death.

But what is left after the occurrence of death when pre-existent life is forfeited? A state of death is introduced. A state of death which is the total absence of life.

By way of illustration, consider a person who is lying in the street after being struck by a car. The doctor comes and examines the body. He does not look for death. He uses every bit of knowledge and skill he possesses with all the resources of modern medicine available to him to look for signs of the presence of life. If the doctor finds just the faintest tiniest evidence of life, the person is not dead. But if the doctor does everything he knows and still can find no evidence of life, he will pronounce the person dead. He cannot find life. That is the nature of death.

There is an occurrence of death and following that there is a state of death which then exists. By way of another illustration, I may take my ink pen from my pocket, hold it up and declare, "This pen is dead." And, in the common vernacular, most would respond, "Duh. That is obvious." But you would have to agree that my pen is dead. It does not possess life. It does not grow. It does not meet a cute little pen, fall in love, get married and have a bunch of little baby pens. To say that my pen is dead is a valid statement.

But, suppose I were to tell you that my pen died three days ago. Very sad, it was. My pen died. You might be inclined to disagree with me and say that it is nonsense to say that my pen died. And you would be right. Why? For the simple reason that death cannot occur except in the presence of pre-existent life. The occurrence of death demands that life be present before death occurred. Without pre-existent life, death cannot occur; but a state of death may exist.

This difference between the occurrence of death and the state of death can be seen in yet another illustration. A man goes for a walk by himself in unfamiliar terrain one afternoon. Not being familiar with the terrain, he is unaware of a high cliff just beyond some brush. In his attempt to keep going, he presses through the brush only to step over the cliff. He does so in a state of life. As he falls, he remains in a state of life until he reaches the bottom of the ravine. Upon being reunited with the earth, but at a fatal speed, he is instantly killed. Since he was alone, no one knew where he was and was not missed for quite some time. A search party is launched several days later. After the body is found, a doctor very quickly ascertains that he is in a state of death. You slip up beside the doctor and ask him when did death occur. In other words, you are not arguing that the man is dead, in a state of death. But when did that state begin? When was it precipitated? When was the exact moment the man went from a state of life to a state of death, death occurring? That is the essential difference between the occurrence of death and the state of death.

Back to Romans chapter five. The Bible makes clear: by one man sin entered into the world, and when by that one man sin entered into the world, death occurred. What happened when death first occurred in the first Adam? Did he die physically? No. But he did die.

But for death to occur presupposes the pre-existence of life and the forfeiture of that life that was pre-existent. God said to Adam, in the day that you eat thereof you shall surely die. It was this fact that the devil challenged. But Adam did not die physically. So, in the day that death occurred in Adam, he did not forfeit physical life. He did forfeit physical life later as a secondary consequence of sin. But his physical death was not the primary consequence of his sin.

If in the day that Adam sinned he died, then he forfeited life. And if that life was not physical life, what then was the life that Adam forfeited in the day that he died for his sin? The answer is simple: God's life; the life of God. Because when God made man and breathed into his nostrils the breath of life, and man became a living soul, man became alive both physically and spiritually with God indwelling the man through the Holy Spirit. God made man in His own image. God imparted His life to man to share that life with man so that God could be in man the origin of His own image, the source of His own activity, the dynamic of His own demand, and the cause of His own effect.

God, from the very beginning, taught man that it takes God Himself to be a man as God created man to be.

In the Garden, God told Adam that, in that day, Adam, when you repudiate this principle, and you reject that moral relationship of your love for me that demands your dependence on me and your obedience to me, in that day I will withdraw my Holy Spirit from your human spirit and you will be left physically alive, soulishly functional, but spiritually destitute. In that day, you will die.

That is when death occurred.

This death was the forfeiture of the life of God. In Him, the Word, the creative Word, the Logos, in Him was life. This life alone was the light of men. Only the life of the Logos, only the life of the Word, only the life of God Himself within a man could set that man alight. And the moment that that life was forfeited, there was death.

Now, death does not destroy life, just as darkness does not destroy light. And for the same reason. Light and darkness cannot mutually co-exist. Where there is light, there is not any darkness. There is now no darkness in this room at the moment because there is light. And so long as there is light, there will not be darkness and no amount of darkness can try to invade this room and destroy light.

When does darkness occur? Darkness occurs when the pre-existent light is removed. And when the pre-existent light is removed, what is left? Darkness. In other words, darkness is the residue when light is forfeited.

In the Lord Jesus is life. This life in man was the light. Remove the life and all that is left as a residue is death. But that life was the light of men, so if you take out the life you also take out the light. What is left is the residue, darkness. The moment death occurred in Adam, darkness occurred. The day that Adam fell into sin, he was plunged into spiritual death and spiritual darkness. He became a child of the night. He was by nature a child of wrath. He was totally destitute of that divine content which alone makes a man competent for the purpose that God made man. That is the nature of death occurring.

But we are told further in Romans 5:12 that as by one man sin entered into the world, and death by sin, so this state of death, that was precipitated by the occurrence of death in the forfeiture of life in Adam, was passed upon all men. By the occurrence of death in Adam, all men entered into a state of death. First Corinthians 15:21 states that death came by man.

> *For since by man* came *death, by man* came *also the resurrection of the dead.*

"Since by man came death, by man came also the resurrection." But verse 22 gets very specific. As in Adam, how many died? All died. Every man, woman, boy, or girl that has ever lived since Adam died in Adam.

> *For as in Adam all die.*

In 2 Corinthians 5:14, we read,

For the love of Christ constraineth us; because we thus judge, that if one died for all, then were all dead.

Why did one die for all? Because all were dead. In other words, if the Lord Jesus died vicariously for all men in all time, there is only one good reason according to the Apostle Paul. He only died for all because all are dead. How is this so? In the day that death occurred in Adam, a state of death passed upon all men. And every man, woman, boy, or girl that was ever born into this world since Adam fell was and is born in a state of death that was precipitated when death occurred first in Adam.

Since in Adam all are dead and born that way, in a state of death (total spiritual lifelessness), it means that no man, woman, boy, or girl ever born on earth since Adam fell can ever under any circumstances die for their sins. And yet congregations are constantly being bombarded with preaching that says that people will die for their sins if they do not get saved. That just is not true.

Why is that not true? It is not true because dead men cannot die! The occurrence of death presupposes the existence of life to be forfeited. And the moment you tell someone that they will die for their sins, you are presupposing that they were born in a state of spiritual life. And that is diametrically opposed to what the Bible teaches.

The Bible teaches that we are all born spiritually destitute, alienated (cutoff) from the life of God.

17 *This I say therefore, and testify in the Lord, that ye henceforth walk not as other Gentiles walk, in the vanity of their mind,*

18 *Having the understanding darkened, being alienated from the life*

of God through the ignorance that is in them, because of the blindness of their heart. (Ephesians 4:17-18

Remember that here in this passage, Paul is writing to those who have already experienced a spiritual resurrection. They have been born again. They were saved. This is seen in Ephesians 2:1:

And you hath he quickened, *who were dead in trespasses and sins.*

"You" were in a state of death. "You" were born in that state of death. But a resurrection has taken place so that Paul was now addressing those who were dead but who have been brought to life again. Not physically, but spiritually. The life of God restored to the soul of man.

In verse seventeen of the fourth chapter of Ephesians, Paul says this to those who have been born again: This I say therefore and testify in the Lord, that you from now on walk (or behave, because the word walk in this verse means to behave), not as other Gentiles walk or behave. Since those to whom he is writing have been born again, spiritually raised from the dead and come alive in Christ, having the very life of God reinstated in their soul, they should not behave as those who are still dead in their trespasses and sin. They should not act like those who do not have the life of God reinstated to them, those who are unregenerate, still walking and behaving in the vanity of their mind, conceited, ego-centric, self-sufficient, all of which is characteristic of those who are unregenerate. To those who have not come alive in Christ, self is still on the throne and they perpetuate the old satanic lie that man can be good enough without God.

The unregenerate man continues to strut around in the vanity of his mind, constantly congratulating himself that he has what it takes to be a man. But their understanding is darkened, verse eighteen. And why is their understanding darkened? Because of the blindness of their heart. Of course, heart refers to the soul of man, his mind, emotion, and will. The soul can be called his behavior mechanism. It is his mind, emotions, and will that are the origin of what he is and what he does. And these are unenlightened, darkened if you will. And the natural man, the unregenerate man, the man who is still the way he was born, does not receive the things of the Spirit of God because they are foolishness to him and he is unable to understand them.

Now that is the state of death in which all of us were born. And any man, woman, boy, or girl in that state of death and spiritual destitution cannot under any circumstances die for their sins. They are already dead. This was the case for the Pharisees in John's Gospel.

> 23 *And he said unto them, Ye are from beneath; I am from above: ye are of this world; I am not of this world.*
>
> 24 *I said therefore unto you, that ye shall die in your sins: for if ye believe not that I am* he, *ye shall die in your sins. (John 8:23-24)*

Notice carefully what He said. Did He say that they would die *for* their sins? No. He said very clearly that they would die *in* their sins. And he said it twice, including the qualification that to avoid dying in their sins they must believe upon Him. But if they do not believe on Him, then they will die physically in the condition in which they were born spiritually; and that is spiritually dead. Then they will be twice dead. They will be physically dead and they will continue to be spiritually dead. They will be destitute of physical life and they will be destitute of spiritual life.

In other words, if a person does not repent of his sins and have faith in Jesus Christ, when he dies physically there will be perpetuated for eternity the state in which he was born spiritually, and that is spiritually dead. This is not talking about annihilation. The essential difference between the animal soul and the human soul is that the human soul is inextricably identified with the human spirit that gives the human soul a capacity to endure forever, remaining morally responsible to God. When the animal dies, the animal soul disintegrates with the animal body because the animal is not morally responsible to God.

When the human body dies, the human soul identified with the human spirit remains morally responsible to God and will be judged. It is this moral responsibility of the human soul that the political and religious liberals deny. It is this moral responsibility that the evolutionists deny and in fact fear. But the Bible says that it is appointed unto men once to die, physically, and after that the judgement.

Death has only occurred twice as a result of sin in all human history: only twice. And it will never, never, never occur again. It occurred for the first time in the person of the first Adam in the day that he fell into sin. It occurred for the second and last time in the person of the last Adam, the Second Man, our Lord Jesus Christ.

> **45** *And so it is written, The first man Adam was made a living soul; the last Adam* was made *a quickening spirit.*
> **46** *Howbeit that* was *not first which is spiritual, but that which is natural; and afterward that which is spiritual.*
> **47** *The first man* is *of the earth, earthy: the second man* is *the Lord from heaven. (1 Corinthians 15:45-47)*

The first Adam, who was made a living soul, died. Death occurred. The Last Adam was made one who could quicken, restore life, raise the dead. The first man is of the earth, the Second Man is the Lord from Heaven. The Second Man is the only other man that has ever walked this earth as man as God created man to be. No other man has ever been man upon the earth apart from Adam before he fell and the Last Adam, the Lord Jesus. There has never ever been any other man who has been man the way God created man to be in holy satisfaction to Himself.

In order to fully understand death in its occurrence and state, it is necessary once again to go back to the beginning and come forward.

When God created Adam, He said good, very good. And, until Adam fell, turning his back on that principle that relates the life of God to the soul of man, until that time he fulfilled the purpose for which he was made to God's moral and functional satisfaction. Then Adam fell into sin. He lost the life of God and the light in his soul went out and he and all his progeny were cast into darkness and blindness of heart. And not until the Lord Jesus walked this earth was there ever another man who fulfilled the purpose for which God made man: to please Him.

How is that purpose accomplished? God created man to provide a physical, visible, and audible image of an invisible God. The subject of this book is the blood, this chapter is about death, and time nor space shall be taken here to expand on this subject of God's purpose in creating man. But a short overview is important in order to understand the necessity of redemption so that God's purpose and plan not be frustrated. And that redemption was accomplished through His Son the Lord Jesus by means of death through His blood. It all ties together and to miss one point is to jeopardize understanding fully what God was doing at Calvary and what God is doing today in your life if you are truly born again.

No man has ever seen God at any time. This we are told in John 1:18. We are also told in this passage that Jesus, the Second Man, has brought the Father once more out into the open and placed Him where He may be seen.

> *No man hath seen God at any time; the only begotten Son, which is in the bosom of the Father, he hath declared* him. *(John 1:18)*

In this verse, when it says that he "hath declared him," it does not mean that Jesus just preached sermons about the Father. It means that the totality of the humanity of Jesus Christ, everything He was, said, or did, for 24 hours in every day, seven days a week, every moment of every day was a declaration about the Father. That is why the Lord Jesus could say that he that has seen me has seen the Father. In other words, our Lord said, "I am what my Father is." Yet, we are told that no man has seen God at any time. But those who walked with the Lord Jesus looked into His face, saw all that there was to be seen of God, and never saw Him except in the form of a man.

> *For he hath made him* to be *sin for us, who knew no sin; that we might be made the righteousness of God in him. (2 Corinthians 5:21)*

Death occurred in the first Adam for the first time on the basis of committed sin and disobedience. Death occurred for the second time in the Second Man, the Last Adam, on the basis of imputed sin and obedience. He did not die for His sin because He was and is without sin, perfect, holy and righteous. God imputed our sin to Him; in other words, our sin was laid to the account of the Lord Jesus and He was actually made to be sin there upon the cross of Calvary. And He was obedient unto death, even the death of the cross. And that death of the Lord Jesus was designed by God to kill death dead. He died for all because all were dead. So that in the place of the all who were dead, the Lord Jesus accepted vicariously the inevitable consequence of man's sin. And then God, without doing violence to His own righteousness, holiness, or justice, could on the basis of that vicarious sacrifice restore to man exactly that which was forfeited in Adam — the life of God.

Since by man came death, the first Adam in which death occurred and the state of death was initiated upon all his progeny, so by man came also the resurrection of the dead, by the Second Man, the Last Adam, the Lord Jesus. Now, we are beginning to understand the significance of spiritual new birth which is not to be confused with redemption.

Maj. Ian Thomas uses an illustration on this point that is very good and easy to understand.

If you were to go into your room and turn on the switch, and the light bulb did not come on, you would remove the bulb from the socket to check it out to see if it was good. You do so and find that the bulb is just the way it is supposed to be and the filament is not broken. Returning to your room, you replace the bulb back into the socket, turn on the switch, and the bulb still does not light up. After determining that there is electrical current to the switch and socket, you examine the bulb more closely. Upon close examination, you discover that a tiny speck of dirt is on the base of the bulb and it is positioned so that in the socket contact cannot be made between the socket and the bulb. Because the dirt has come in the life has to stay out. In this case, the life is the electricity. Well, what do you do about it? Simple; remove the dirt.

The chronological order of events is: the dirt came in, the life went out, the light went off. And that is the fall of man into sin. As by one man sin, the dirt came in, the life went out, death, and the light went off, darkness. No longer in the image of God in which man was created. For, you see, the image of God requires God's presence as the source.

What is the solution? If when sin came in the life went out and the light went off, quite obviously God's remedial measure will involve taking the dirt out, letting the life in and putting the light on. And that is the Gospel.

You get some fine grit sandpaper and you clean the dirt off of the bulb and declare that now the dirt is gone. And you just lay the bulb on the table. What have you accomplished? Well, all you have is a nice clean bulb. That is all. Nothing more. Just a clean bulb. But do you have any light? No. Why? Because, although you have taken the dirt out you have not let the life in and therefore the light has not been put on.

Application of this illustration can be made to preaching today. When a preacher preaches redemption through the shed blood of Jesus simply as a means whereby men escape the punitive consequences of their guilt (Hell), and say that they are cleansed, their sins forgiven, they are free, emancipated, and that is all Jesus ever came to do for them — He came to take away their sin and make them clean and leave them fit for Heaven — and then just stick them on the table, who knows the difference?

The person may have genuinely decided to receive Christ as their redeemer and is now rejoicing in the fact that their sins are forgiven and they are on their way to Heaven and not Hell. But nobody has told them that the purpose for which Christ has redeemed them from the curse of the law, by being made a curse for them, is that they might receive the promise of the Holy Ghost by faith and receive eternal life, the very life of God. In other words, if the Lord Jesus came upon the cross through His shed blood to take the dirt out (sin), there was only one intelligent purpose in God's mind, and that was, having taken the dirt out (sin) to let once more the life in so that the life of God through the human spirit might flood the human soul, once more coming under the sovereignty of God and a man would be restored to his true function — the life in, the light on: restored to the image of God as created by God in the beginning.

That is the Gospel. Only when the Gospel is presented with the full claims of Jesus Christ, not only as the one who died redemptively but also as the one who rose again from the dead to inhabit our humanity in the person of His other self, the Holy Spirit, in spiritual regeneration, only then have people been led to the true word of life. The Gospel invites dead men to be raised to life again.

> 8 *Be not thou therefore ashamed of the testimony of our Lord, nor of me his prisoner: but be thou partaker of the afflictions of the gospel according to the power of God;*
>
> 9 *Who hath saved us, and called* us *with an holy calling, not according to our works, but according to his own purpose and grace, which was given us in Christ Jesus before the world began,*
>
> 10 *But is now made manifest by the appearing of our Saviour Jesus Christ, who hath abolished death, and hath brought life and immortality to light through the gospel: (2 Timothy 1:8-10)*

Notice in the middle of verse 10, *"who abolished death."* How does God abolish death? Since death is a residue after life has been forfeited, there is only one way to abolish death and that is by reintroducing life. That is the only cure for death. Christ has abolished death and brought life and immortality to light through the Gospel. He abolishes death by introducing life that the life might become obvious in light. This is the redemptive work of God through the Gospel of Christ. Abolish death and bring life and immortality to light.

As a consequence, it becomes powerfully obvious to all everywhere that a person in repentance toward God and faith in the Lord Jesus Christ, a person now cleansed in the blood of Jesus and reinhabited by His risen Lord, is now available to Him to clothe His divine activity with their humanity. In that person's presence, everyone is convinced that Jesus is alive. And that is the message of the Gospel.

It is referred to as being added to the Lord, a living member in particular of the body corporate through which Jesus Himself now lives on earth in their humanity exactly the same quality of life He lived then in the humanity God provided Him that day in Bethlehem. The same quality of life is lived by Him now in us that He lived then in His own body. And that is the nature of the Christian life.

The Christian life is the life He lived then lived now by Him in us — if we simply let Him. This is the invitation that should be taken to those who are without Christ. Christians should not try to present people with a plan of salvation; they should present Christ, and invite them to accept Him, not a plan. The world still cries out "Sir, we would see Jesus."

Jesus said to the Pharisees that He was come that we might have life. We were dead, we can now come alive with that life that is imparted by God and has its origin in God and present our humanity to become the living temple of the living God.

> **14** *For the love of Christ constraineth us; because we thus judge,*

that if one died for all, then were all dead:

15 *And* that *he died for all, that they which live should not henceforth live unto themselves, but unto him which died for them, and rose again. (2 Corinthians 5:14-15)*

In other words, the love of Christ urges and compels us because we are of the conviction that if Jesus died for all, then all were dead, and that without exception. And since all were dead, all needed life restored to abolish death. For life to occur (be reintroduced) presupposes the pre-existence of a state of death which is the absence of life. And we are quickened together with Christ, lifted out of a state of death, made alive unto God, life reintroduced to abolish death. So that when Christ redeems you, He does not do so simply to save you from the future consequences of your sin which is death in its continual state for eternity, He saves you out of a state of death and restores you to a state of life. And that spiritual resurrection, the reimparting of the Holy Spirit to your spirit, as the seal of your redemption, is what the Bible calls the new birth, being born again.

But notice in verse 15 the end to which we are saved. He died for all, so that all who do live, who have received this free gift of salvation, should live no longer for and to ourselves. We should cease to be ego-centric, cease to deify self, cease to reckon only with ourselves, but live to and for Him who died for us to abolish death and was raised again that He may come by His Holy Spirit to indwell us. To live to and for yourself is to walk after the flesh. To live to and for Jesus Christ is to walk after the Spirit.

Wherefore henceforth know we no man after the flesh: yea, though we have

> *known Christ after the flesh, yet now henceforth know we* him *no more. (2 Corinthians 5:16)*

This verse gives the full impact of Paul's argument. From now on, we estimate and regard no one from a purely human point of view. Even though, says Paul, we once did estimate Christ from the human point of view and as a man only; yet, now, we have such knowledge of Him, that we know Him no longer in terms of the flesh.

Please do not miss this most important point. Christ died for you, shed His blood to cleanse you from sin, so that He Himself in the person of the Holy Ghost, might come and reinhabit your humanity, putting the very life of God back in, to put the light of God back on. And ye are the light of the world.

So, Paul says, having understood all this: having understood that Jesus did not come to be a doormat over whom I walk into Heaven; He did not simply come as a spiritual convenience so that I may avoid the punitive consequences of my sin, I see now what it is really all about. It is to get God back into the man.

From now on, we regard no one from a purely human point of view, from natural standards of value. Paul says that we did once estimate Christ that way. How was that? As a Pharisee, Saul of Tarsus (Paul) estimated Christ on the normal standards of man.

First, how much money did Christ have? Well, He did not have any money at all. From Saul's perspective as a Pharisee, Christ could have been considered an incorrigible scrounger, living under somebody else's roof, sitting at somebody else's table the whole time. And so, in Saul's estimation, on a perfectly normal human standard, Christ was worth nothing financially. Saul of Tarsus would not have even crossed the road to invite Him into his synagogue. And he certainly would not have given Him any responsibility in the synagogue. Financially, He was worth nothing.

Saul of Tarsus also would have believed, as was believed by all his ecclesiastical colleagues, that Jesus, in their opinion, was the illegitimate child of a faithless woman. Socially, He was worth nothing.

Jesus went about preaching. How dare He preach? What was He worth ecclesiastically? What was He worth theologically? Absolutely nothing. He was totally repudiated by the religious leaders of His day. All the big name preachers and teachers that made theological news rejected Him out of hand. He never had any of His sermons printed in the religious papers of His day! How dare He preach? He was worth nothing ecclesiastically.

What was He worth scholastically? He only went to a village school. All He ever learned was His craft as a carpenter. The only thing He ever did was fix windows and doors. How much was He worth intellectually, scholastically? Nothing.

Saul of Tarsus' evaluation of Christ, on a purely human perspective by normal human standards would have been: He was worth nothing financially, socially, ecclesiastically, scholastically, intellectually. That was his evaluation of Jesus' worth as a man.

Then something happened. Saul of Tarsus met Jesus on the road to Damascus. There was Saul, breathing out threatenings and slaughter against the children of God, the followers of Christ. He had letters of authority from the high priest, he was the representative of the highest and noblest theological trends of his day and generation, he was promoted above many of his own equals.

Saul then saw a light that was brighter than the noon day sun. He was blinded. He heard a voice, "Saul, Saul, why persecutest thou me?" Saul said, "Who are you, Lord?" The answer came back. I am Jesus, financially worth nothing in your opinion, ecclesiastically repudiated by you and your colleagues, socially an outcast from my own people, and without any background that would impress you scholastically. I am Jesus whom thou persecutest.

And Saul of Tarsus, there on that road to Damascus, yielded to Christ as Lord and now says, "I know Him in an entirely new way." On that day, Saul had to reassess his terms for evaluating a man's worth. For, after looking into the face of Jesus, Saul recognized that he saw in Him all that can ever be seen of God. And at that moment, he discovered just how much a man is worth. A man is worth no more than what can be seen of God in him. That is a man's worth.

And this is a very hard thing to discover, not only for Saul of Tarsus, but for us. We might go to church, as many do, and look across the room. We might see someone of interest and ask the person next to us, How much do you think that person over there is worth? Well, they answer that if he is worth a nickel he is worth a million. And our response would be, Pardon me, I did not ask you how much money he has, I asked how much he was worth.

We might ask of the preacher, How much is he worth? Well, you should see the list of degrees he has after his name. He has an honorary doctorate. We call him Doctor. You should see the church **he** has built. You should hear **his** reputation. Why, do you know how many buses **they** run on Sunday morning? Do you know how long it has been since they had a Sunday when no one was baptized? Haven't you heard **his** numbers? Don't you know who **HE** is? We would respond, Excuse me, I did not ask all that. I asked, How much is he really worth.

How much are you worth?

You are worth no more to God or man, to your children or your neighbors, to your church or congregation as a preacher, or the masses as an evangelist, or as a Bible teacher in a college, you are worth absolutely no more than what can be seen of Jesus Christ in you 24 hours a day, seven days a week, every moment of every day. Not just on Sunday for a few hours, all dressed up and rehearsed. Not when you are on display, but in the day to day moment by moment process of living the Christian life. That life is lived by His presence, exercising His divine sovereignty through the Holy Ghost in every area of your personality, in the process of being what you became in the day you were born again. That is how much you are worth. No more. No less.

That is the discovery that Saul of Tarsus made and every one makes who in genuine repentance toward God and faith in the Lord Jesus Christ invites Him into their lives to abolish death by the reintroduction of eternal life, who is Christ Himself — a person — indwelling each believer.

Death occurred twice that for those who accept Christ life might be reintroduced.

That is the nature of death and provides some insight into the purpose of His shed blood. He shed His blood for us, giving His life for us. He rose from the dead to give His life to us so that He could communicate that life through us: if only we would let Him.

CHAPTER SIX

LIFE

"I am the ...life" John 14:6

Death is meaningless apart from life. You can say of a pine 2 x 4, "That piece of wood is dead." And you would certainly be correct. However, you cannot say of a brick, "That brick is dead." The brick does not have the capacity for life; therefore, it was never alive, nor indeed could be. Therefore, a brick cannot die. It cannot forfeit a life that it never had. We recall from the previous chapter that death is a residue, it is what is left over after life has been forfeited.

We also learned that if Adam was capable of death while remaining physically alive, it can only mean that he possessed life in a quality other than physical life while in his innocency. And under certain circumstances he could forfeit that life without physically dying. This he did when death occurred in Adam when he fell.

What was that life which Adam forfeited when he determined to eat the fruit of the tree of the knowledge of good and evil? It was spiritual life: the very life of God Himself.

In this chapter we will explore in greater detail the subject of life. For, if we do not know what life is, or at least have a close approximation of what life is, we cannot understand what it is that has been forfeited in Adam and reinstated in Christ. At first blush this will seem to be an attempt to ponder the imponderable. Life cannot be empirically investigated nor life itself observed by scientific means. Upon little reflection we can deduce that what is observable is only the physical manifestations of life present in that which is alive.

We shall not spend time on studying these manifestations. Our effort will be directed toward an attempt to understand what life itself is and what its origin is. In understanding this, to some small degree, we shall then understand the significance of death and the significance of what Christ did on the cross where He shed His blood. The significance and importance of the blood in this entire transaction of redemption will become evident in later chapters.

Usually a good place to start a discussion of a subject is by examining the definition of the term. One place NOT to turn is the *Encyclopedia Britannica.* The discussion of life rambles on for page after page of humanistic reasoning that attempts, but fails, to discuss life on the scientific level only. Of course it is obvious that the authors of the article were or are atheists. So, no real definition or explanation could be found there. However, in turning to the dictionary another story can be told.

In Webster's dictionary, the definition is a lengthy one and includes references to the Bible and to God. This is a necessity, as we shall see, to any attempt to understand life. Some of the nearly two dozen definitions of life include:

> animate being: the quality that distinguishes a vital and functional being from a dead body or purely chemical matter (life is the immediate gift of God — William Blackstone);
>
> the principle or force by which animals and plants are maintained in the performance of their functions and which distinguishes by its presence animate from inanimate matter;
>
> the earthly state of human existence as distinguished from the spiritual state after death; a spiritual form of eternal existence transcending physical death (he who hears my word…has passed from death to life Jn 5:24(RSV))
>
> something held to be essential to animate existence or to a livelihood (the words that I have spoken to you are spirit and life (Jn 6:63 (RSV))
>
> conscious existence supposed to be a quality of the soul or as the soul's nature and being.

(Inclusion of references to the RSV in no way implies an endorsement of that version. They are quotes from Webster's dictionary and included to show the use of and reliance upon the Bible in defining what life is.)

It is insufficient to define the English word "life" in an attempt to understand what the Bible is talking about when it refers to life. We must go back to the original languages to find the words used by the Holy Ghost as the original manuscripts were written. This is not going to be a course in Greek and Hebrew. But we understand the Bible more richly and plumb its depths more deeply when we endeavor to understand the meanings of the original words.

The real difficulty can be illustrated by the fact that the King James Version uses over 28 different English terms for one Hebrew word, *nepes.* This word is variously translated soul, self, life. The problem, for example, with the English word "soul" is that there is no direct equivalent found in the Hebrew language. The Hebrew system of thought does not consider soul and body as separate. Man was a unified entity of the whole.

In the Greek language of the New Testament, examples abound of the same difficulty in translating. The same English word may be used in different places but is a translation of two completely different Greek words with different meanings. Some examples.

> *Every good* ***gift*** *and every perfect* ***gift*** *is from above, and cometh down from the Father of lights, with whom is no variableness, neither shadow of turning. (James 1:17) (Emphasis added)*

In this verse the word "gift" is used twice. What is the difference between a good gift and a perfect gift? Both come down from Heaven. If both come down from Heaven, is a perfect gift better than a good gift? No little confusion could result from such an approach. This confusion is eliminated and greater understanding of the passage gained by looking at the two different Greek words translated "gift" in this verse.

The first "gift" is translated from the word *dosis* and refers primarily to the act of giving. The second "gift" is from the word *dorema* and refers primarily to the thing given. Same English word, yet two distinct Greek words in the original that, when understood, shed more light on the passage of Scripture.

Another example is

> 3 *And when they had fasted and prayed, and laid* their *hands on them, they* ***sent*** them *away.*
>
> 4 *So they, being* ***sent*** *forth by the Holy Ghost, departed unto Seleucia; and from thence they sailed to Cyprus. (Acts 13:3-4) (Emphasis added)*

In these two verses the word "sent" is used. Once again we find that they come from different Greek words with different meanings and subsequent ramifications to the impact of the verses. These examples are not for purpose of exposition of these passages of Scripture. Rather, they are used to illustrate that our English words may come from one or more words in the original languages whose meanings shed sometimes a different light on a passage.

The first "sent" of verse 3 is from the Greek word *apoluo*. This word means to let go, bid depart, dismiss, detain no longer. In other words, the church bid them go. The second "sent" of verse 4 is from the Greek word *ekpempo*, to dispatch, send forth. They were dispatched by the Holy Ghost and Holy Ghost authority. There is a difference between being dismissed from the presence of someone or some assembly and being dispatched by authority on a mission. Looking at the original language adds impact to the responsibility of a missionary.

These are just two of many, many examples of the difficulty in going from one language to another. They illustrate the need to look very closely at the original languages concerning our study of what life is: not what life is about; what life is. In addition to looking into the original languages, there must of necessity be an understanding and appreciation of the culture of those whom God chose to write the Bible. That culture is reflected in their language and the use of that language within their culture helps us in understanding the meanings of the original words.

Of the nine original language words that are translated "life," we shall focus only on a couple. Some original language words have only one occurrence of being translated life or are derivatives of another word. Our focus shall be on those that give us as clear an understanding as possible of what the Bible is teaching us concerning life. If we understand what life is, or at least appreciate its scope, nature, origin, and significance, we will better grasp what was done for us on Calvary.

Staying with our first step of defining terms (which was interrupted by examples of language difficulties), we shall first define some terms for life. This is not for the purpose of doing Greek and Hebrew studies. We are attempting to gather an understanding of the concept of life through a study of what these words signify.

The two primary Hebrew words translated "life" in the Old Testament are *chay* and *nephesh*.

Strong's Dictionary defines *chay* as:

1) living, alive
1a) green (of vegetation)
1b) flowing, fresh (of water)
1c) lively, active (of man)

1d) reviving (of the springtime)
2) relatives
3) life (abstract emphatic)
3a) life
3b) sustenance, maintenance n f
4) living thing, animal
4a) animal
4b) life
4c) appetite
4d) revival, renewal
5) community

Strong's define *nephesh* as:

1) soul, self, life, creature, person, appetite, mind, living being, desire, emotion, passion
1a) that which breathes, the breathing substance or being, soul, the inner being of man
1b) living being
1c) living being (with life in the blood)
1d) the man himself, self, person or individual
1e) seat of the appetites
1f) seat of emotions and passions
1g) activity of mind

The three Greek words translated "life" are *bios, psuche,* and *zoe.* They are defined in Strong's dictionary.

bios -
1) life
1a) life extensively
1a1) the period or course of life
1b) that by which life is sustained, resources, wealth, goods.

psuche –

1) breath

1a) the breath of life

1a1) the vital force which animates the body and shows itself in breathing

1a1a) of animals

1a1b) of men

1b) life

1c) that in which there is life

1c1) a living being, a living soul

2) the soul

2a) the seat of the feelings, desires, affections, aversions (our heart, soul etc.)

2b) the (human) soul in so far as it is constituted that by the right use of the aids offered it by God it can attain its highest end and secure eternal blessedness, the soul regarded as a moral being designed for everlasting life

2c) the soul as an essence which differs from the body and is not dissolved by death (distinguished from other parts of the body).

zoe –

1) life

1a) the state of one who is possessed of vitality or is animate

1b) every living soul

2) life

2a) of the absolute fullness of life, both essential and ethical, which belongs to God, and through him both to the hypostatic "logos" and to Christ in whom the "logos" put on human nature

2b) life real and genuine, a life active and vigorous, devoted to God, blessed, in the portion even in this world of those who put their trust in Christ, but after the resurrection to be consummated by new accessions (among them a more perfect body), and to last for ever.

When the Septuagint was translated, the Greek word used most often for the Hebrew words was *zoe*. *Zoe* shall be the word we focus on to see if we can get a feeling for the concept of life.

In classical Greek usage, *zoe* refers to all living things: vegetable, animal, and man. Life was understood to be not a tangible thing to be observed and scrutinized, but a vitality, a force. *Zoe* is therefore not used in the plural; there is just *zoe*, life. To the ancient philosophers and theologians, *zoe* was always something more than and other than what is defined and expressed by scientists in their terms. It has always been held and believed that life in its essence, that which is really life, is unobservable, not able to be measured, evaluated, restricted, or otherwise handled by science.

It appears that only one word is used for life when referring to either vegetable, animal, or human. There is only life. All forms of living things have life. But it is obvious that there must be a differentiation between a carrot, a dog, and a man. We also gather that human life is more than a natural biological process of an organism that takes in food, converts that food to energy, grows, moves, reproduces, etc.

The sort of life that is described as biological functions alone is a close approximation to the word *bios*. But human life is far more than that, and it is still called *zoe*. Human life is experienced in an individual *bios*. By that is meant that human life is not a state of existence, but is a being who is expressed and experienced through a particular organic mechanism we know as the body. It is obvious that each of us only has one body. I have never met anyone who said that they have two bodies. I guess they would keep the second at home for spares or to use while the first is being worked on. There are two car families, but there are no two body people. Those who would make such a claim expose themselves to the possibility of confinement in a facility for those of dubious mental capacity.

Just as each one of us has only one body, each human body has only one of us. Two individuals cannot inhabit the same body. We shall not enter into the mysterious realm of psychiatrists. We will deal strictly with the Bible. All truth is God's truth and His Word is truth.

Any time you hear of a case where it is said that a person has multiple personalities, or that there are really two persons (or more) and it was the "other one" that committed the crime, extreme caution is warranted. If it is true in fact that there is more than one being in a body, it is nothing other than demon possession. And it can be nothing else.

Assume for a moment the absurdity of more than one person occupying one body. For simplicity's sake we shall assume there are only two people in the body. When we talk to the body, it is assumed only one will answer at a time. They may trade off answering which would only add to the confusion. But we speak to the body and converse with person A. Person A seems a nice enough sort and even appears to be rational. Some time later we are interrupted by person B.

Now person B is not nice at all. As a matter of fact person B is rather rebellious, proud and arrogant. We cannot have a decent conversation with person B. The question arises, "Does this body have only one soul or two souls?" If there are in fact two persons in this one body, they must each have their own *psuche*, their own soul. This is unheard of in Scripture and reality. This leaves us with one body, one soul and two persons.

Continuing our illustration a little further, we witness to the body with person A responding and present the Gospel. Person A responds in repentance and faith and is born again. We ask person A to have person B join in the conversation. Person B is totally unresponsive to the Gospel and rejects Jesus Christ.

We face a dilemma. (And you saw this coming, I hope.) When the body dies, does the soul go to Heaven or Hell? And in the resurrection, whose body will it be? Person A or person B? What utter nonsense.

If more than one being is present in one body, it is nothing other than demon possession. And if your are in their presence, you have more problems than a multiple personality disorder! There are no limits to which modern science will travel to excuse man from moral accountability to a holy God.

One body equals one soul equals one being.

Of course, we also observe that a carrot has a body. It has a carrot body. We recognize it by its body. It is distinctive. We are able to tell the difference between a carrot, a potato, a watermelon, or a weed. All have their distinctive bodies given to them by God in creation to serve their individual functional purpose.

But I never heard of a carrot falling in love with the radish three rows over in the garden. The tomatoes do not shun the onions because of their peculiar "body odor." I have never heard of the corn banding together to fight the peas over domination in that particular field. In other words, vegetables do not behave. They do indeed have life and that life was given to them by God. It is a limited life with a specific purpose and function within an intelligent design. Vegetables have a body; but not a soul or behavior mechanism. Behavior is a characteristic of man and animals. The seat of all animal (including man) behavior is the soul.

The greek word for soul is *psuche*. This word is used throughout the New Testament (and the Septuagint) for soul. It corresponds to the Old Testament *nephesh*. In the creation account we learn that animals have *nephesh*, a soul. To keep it very simple, the soul is comprised of the mind, emotions, and will. It is invisible; the body is visible. The soul came from God. This we shall see later.

That man is an animal goes without saying. We eat, drink, breathe, breed, and bleed and die the animal way. That man is not only animal will become clear as we progress, but animal he is. We have a *nephesh* in common with animals. This is clearly seen in the Genesis account of creation.

> 20 *And God said, Let the waters bring forth abundantly the moving creature that* ***hath life****, and fowl* that *may fly above the earth in the open firmament of heaven.*
>
> 21 *And God created great whales, and every* ***living creature*** *that moveth, which the waters brought forth abundantly, after their kind, and every winged fowl after his kind: and God saw that* it was *good.*
>
> 24 *And God said, Let the earth bring forth the* ***living creature*** *after his kind, cattle, and creeping thing, and beast of the earth after his kind: and it was so.*
>
> 30 *And to every beast of the earth, and to every fowl of the air, and to every thing that creepeth upon the earth, wherein* there is ***life****,* I have given *every green herb for meat: and it was so. (Genesis 1:20, 21, 24, 30) (Emphasis added)*
>
> 7 *And the LORD God formed man* of *the dust of the ground, and breathed into his nostrils the breath of life; and*

man became a ***living soul****. (Genesis 2:7)*
(+Emphasis added)

In these verses the same phrase is used in the Hebrew for living creatures and man. Animals have *nephesh* (soul) and man has *nephesh* (soul). Man and animals are living (*chay*). So, the answer to the question, "Do animals have a soul?" is simply, "Yes." And that answer is based upon the authority of the Word of God. Of course, animals do not have a spirit inextricably united with their soul as does man.

Behavior is the exercise of the will under the influence of the mind and the emotions. Of course, behavior need not require the use of the body. The body is only required when you want to give outward, physical and visible manifestation to your inward behavior. Since carrots do not have a soul, thus no behavior mechanism, they just grow. And we eat them. They do not express anything to anybody. They also do not experience fear as they do not see the gardener coming their way with the intention of making them supper. This in itself is encouraging, and we do not have to chase and catch that part of our meal.

But animals, including man, do have a behavior mechanism in the soul. The body provides not only a "house" to dwell in but a means of expressing behavior — or disguising it. The outward, physical communication of your body may not reflect the inward behavior you are experiencing. How many times have you looked at someone who is smiling and you know, you really know, that inside they are seething mad or totally disinterested. The Psalmist puts it very plainly,

> The words *of his mouth were smoother than butter, but war* was *in his heart: his words were softer than oil, yet* were *they drawn swords. (Psalms 55:21)*

When was the last time you sat in church all dressed up in your finest "outdo the Jones's" wardrobe looking in the direction of the preacher acting as if you were really paying attention. But you were really planning you outing for the afternoon that would take you to the lake and keep you there past church time that evening. Or maybe you were seething about Mrs. So-and-So and her new dress. Why, it is just like yours and she really looks better in it than you do!

As a teenager, what exciting times have been had in your mind as you sat there while the preacher preached or the special music was sung. You dreamed of that special someone two rows up and a little to the left. All the while you sat with your body expressing a behavior that to the nondiscerning appeared as one who was hanging intently on every word being preached or sung.

Of course animals do the same thing. Anyone who has had a pet can testify to that. For example, cocker spaniels are an emotional breed of dog. It only takes seconds to discern that there is a mind at work, emotions in action, and a will that is being exercised.

We had a cocker spaniel many years ago named Sandy. Training her was a challenge. She was intelligent and had a memory. I taught her voice commands, hand commands and commands on a whistle. Training went very well. When I would go outside to the back yard, I would call her name, which she recognized, and yell, "COME." She would come to me. As she was running around the yard I would call her name and raise my hand in the air and hold it there. She would hear her name, look at me and see my hand in the air. That meant stop right there and pay attention. She would do just that (most of the time). As I dropped my hand to my side, that was the silent command for COME. She would come running. All this was nice. But then there was the matter of restrictions and privileges.

One of the restrictions was the garbage. She knew, she absolutely knew that the garbage was off limits to her. She would avoid it like the plague while I was out in the yard. She had received enough discipline for disobeying in that regard that she did not want to repeat that violation. But while we were inside and she was on her own, that was a different story. She loved garbage. Garbage was a temptation too great to resist.

There were days when I would go out the back door, call for her, and nothing would happen. No bounding happy dog running to meet me. I would look for her. Then I would see her across the yard, ears very low on her head, tail tucked, head hanging low, and creeping toward her dog house to try to hide. That was a very clear indication to me to walk around the side of the house and "voila" garbage everywhere. SHE KNEW! Guilt was written all over her countenance. She was expressing through her body an inward behavior. Animals have a mind, emotions, and a will. They have a soul.

Contrary to man, however, the animal soul is not inextricably united with an animal spirit. Instead, there is an interlock, if you will, between the soul of the animal and the animal's creator, God. The animal functions as God designed that animal to function and has instilled in that animal an interlock we call instinct. That is the driving force behind animal behavior and that animal behavior, absent the curse from the fall of man, is exactly what God intended and is functionally satisfying to God. He made the animal that way.

But when an animal behaves in the course of its life, it is not expressing anything to its creator. It does not say by its behavior, "God, I love you" or "God, I could not care less." The animal is not morally responsible to God. The animal shall not stand before God after death and give account for its behavior. When an animal dies, it goes back into the ground from which it was made and ceases to exist.

So if we put man in this category, man ceases to be morally responsible to God, he ceases to exist after death, has no eternal destiny, and can behave as he sees fit. Of course that behavior is not like an animal but it is far worse than an animal. The basic reason for man to hang on to a bankrupt theory of evolution is to be morally free from accountability to God. It is rebellion; the same rebellion demonstrated in the garden of Eden by Adam.

Of course, if you hold that philosophy you have no problem butchering babies in the womb or even out of the womb. They are just "animals" in your sight and even less than animals. The same people who want to save baby eagles or baby seals do not care a wit about baby humans.

Man acts like an animal, but man is not an animal. What is the essential difference between man and the rest of the animal kingdom?

If we are to understand what happened when Adam sinned, what happened upon the cross of Calvary, what happens at salvation, and what God expects of us after being redeemed, it is necessary for us to understand the nature of man, how man was made by his creator, and how his creator restores man to full function and purpose as He as God intended when He made man.

Just to keep things simple, but foremost to keep the discussion Biblical, our investigation into the nature and makeup of man begins in 1 Thessalonians 5:23,

> *And the very God of peace sanctify you wholly; and* I pray God *your whole* ***spirit*** *and* ***soul*** *and* ***body*** *be preserved blameless unto the coming of our Lord Jesus Christ. (Emphasis added)*

At first glance we learn from this verse that man is composed of three parts: spirit, soul, and body. This is called the trichotomy of man. This simply means constituted of three parts. I know that since time immemorial the debate has been on between the "trichotomists" and the "dichotomists." A dichotomist believes that man is only two parts: the visible and the invisible, lumping soul and spirit together. I do not intend to debate the issue nor even resolve it for all time. Quite simply, whichever side a coin falls on, it is still a coin.

The fact that the body is a physical, visible, tangible part of man is beyond dispute. The fact that soul and spirit are intangible and invisible is also beyond dispute. But let us also keep in mind that without a doubt and beyond controversy is the fact that we now see through a glass darkly and in our limited human capacity do not completely understand the infinite and eternal things of God.

However you want to cut it, the Bible is quite clear in this passage. Three different Greek words are used to describe man. These three different Greek words are correctly translated into three different English words. The first is *pneuma*. It is correctly translated as spirit and is distinct from the second word *psuche* translated soul, which we have already looked at briefly. Of course the third word is *soma* translated body.

So, we are comprised, according to the inspired Word of God, of *pneuma, psuche,* and *soma*. We may not be able to understand the exact and full relationship between spirit and soul, but we must accept the Bible at face value even when and where we do not understand fully.

> *For the word of God* is *quick, and powerful, and sharper than any twoedged sword, piercing even to the dividing asunder of soul and spirit, and of the joints and marrow, and* is *a discerner of the thoughts and intents of the heart. (Hebrews 4:12)*

Couple with that verse Leviticus 17:11 where we are told that the life of the flesh is in the blood. Major Ian Thomas gives a good illustration and explanation of this in his book, *The Mystery of Godliness.*

> "It is a physiological fact that the blood is manufactured in the marrow, and this 'source of life,' being of such paramount importance to the body as a whole, is buried and protected deep within the joints and the bones. The 'joints' provide a unique 'behavior mechanism,' but it is ultimately from the 'marrow' that there flows the life which *motivates the mechanism*, and this in turn gives *expression* to the life which does the motivating!
>
> This is a beautiful illustration given to us by the Holy Spirit! The joints and the marrow are interdependent if they are both to function properly, and the one is buried deep within the other. Together they form one entity, yet each remains distinct; they may not safely part company, but the one must not be mistaken for the other, and the final paradox is this, that the marrow itself lives only as there flows *through* it the very life that stems from it — the blood! '...for the blood is the life' (Deuteronomy 12:23) — not the marrow!
>
> This is why the blood is sacred in the Bible. It represents the *very life of God Himself* — the Spirit of God *within* the human spirit, as the blood flowing

> through and from the marrow, imparting the very Life of God *to* the human spirit, from whence this Life must flow to activate the 'joints' within the human soul, and produce that pattern of behavior which enables man to bear the image of the Invisible, and give expression to the Indwelling, Quickening, Motivating Life of God."

If we consider man as consisting of spirit, soul, and body, each with specific functions, purpose, and capacity, much of the Bible will make sense that did not make sense before and those passages will mean more to the reader.

We are most familiar with the body since it greets us every morning when we awake. We spend much effort in the maintenance of the body giving only passing thought to the soul. One thing we are sure of: if we do not keep the body and soul together, tradition dictates putting the body in the ground. This would be an untoward circumstance if it should happen and we be unprepared.

The third but most important part of man is his spirit. The human spirit was given by God simultaneously with the human soul and physical life when He breathed into Adam the breath of life. It is this spirit, the human spirit, that distinguishes man from animal. The spirit and the soul are inextricably inseparable. But they should not be confused the one for the other. We may not understand exactly what the difference is or understand completely how they operate together and individually, but that does not change the fact of their existence. It is the spirit that is eternally united to the human soul that gives that soul the ability to survive after physical death and imparts with that its moral responsibility to God.

It is the human spirit that is the unique capacity that God has put in man that enables man to receive and enjoy the very life of God, God Himself being present in the man by the Holy Spirit. This ability and capacity from God to be indwelt by God Himself and receive His life which is eternal in its character and quality is that which distinguishes man from animal. And the only logical conclusion that can be drawn at this point is that God must be present in man, imparting His life to man, sharing His life with man, so that He may communicate that life through man to all of His creation. And that was His original intent in creation. Man was created as a whole being: spirit, soul, and body completely indwelt by God and motivated by love for God and dependence upon God which results in and is manifested by obedience to God.

This chapter thus far has laid the groundwork and structure to continue examining *zoe*, or life. It has been a bit tedious and maybe even laborious, but it is toward an end. We are attempting to build a wall from the foundation up. The bottom stones must be placed first, then the second, and so on. Hopefully, this will all come together soon.

The words *zoe* and *nephesh* when used and translated as life are regarded as something in man or more specifically in his blood. This we have seen in Leviticus 17:11. From this we may observe that life is transcendent and not subject to the control of man. This is seen from creation.

> *And the LORD God formed man* of *the dust of the ground, and breathed into his nostrils the breath of life; and man became a living soul. (Genesis 2:7)*

God created man of the dust of the ground. At that exact point the body of man was lying upon the ground motionless, devoid of any life. It was the body and the body only. The Apostle Paul calls it "our earthly house." Man's body, created by God was prepared and ready, but man was not yet man.

Man did not become a living soul until God breathed into him the breath of life. At that point man became everything God wanted him to be and possessed life as only God could provide. Man has life only because God gave it to him and God gave it to him on a conditional basis. Life remains solely under God's control. God is the origin and source of life. There is no other origin and there is no other source. He is life eternal.

God is the self-sufficient, self-existent One who alone possesses and is eternal life. Life as given by God to man is from and unto God and is sustained by God.

This life was and is all encompassing. In other words, when God breathed into Adam the breath of life, man became a living soul. He came alive physically. His body began to function. He came alive soulishly: mind, emotion and will. He was self-conscious and aware of his surroundings. He also came alive unto God spiritually by means of the Holy Spirit inhabiting his human spirit. God was present in the man and thus imparted to man certain eternal qualities along with fellowship with God.

A distinction is thus made at this point that life may be considered to possess various qualities. This is a difficult part of the examination. We refer to qualities of life rather than types of life, portions of life, components of life, etc. We must keep in mind that there is just "life." We may refer to different kinds of life: e.g. vegetable life, animal life, human life.

We do not see anywhere in creation all of life as life is found in God. That is impossible. God is life eternal, infinite. He is the source and He is the origin. At His command and in accordance with His will and desire, He imparted life to creation in various qualities. We would not dispute that the quality of life led by a carrot is less than that of the puppy lying so comfortably by the chair and who responds to you in adoration and a desire to please. Eating a carrot is not the same as eating the puppy. The quality of life is different; but life nonetheless is life.

This does not mean we should not eat carrots. Although I can hear a loud crescendo arising from young people around the world in support of the Save the Carrot Movement. By the way, it also does not mean we should not eat the dog. In societies less civilized than our own (not said in any pride or arrogance), dog is a normal fare for dinner. That does not make it right or wrong. We choose the meat we eat based upon our culture. But eating meat is absolutely acceptable because it is God's plan.

> *Every moving thing that liveth shall be meat for you; even as the green herb have I given you all things. (Genesis 9:3)*

There is no prohibition from God against eating the meat of animals. There is a prohibition against eating the blood of the flesh. That subject will be covered in a later chapter. When a carrot dies, life is forfeited. When a dog dies, life is forfeited. We observe a difference in the quality of life given by God at creation between a carrot and a dog.

Although a dog has a soul and a quality of life better than that of a carrot, a dog is not equipped with a capacity to know God by His indwelling Holy Spirit. Man has that capacity.

When we first observe the use of the Greek word *zoe*, we see that its first use is in reference to the natural life of man. Then as we progress it is used to refer to more than the physical processes of the human body we call life. It refers to that quality of life that results from a mind, emotions, and will engaged in enterprise to achieve possibilities. Then we observe its use to refer to our present life in Christ. And finally, it is used to denote True Life which is none other than the Life of God.

All these referred to by the use of only one word. Why? Because life is simply that: life. It may be observed in various qualities (we may even say degrees of life but we choose the term qualities for now). These various qualities will range from the simple plant life of creation to the highest form of physical life, man. Life is that vitality that derives from God as the origin and is derived from God as the source. Man may feed his body to maintain continuance of life, but that continuance is dependent solely upon God who is the life-giver and sustainer of all life.

At this point let us consider when life began so that we can understand when life begins. "In the beginning God…" That was all. As my grandson said when he was four years old, "Grandpa, before God created the world and everything, there was just God."

May he never forget that simple yet deep theological truth. He also informed me one day, while we were driving to the home improvement center to play on the garden tractors, that the Pharisees didn't kill Jesus. I asked him why was that. He said that Jesus let them do it.

By the way, at the age of four and a half he was born again. He completely understood the plan of salvation, he knew who Jesus was, he knew that he was a sinner and the only way to Heaven was to be saved. His Daddy questioned him, I questioned him, his pastor questioned him. He was not to be deterred. Oh, that adults would exercise the simple faith of a child. And a child understood the fact that before God created the universe there was just Him.

And He is eternal life. He is self-sufficient. His life is never ending. In God and God alone is life eternally inherent: eternally pre-existent, self-existent, and self-perpetuating.

And this life was breathed into the nostrils of man and man became a living soul on the sixth day of creation.

From our perspective as man and considering man, that is when life began. And since that time, life has only been passed on from generation to generation by the act of reproduction; an act created by God for that specific purpose.

Life began in Adam. Life does not begin at conception. This will throw a whole new light on the so-called abortion debate. Immediately upon conception, life is passed on to a new and unique individual with a soul and a spirit whose body consists of only one cell at the time. Life is passed on.

The life that began in Adam, received directly from God was of a quality that was much more than a vegetable, and much more than an animal. Having placed within the human soul a human spirit capable of receiving the life of God, God Himself imparted to man His very own life. Man was created a whole. Spirit, soul, and body: indwelt by God Himself.

This quality of life that allowed man to share the life of God and have fellowship with God was what was forfeited when Adam fell. Adam retained the rest of it, being able to function physically, intellectually, emotionally, and volitionally. But Adam was dead to God. Alienated from the life of God. The Holy Spirit had been removed who is the link through which that life is shared.

And it is that very life of God that is restored to the soul of man upon genuine conversion. And man can enjoy that quality of life that God intended for man to enjoy when He created man. And that life is eternal life. Of course we are still in the present at home in a fallen, sinful body, so that the degree to which we allow that life to be communicated and the degree to which we share that life is dependent upon our yielding to the Holy Spirit and not to the fleshly lusts of this fallen nature.

The concept of life remaining after life has been forfeited is made difficult to understand because of the multiple use of a single word, life. But *zoe* encompasses more than a single abstract quality of life.

That is how we can say and understand that Adam died in the day he ate the fruit and then died physically many years later. That is how we can say and understand that any man, woman, boy, or girl born into this world since Adam fell is born physically alive but spiritually dead. That quality of life that reunites the Holy Spirit with the human spirit is absent. Dead men walking!

That is how we can talk about coming alive in Christ Jesus, of being quickened, of being raised from the dead. And this life of which we speak, this quality of life that restores to man the Holy Spirit of God and reunites the lost sinner with his creator, this life is the very life of God.

And "the life of the flesh is in the blood."

And Jesus was a man.

And Jesus had blood.

CHAPTER SEVEN

THE LIFE OF THE FLESH

"For it is the life of all flesh" Leviticus 17:14

In this and following chapters, the theological significance and importance of the blood, the necessity of sacrificial blood and its use in atonement, and the practical application of these truths to the lives of believers will be presented. Once again, it is necessary to take a look at some details concerning the word blood.

The English word blood is found in 375 locations in the King James Version of the Bible. The first appearance of this word is in Genesis 4:10 and the last appearance is in Revelation 19:13. From the very beginning of the Word of God, throughout its entirety and unto the very end, blood is not only mentioned but is a central tenet of God's system of dealing with fallen man.

Although the first mention of the word blood is not found until Genesis 4:10, the presence of blood is found by inference earlier. In Genesis chapter two when God formed man of the dust of the ground, man's body was complete; the only thing missing was life which came from God. As man lay upon the ground from which he was made, before God breathed into him the breath of life, his body had blood in it; just as it had all the organs and bones and skin and everything to make the body complete. Blood was present in man from the formation of man from the ground and will be present through the end of the Revelation.

Of course, animal blood had appeared earlier when God made those animals in which there was life.

> 20 *And God said, Let the waters bring forth abundantly the moving creature that hath life, and fowl* that *may fly above the earth in the open firmament of heaven.*
>
> 21 *And God created great whales, and every living creature that moveth, which the waters brought forth abundantly, after their kind, and every winged fowl after his kind: and God saw that* it was *good.*
>
> 22 *And God blessed them, saying, Be fruitful, and multiply, and fill the waters in the seas, and let fowl multiply in the earth.*

23 *And the evening and the morning were the fifth day.*

24 *And God said, Let the earth bring forth the living creature after his kind, cattle, and creeping thing, and beast of the earth after his kind: and it was so.*

25 *And God made the beast of the earth after his kind, and cattle after their kind, and every thing that creepeth upon the earth after his kind: and God saw that* it was *good. (Genesis 1:20-25)*

The Hebrew words used in connection with creation of animal life are the same words used in connection with the creation of man. The same word, *nephesh*, translated soul in Genesis 2:7 with regard to man is also used in 1:20-25 with regard to the beasts of the field. Both man and beasts have blood, wherein is life, as well as a soul. The difference lies in the manner of creation. Animals were created and endued with a living soul; they were alive. When God created them, He created them alive.

Man, on the other hand, received his life directly from God when God breathed into him the breath of life. At this point, man received not only his physical, animal life, but also his spiritual life and was indwelt by the Spirit of the living God and was alive unto God.

That is a dividing line between man and animals in creation. Animals are not God-conscious, expressing an attitude toward God with their behavior. They behave based upon instinct received from their Creator. Man, though, is God-conscious, demonstrating an attitude toward God with and by his behavior; either an attitude of love for and dependence upon God demonstrated by his obedience to God, or an attitude of rebellion against and independence from God demonstrated by his disobedience of God.

Clearly seen in creation is the fact of the blood being the seat of life in man and animals. Both man and animals have a soul (*nephesh*). This soul, although it may not be in actuality located in the blood, is, however, inextricably united with the blood. Remove the blood from the animal or man and life is removed. When life is removed the soul departs. And when the soul departs, only death remains.

> *And it came to pass, as her soul was in departing, (for she died) that she called his name Benoni: but his father called him Benjamin. (Genesis 35:18)*

The term living soul indicates the union of the soul and the blood in man and animals. Both have life. The significance of this union in both man and animal shall be seen in an examination of the atonement.

In Genesis 3:21, God made coats of skins with which a fallen and sinful Adam and Eve were to be clothed. It is indeed quite obvious that in order to get the skins off of the animals, death occurred. In the process, life was forfeited. This is not explicitly stated, but is implicitly clear through reason, revelation in nature and our knowledge of the animal world. Blood was poured out in death that man might be clothed and once again be able to approach God and have fellowship with God. To restore the broken fellowship between the Creator God and man, life had to be given up. That life that was given up was the life of an acceptable substitute.

Of the 375 occurrences of the word blood in the Bible, in the Old Testament it occurs most often in Leviticus (88 times); followed by Ezekiel (55 times), Exodus (29 times), Deuteronomy (23 times), and Psalms (21 times). In the New Testament, blood occurs most often in Hebrews (20 times) followed by Revelation (17 times), and occurs only three times in Romans, twice only in reference to the blood of Christ.

When the word blood appears, it is generally used in one of two contexts: (1) shedding of blood through violence resulting in death; e.g., war or murder; or, (2) shedding of blood, always resulting in death, in a sacrifice to God.[1] When blood is mentioned or is the subject of the text, it is commonly associated with shedding of that blood resulting in death. This does not refer to the mere act of bleeding, but something of much, much more significance and extent. The two go together, shedding of blood and death.

This usage is still present today. When reference is made to those who fought and died in previous wars for our country, they are spoken of as shedding their blood in defense of their country. By that is meant that they died defending their country. So it is not an unfamiliar usage to equate shedding of blood with death.

The Hebrew word for blood is *dam* (pronounced *dawm, as in dawn)*. This word is used to denote the blood of animals, birds, and men; but, never used in reference to fish, although fish have blood as we think of it biologically. *Dam*, as used in the Old Testament, carries several shades of meaning. First, it can mean "blood shed by violence."

> *So ye shall not pollute the land wherein ye* are*: for blood it defileth the land: and the land cannot be cleansed of the blood that is shed therein, but by the blood of him that shed it. (Numbers 35:33)*

As a result of the application of this usage, it can mean death.

So will I send upon you famine and evil beasts, and they shall bereave thee; and pestilence and blood shall pass through thee; and I will bring the sword upon thee. I the LORD have spoken it. *(Ezekiel 5:17)*

Next, *dam* may indicate the act by which human life is taken, or blood is shed.

If there arise a matter too hard for thee in judgment, between blood and blood, between plea and plea, and between stroke and stroke, being *matters of controversy within thy gates: then shalt thou arise, and get thee up into the place which the LORD thy God shall choose; (Deuteronomy 17:8)*

Another way of referring to murder is to call it "shedding of blood".

Whoso sheddeth man's blood, by man shall his blood be shed: for in the image of God made he man. (Genesis 9:6)

"Shedding of blood may also mean the killing of a sacrificial animal which is then not brought as an offering.

3 *What man soever* there be *of the house of Israel, that killeth an ox, or lamb, or goat, in the camp, or that killeth* it *out of the camp,*

4 *And bringeth it not unto the door of the tabernacle of the congregation, to*

offer an offering unto the LORD before the tabernacle of the LORD; blood shall be imputed unto that man; he hath shed blood; and that man shall be cut off from among his people: (Leviticus 17:3-4)

Another use of this word is the judicial import associated with the life of man. In Leviticus the principle is found that to "stand against one's blood" means to stand before a court against an accused as a plaintiff, witness, or judge.

Thou shalt not go up and down as *a talebearer among thy people: neither shalt thou stand against the blood of thy neighbour: I* am *the LORD. (Leviticus 19:16)*

When the Bible refers to "his blood be upon his head," it does not mean a literal placing of the blood upon the head. Rather, it means that the guilt and punishment for a violent act is to be placed upon the guilty perpetrator.

For every one that curseth his father or his mother shall be surely put to death: he hath cursed his father or his mother; his blood shall be *upon him. (Leviticus 20:9)*

Throughout the Bible, when it refers to someone's blood being upon another's head, it refers to guilt for an action and not to actual literal blood being placed upon that individual. It is symbolic. Responsibility for the life, or death, of someone can be referred to by the statement, "His blood be upon your head." In other words, the guilt associated with the death, or loss of life, of someone is assigned judicially by referring to the blood.

The Greek word for blood in the New Testament is *haima* (pronounced *hah' ee-mah*). As used in the New Testament, *haima* can refer to man or human beings, as in "flesh and blood."

> *And Jesus answered and said unto him, Blessed art thou, Simon Barjona: for flesh and blood hath not revealed* it *unto thee, but my Father which is in heaven. (Matthew 16:17)*
>
> *Now this I say, brethren, that flesh and blood cannot inherit the kingdom of God; neither doth corruption inherit incorruption. (1 Corinthians 15:50)*
>
> *To reveal his Son in me, that I might preach him among the heathen; immediately I conferred not with flesh and blood: (Galatians 1:16)*
>
> *For we wrestle not against flesh and blood, but against principalities, against powers, against the rulers of the darkness of this world, against spiritual wickedness in high* places. *(Ephesians 6:12)*
>
> *Forasmuch then as the children are partakers of flesh and blood, he also himself likewise took part of the same; that through death he might destroy him that had the power of death, that is, the devil; (Hebrews 2:14)*

In John 1:13, blood is used to refer to human generation. A third meaning of the word *haima* refers to blood shed by violence resulting in death.

> *That upon you may come all the righteous blood shed upon the earth, from the blood of righteous Abel unto the blood of Zacharias son of Barachias, whom ye slew between the temple and the altar. (Matthew 23:35)*
>
> *And I saw the woman drunken with the blood of the saints, and with the blood of the martyrs of Jesus: and when I saw her, I wondered with great admiration. (Revelation 17:6)*

Another use of blood is in reference to the actual blood of sacrificial victims.

> *But into the second* went *the high priest alone once every year, not without blood, which he offered for himself, and* for *the errors of the people: (Hebrews 9:7)*

As is readily seen from both the Hebrew word and the Greek word, the English word "blood" in our Bible more often than not has an expanded and deeper meaning than simply referring only to that red fluid flowing through the circulatory system of man and animals. It often represents, symbolically, typologically, and literally, not only the actual blood but the death that resulted from the shedding of that blood. The two terms, shedding of blood and sacrificial death, are quite often interchangeable because they are inextricably united in the act of atonement. The sacrificial death is inadequate without the shedding of the blood. And the shedding of the blood is inadequate without the accompanying death. They are indivisible yet distinguishable.

There is no doubt as to the theological significance of the blood in the Bible. It is present from the beginning to the end of the Scriptures. Its import is seen in reference to man and man's life. God places a high value upon the life of man. This is seen in the Levitical law. But a debate arises due to the symbolic and typological usage of the word blood.

When does it mean only the actual, literal fluid?

When does it refer to death?

When does it mean guilt associated with the death of a person or animal?

When does it refer to the life of a man or animal poured out in death?

These questions and their answers can cause confusion if proper hermeneutical principles are not applied. The solution, of course, is that the meaning is always to be drawn from the context of the text and compared with other Scripture on the same subject. Slight departures from the simplicity of the clear Scriptural statements on the matter of the blood are fraught with grave danger and call for eternal vigilance and earnest resistance. Text out of context is pretext.

A debate today in Christianity seems to center around the significance of the blood and what is thereby symbolized in the context of sacrifice. In attempts at presenting one side as opposed to another, one man's opinion against another man's opinion, this school of thought compared to another school of thought, one interpretation or another, an exhibition of a tendency to give way to learned and unimportant minutia, which is out of place in a serious discussion of the topic at hand, may actually imperil the great principles associated with the doctrine of the blood. The debaters quite often become too smart by half and reduce the arguments to the ridiculous with emphasis placed upon that which is not direct and explicit in Scripture but, rather, is derived and inferred from certain readings of passages of Scripture, quite often in isolation from parallel or enlightening passages elsewhere.

The many suggestions and attestations offered up in discussions and publications concerning the blood may be summarized in three general statements: (1) Blood symbolizes life; (2) Blood, especially in the Old Testament, denotes life offered up in death; and, (3) Blood simply and only means just that, the literal fluid flowing through the flesh of man and animal.

On the surface, the first two appear to be very similar if not the same idea simply restated. This is not the case. The third seeks to limit the meaning of the word blood to a very narrow definition not found in the Hebrew and Greek languages used to pen the Word of God under inspiration of the Holy Ghost. This third position is unsupportable in linguistics as well as theology. For, to make too much of the literal blood itself is to make too little of the blood. This shall be made clearer later in the study. And to make too much of the literal blood itself is borderline idolatry. This also shall be clearer.

In the first instance, where blood symbolizes life, the blood of the sacrificial victim is the life that has passed through death. This position derives from several Old Testament passages.

> *But flesh with the life thereof,* which is *the blood thereof, shall ye not eat. (Genesis 9:4)*
>
> *For the life of the flesh* is *in the blood: and I have given it to you upon the altar to make an atonement for your souls: for it* is *the blood* that *maketh an atonement for the soul. (Leviticus 17:11)*

Only be sure that thou eat not the blood: for the blood is *the life; and thou mayest not eat the life with the flesh. (Deuteronomy 12:23)*

Carrying this position from the Old Testament into the New Testament leads to the conclusion that to say that one is saved by "the blood of Christ" means that one is saved by Christ's life, by participating in his life.

The second position, that of the blood denoting the life poured out in sacrificial death, does not abandon the three passages above that speak of the life of the flesh being in the blood. These passages do not say that blood is the actual life. They simply refer to blood as the source of life, the seat of life, or the means whereby life is perpetuated. In other words, removing the blood will result in a termination of life. It does not remove life, but does cause life to be removed.

This can be demonstrated and seen in modern medicine during certain surgical procedures, especially during heart transplants. The symbolic nature of Biblical language takes on greater dimension in these cases. For example, the symbolic use of the phrase the "heart of man."

After a heart transplant, the receiving patient is not a "new man" or different person. Similarly, blood transfusions, removal and replacement of blood for certain medical operations, etc., demonstrate that life is far more than actual blood. Also, after a person dies, life departs the body, the blood remains. The blood doesn't disappear with the life.

Since the blood is the seat of life, or that by which lifc is perpetuated in man, and is inextricably associated with the soul of man, it has significance in God's sight resulting in three distinct principles concerning blood that are very specific.

The first principle is the sanctity of life. The import of this can only be understood if life itself is seen in proper perspective.

In the battle today for the life of the unborn, many hold that life begins at conception. This accepted, to abort a baby is to murder. One thing is certain, abortion is premeditated murder of the most heinous description. However, the premise that life begins at conception is incorrect. Life does not begin at conception, but is passed on at conception. Life began in man when God breathed into Adam the breath of life. From that point forward, life was and is passed on through conception. Medical science aside, which completely supports the proposition of passing on life, the Bible gives indication of this when referring to individuals before their birth as being in the loins of their father. Man's limited understanding of genetics and DNA notwithstanding, science and the Bible are in harmony on this when individuals are considered in light of genetic traits and abilities. This point, however, is not a major focus of this book, but is mentioned again to emphasize the importance of life in God's eyes. Life is a gift directly from God to and through Adam and man is accountable for his stewardship of it.

We must be careful in our terminology. Christians have adopted the world's words and phrases relating to life and reproduction. For example, quite often you hear reference to a woman who is pregnant as being an expectant mother. This seems to be a common usage. But consider for a moment the impact of such a phrase and the derivative positions taken on abortion.

The term "expectant mother" may imply that the woman is expecting to become a mother when the baby is born. Of course this is not true for she already is a mother. Immediately upon conception, she became a mother of an individual known to God. She is a mother. The Bible refers to this as being with child. Care must be exercised in choosing our words in order to carry the exact and unquestionable meaning we intend. At conception life is passed on and the woman is with child and a mother. To kill the baby, at any stage in any trimester, is killing an innocent human for which those who are involved will stand before a holy God and give account. They are guilty of murder.

This first principle, the sanctity of life, is seen in the prohibition in Scripture that man may not shed the blood of another man. God pronounced the death penalty upon those guilty of shedding another's blood.

> *The revenger of blood himself shall slay the murderer: when he meeteth him, he shall slay him. (Numbers 35:19)*
>
> *Then the elders of his city shall send and fetch him thence, and deliver him into the hand of the avenger of blood, that he may die. (Deuteronomy 19:12)*

Further, an individual who committed an infraction of the moral law necessitating the death penalty is described as a person whose "blood is upon" or "his blood shall be upon his head." These passages clearly indicate that life is the subject while blood is the word used symbolically.

> 9 *For every one that curseth his father or his mother shall be surely put to death: he hath cursed his father or his mother; his blood* shall be *upon him.*
>
> 11 *And the man that lieth with his father's wife hath uncovered his father's nakedness: both of them shall surely be*

put to death; their blood shall be *upon them.*

12 *And if a man lie with his daughter in law, both of them shall surely be put to death: they have wrought confusion; their blood* shall be *upon them.*

13 *If a man also lie with mankind, as he lieth with a woman, both of them have committed an abomination: they shall surely be put to death; their blood* shall be *upon them.*

16 *And if a woman approach unto any beast, and lie down thereto, thou shalt kill the woman, and the beast: they shall surely be put to death; their blood* shall be *upon them.*

27 *A man also or woman that hath a familiar spirit, or that is a wizard, shall surely be put to death: they shall stone them with stones: their blood* shall be *upon them. (Leviticus 20:9, 11-13, 16, 27)*

And it shall be, that *whosoever shall go out of the doors of thy house into the street, his blood* shall be *upon his head, and we* will be *guiltless: and whosoever shall be with thee in the house, his blood* shall be *on our head, if* any *hand be upon him. (Joshua 2:19)*

For it shall be, that *on the day thou goest out, and passest over the brook Kidron, thou shalt know for certain that thou shalt surely die: thy blood shall be upon thine own head. (1 Kings 2:37)*

By way of aside on the matter of the death penalty. It is just that, a penalty. It is punishment for a specific infraction of the law. It is not a deterrent in God's eyes. It is the penalty for the crime. Sin always will and must be punished. The administration of the death penalty is divinely appointed to civil government.

The second principle regarding the blood and its relationship to life is seen in the requirements dictated by God for the offering of animal sacrifice. All of the blood of the animal must be drained and disposed of either on the altar, the ground, or elsewhere.

> *And he shall kill the bullock before the LORD: and the priests, Aaron's sons, shall bring the blood, and sprinkle the blood round about upon the altar that* is by *the door of the tabernacle of the congregation. (Leviticus 1:5)*
>
> 6 *And the priest shall dip his finger in the blood, and sprinkle of the blood seven times before the LORD, before the vail of the sanctuary.*
>
> 7 *And the priest shall put* some *of the blood upon the horns of the altar of sweet incense before the LORD, which* is *in the tabernacle of the congregation; and shall pour all the blood of the bullock at the bottom of the altar of the burnt offering, which* is at *the door of the tabernacle of the congregation. (Leviticus 4:6-7)*
>
> *Thou shalt not eat it; thou shalt pour it upon the earth as water. (Deuteronomy 12:24)*

The third principle is the prohibition of eating or drinking blood.

> *But flesh with the life thereof,* which is *the blood thereof, shall ye not eat. (Genesis 9:4)*
>
> It shall be *a perpetual statute for your generations throughout all your dwellings, that ye eat neither fat nor blood. (Leviticus 3:17)*
>
> 10 *And whatsoever man* there be *of the house of Israel, or of the strangers that sojourn among you, that eateth any manner of blood; I will even set my face against that soul that eateth blood, and will cut him off from among his people.*
>
> 11 *For the life of the flesh* is *in the blood: and I have given it to you upon the altar to make an atonement for your souls: for it* is *the blood* that *maketh an atonement for the soul.*
>
> 12 *Therefore I said unto the children of Israel, No soul of you shall eat blood, neither shall any stranger that sojourneth among you eat blood.*
>
> 13 *And whatsoever man* there be *of the children of Israel, or of the strangers that sojourn among you, which hunteth and catcheth any beast or fowl that may be eaten; he shall even pour out the blood thereof, and cover it with dust. (Leviticus 17:10-13)*
>
> 31 *And they smote the Philistines that day from Michmash to Aijalon: and the people were very faint.*

32 And the people flew upon the
spoil, and took sheep, and oxen, and
calves, and slew them on the ground:
and the people did eat them with the
blood.
33 Then they told Saul, saying,
Behold, the people sin against the
LORD, in that they eat with the blood.
And he said, Ye have transgressed: roll
a great stone unto me this day.
34 And Saul said, Disperse
yourselves among the people, and say
unto them, Bring me hither every man
his ox, and every man his sheep, and
slay them here, and eat; and sin not
against the LORD in eating with the
blood. And all the people brought every
man his ox with him that night, and slew
them there.
35 And Saul built an altar unto the
LORD: the same was the first altar that
he built unto the LORD. (1 Samuel
14:31-35)
25 Wherefore say unto them, Thus
saith the Lord GOD; Ye eat with the
blood, and lift up your eyes toward your
idols, and shed blood: and shall ye
possess the land?
26 Ye stand upon your sword, ye
work abomination, and ye defile every
one his neighbour's wife: and shall ye
possess the land?
27 Say thou thus unto them, Thus
saith the Lord GOD; As I live, surely
they that are in the wastes shall fall by
the sword, and him that is in the open

field will I give to the beasts to be devoured, and they that be *in the forts and in the caves shall die of the pestilence.*

28 *For I will lay the land most desolate, and the pomp of her strength shall cease; and the mountains of Israel shall be desolate, that none shall pass through.*

29 *Then shall they know that I* am *the LORD, when I have laid the land most desolate because of all their abominations which they have committed. (Ezekiel 33:25-29)*

20 *But that we write unto them, that they abstain from pollutions of idols, and* from *fornication, and* from *things strangled, and* from *blood.*

29 *That ye abstain from meats offered to idols, and from blood, and from things strangled, and from fornication: from which if ye keep yourselves, ye shall do well. (Acts 15:20, 29)*

This prohibition of eating or drinking the blood, instituted immediately following the flood, has not been revoked or lifted. The early Christians in Acts continued this prohibition, and for very good reasons. Atonement for sin was made by the sacrifice of the life of animals as a substitution for one's own life; and the shedding of blood, the pouring out of that life in sacrifice for another, was the most important element in the expiation of sin. The blood was and is too sacred for man to handle in such fashion. This prohibition and regard for the blood of man and animals, having never been lifted by God, remains in effect today and man would be well advised to abide thereby.

We do not and should not worship the blood — not even the blood of Christ. We worship God. But the blood must be held by man in the highest regard given it by God Himself.

Why?

Because the life is in the blood.

---

[1] Theological Wordbook of the Old Testament: 4360

CHAPTER EIGHT

THE BLOOD ATONEMENT

"for it is the blood that maketh atonement for the soul."
Leviticus 17:11

The importance of a proper Biblical understanding of the blood is obvious. Not only is the blood central and vital to our life as man, but more importantly the blood is at the center of the atonement and the atonement is at the center, and in fact is the heart of, Christianity. Redemption and regeneration by atonement is a distinguishing mark of

Biblical Christianity. Without atonement, Christianity is just another religion of man.

No one can clearly comprehend the great theme of atonement who is not at once prepared to take Scripture at face value and treat the Word of God as the final authoritative source of knowledge of this or any other doctrine. Furthermore, the student of this doctrine of atonement and the blood must be prepared to be led of the Holy Ghost into this knowledge. The unsaved cannot, the carnal Christian cannot, the lazy student cannot expect to receive of God that which enlightens the understanding in this matter.

Scriptural views of the atonement, and therefore of the blood, cannot be deduced from non-Biblical conceptions or perceptions of the person of Christ. The importance of the studies earlier in this book of the incarnation of Christ, His virgin birth, and the hypostatic union and their relationship to a proper understanding of the atonement and the role of the blood therein can be readily seen.

Of course, a point of beginning must be the doctrine of the Trinity: God the Father, God the Son, and God the Holy Ghost. The eternality of the Son, co-equal with the Father, is imperative. These facts are fundamental and non-negotiable.

A basic study of the Old Testament reveals that under the system given to the patriarchs by God there could be no access for fallen man, a sinner, into the presence of the Holy God without an atoning sacrifice. In order to worship God there must be acceptance by God. Before there is acceptance by God of sinful man there must be atonement for man's sin. This atonement for sin was achieved in a manner of divine origin. God Himself dictated the terms of man's approach to and restoration of fellowship with God. Those terms were the shedding of blood.

Note that the terms and conditions for atonement consisted not only of blood itself, but also that the blood must be shed. This shedding of blood was an effusion of life (a pouring out completely) — for the life of the flesh is in the blood. The focus then was not on the blood itself but through the blood onto the life that was therein. The two were and are inseparable. The blood and the life are inseparable in atonement.

The blood that was to be shed in atonement for sin was to be the blood of a substitutionary representative that was to be ceremonially without blemish.

> *Your lamb shall be without blemish, a male of the first year: ye shall take* it *out from the sheep, or from the goats: (Exodus 12:5)*
>
> *But with the precious blood of Christ, as of a lamb without blemish and without spot: (1 Peter 1:19)*

The first four chapters of Leviticus explain the substitutionary sacrifice very clearly.

The death of the vicarious or substitutionary victim, represented by the blood poured out (shed), was an acknowledgment by the sinner of the guilt of his sin, the penalty for sin, and payment for that penalty. That penalty for sin was, and is, death. Always has been. Always will be.

> *But of the tree of the knowledge of good and evil, thou shalt not eat of it: for in the day that thou eatest thereof thou shalt surely die. (Genesis 2:17)*
>
> *For the wages of sin* is *death. (Romans 6:23)*

The penalty for sin was not blood. The penalty was death and could only be satisfied by death of the guilty sinner or a substitute acceptable to God. The blood of the substitute could not atone for the sinner's sin apart from death. It was so ordered by God.

God was very specific in the details. There must be the death of the sacrificial substitute **and** that death must be by the shedding of blood. That blood then **must** be presented before God, the blood speaking of the life that was poured out in death as payment for the penalty of sin. The blood represented to God and man the life that was poured out in satisfaction of His holy demands.

The word "shed" comes from the Hebrew word *shaphak* (pronounced *shaw-fak'*). Its meanings are given as pour out, shed (blood), cast, gush out. It is used 115 times in twenty four books of the Old Testament. It is used in both the physical and metaphorical sense. This word is the common verb used to describe a pouring out of a variety of materials. However, the pouring out of blood constitutes the single most frequent use of the verb in Scripture.

In studying the shedding of blood, the principle of interpretation known in Hermeneutics as the First Mention Principle applies. That is the principle whereby God indicates in the first mention of a subject the truth with which that subject stands connected in the mind of God. This principle "will serve as an unfailing guide to what was in the mind of God."[1] Dr. A. T. Pierson has said, "This is a law we have long since noted, and have never yet found it to fail. The first occurrence of a word, expression, or utterance, is the key to its subsequent meaning, or it will be a guide to ascertaining the essential truth connected with it."[2] The first time a subject, concept, principle, precept, etc., is mentioned in Scripture it will then carry with it that meaning throughout the Word of God.

There is in fact only one speaker through all of Scripture, but many mouths and many pens. There is only one providing, governing, and controlling mind: God, who spoke through holy men of old. No matter when, where, or how the message is given, God is the speaker and as such He knows from the beginning what He is going to say, and so He shapes the first utterances as to forecast everything that is to follow. He is able to do that, He is God.[3] God says what He means, means what He says, and has the absolute right to say it. Applying the First Mention Principle to this point of the study gives indication and forecast concerning the meaning and implications of the shedding of blood.

The first occurrence of this word in Scripture is found in Genesis 9:6,

> *"Whoso **sheddeth** man's blood, by man shall his blood be **shed**." (Emphasis added)*

In this first use in the Old Testament, it is part of the general principle concerning the taking of human life. This concept is to be used throughout the rest of Scripture to understand the truth underlying the shedding of blood and the true focus that should be maintained. The whole thrust of this first occurrence is not concerned with the actual blood, but that wrongful, deliberate death has occurred. Our focus should be adjusted to coincide with this first mention and applied throughout the study of the shedding of blood and the significance it carries in the mind of God.

The system given by God in the Old Testament for atonement and reconciliation to God was designed to teach His people about the holiness of God, their own sinfulness with the personal guilt and responsibility that must be borne, and especially to demonstrate that God would forgive them not based upon any merit of their own or any act they might undertake for that end. Forgiveness by God was to be based solely on the undeserved grace of God obtained through the death of an innocent substitute, whose literal shed blood represented the substitution of an innocent life for a guilty life in payment of the penalty due. And do not forget, the penalty that was due was death.

This system, designed by God, delivered to man, and instituted by man was temporary and imperfect.[4] It was intended by God for man to learn just how holy He is and how wicked man is and deserving of death, which is the wages of sin. It was also typical and prophetic at the same time, giving hope to the faithful of a coming kinsman redeemer and the actuality of an atonement that could satisfy God completely. It taught the people of God about the One who was to come and be the Lamb of God, slain from the foundation of the world.

In the New Testament, there is an unprecedented and unique prominence given to the death of Christ in the four Gospels and the Epistles. None of the patriarchs, prophets, or great men of the Old Testament had any significant value or benefit to men associated with their death. None were able to give life by dying.

A cursory reading of the New Testament quickly reveals that the purpose of the incarnation of Jesus Christ was His death by crucifixion. He came to die. His mission to earth was to die. His death overshadowed all that He did. He came to give His life a ransom for man.

Not only did He come to earth with the intent and purpose to die, the object of His death was the forgiveness of sins. More than forgiveness, a complete and irrevocable remission of sins. His death was the means whereby men should and could obtain eternal life. The singular theme of the death of Christ throughout thc entirety of the New Testament is that Christ did not die a martyr's death, did not die by accident, but died according to the predeterminate will of God. He did so of His own volition, according to the prophets, was completely innocent and undefiled; and His death was substitutionary, sacrificial, atoning, reconciling, redeeming, and fulfilling the law. He paid the penalty in full once and for all.

> *No man taketh it from me, but I lay it down of myself. I have power to lay it down, and I have power to take it again. This commandment have I received of my Father. (John 10:18)*
>
> *Him, being delivered by the determinate counsel and foreknowledge of God, ye have taken, and by wicked hands have crucified and slain: (Acts 2:23)*
>
> *Whom God hath set forth* to be *a propitiation through faith in his blood, to declare his righteousness for the remission of sins that are past, through the forbearance of God. (Romans 3:25)*
>
> 6 *For when we were yet without strength, in due time Christ died for the ungodly.*
>
> 9 *Much more then, being now justified by his blood, we shall be saved from wrath through him. (Romans 5:6, 9)*
>
> *For I delivered unto you first of all that which I also received, how that Christ died for our sins according to the scriptures. (1 Corinthians 15:3)*
>
> 15 *And* that *he died for all, that they which live should not henceforth live unto themselves, but unto him which died for them, and rose again.*
>
> 19 *To wit, that God was in Christ, reconciling the world unto himself, not imputing their trespasses unto them; and*

hath committed unto us the word of reconciliation.

21 *For he hath made him* to be *sin for us, who knew no sin; that we might be made the righteousness of God in him. (2 Corinthians 5:15, 19, 21)*

14 *How much more shall the blood of Christ, who through the eternal Spirit offered himself without spot to God, purge your conscience from dead works to serve the living God?*

26 *For then must he often have suffered since the foundation of the world: but now once in the end of the world hath he appeared to put away sin by the sacrifice of himself. (Hebrews 9:14, 26)*

Atonement for sin, from the beginning of the Bible until the antitype Himself fulfilled the prophecy, has been by the death of an innocent substitute. But, a very specific death is determined, that by shedding of blood, which must be presented to God in the prescribed manner representing the life poured out in substitutionary death in payment for another's sin penalty.

"The wages of sin is death" and the death that is to pay those wages must be by the pouring out of innocent life by the shedding of blood. The payment was death, the method or process of that death was by shedding of blood.

Schofield's notes on atonement in Leviticus 16 are instructive and an excellent summary presented here before going on with our study of shedding of blood.

> The biblical use and meaning of the word must be sharply distinguished from its use in theology. In theology it

> is a term which covers the whole sacrificial and redemptive work of Christ. In the O.T. atonement is the English word used to translate the Hebrew words which mean "cover," "coverings," or "to cover." Atonement (at-one-ment) is, therefore, not a translation of the Hebrew, but a purely theologic concept. The Levitical offerings "covered" the sins of Israel until, and in anticipation of the Cross, but did not "take away" (Heb. 10:4) those sins. These were the "sins done aforetime" ("covered" meantime by the Levitical sacrifices), which God "passed over" (Rom. 3:25) — for which "passing over" God's righteousness was never vindicated until, in the Cross, Jesus Christ was "set forth a propitiation. ...It was the Cross, not the Levitical sacrifices which made "at-one-ment." The O.T. sacrifices enabled God to go on with a guilty people because they typified the Cross. To the *offerer* they were the confession of his desert of death, and the expression of his faith; to God they were the "shadows" (Heb 10:1) of which Christ was the reality.

In the Old Testament system of worship and atonement for sin, the altar of burnt-offering obtained its importance and significance from the connection in which it stood with the presentation before God of the blood of the slain vicarious victim. The altar was the place, but the actual presentation of the literal blood was the focal point of the whole ceremony. The blood must of necessity be presented before God. The proper Biblical account of the institution of sacrifice by blood had a direct bearing upon the Old Testament worshippers and a prospective bearing upon New Testament Christians. There are great principles involved in the doctrine of vicarious atonement and the typology of the symbols bears directly upon the antitypes of the New Testament.

The divine reason for the singular place and primary significance given to sacrifice by blood, as given by God through Moses to His people, is explained in the Epistle to the Hebrews where it is stated that "without shedding of blood there is no remission."[5] The great significance and import of this statement is that there is no peace or fellowship with God, no approach in worship, no acceptance of the sinner, in fact no hope for lost mankind without the shedding of blood. There is no entrance into Heaven or God's presence without the shedding of blood on the part of a substitute sacrifice and acceptance of that sacrifice by the guilty sinner.

Why should God have designed such a system and employed the use of the blood in such a symbolic way?

This principle of divine origin can be found in the writings of Moses under the inspiration of the Holy Ghost and a very careful study and consideration of the passages must be made to understand to some degree what was in the mind of God in instituting such a system. The key passage on this point is Leviticus 17:11. It reads,

> *"For the life of the flesh is in the blood: and I have given it to you upon the altar to make an atonement for your* ***souls****: for it is the blood that maketh an atonement for the* ***soul****." (Emphasis added)*

The sense of this most decidedly theological and distinctively meaningful passage is not easily misunderstood. However, its precise and definite meaning is generally obscured by not perceiving and understanding the application of the terms soul and life in this verse.

In Leviticus 17:11, the English words soul and life are from the same Hebrew word, *nephesh* (pronounced *neh' -fesh*) which we saw in an earlier chapter of this book. Of the 753 occurrences of this word in the Old Testament, it is translated soul 475 times, life 117 times, person 29 times. The definition is: soul, self, life, creature, person, appetite, mind, living being, desire, emotion, passion; that which breathes, the breathing substance or being, soul, the inner being of man; living being (with life in the blood).

A correct rendering of the passage from the Hebrew can be thus:

> *"For the* ***soul*** *(*nephesh*) of the flesh is in the blood, and I have given it to you upon the altar, to atone for your* ***souls*** *(*nephesh*), for the blood atones* <u>*through*</u> *the* ***soul*** *(*nephesh*)."*[6]

The *soul* at the end of the verse refers back to the *soul* at the beginning of the verse, and expresses the principle seat of life, not in him who is to be atoned for, but in the creature, the substitute, by which the atonement is made for the offeror.[7] The importance and impact this verse has on the doctrine of the blood is seen in the prohibition against eating the blood and can be thusly represented:

> *"You must not eat the blood, because God has appointed it as the means of atonement for your sins. But it is the means of atonement, as the bearer of the soul. It is not, therefore, the*

> *matter of the blood that atones, but the soul or life which resides in it; so that the soul of the offered victim atones for the soul of the man who offers it."*[8]

The problem in interpretation into English lies in the word *for* at the end of verse eleven where we read "*it is the blood that maketh an atonement for the soul*," and can best be illustrated with the following example: "He is wanted for murder."

In this statement, one interpretation could be, "He is wanted *because of* murder." In other words, he committed murder and now he is being pursued by authorities. However, another interpretation could be, "He is wanted *with the aim or purpose of* murder." Said another way, "I want him to murder someone." Both definitions are within the scope of the word *for*, but are not necessarily correct in a given context.

This is the case at the end of verse eleven. The Hebrew preposition invariably denotes *that by which the atonement is made*; hence, the rendering "through the soul" or "by reason of" the soul or life of the victim.

This verse is rendered in "The Holy Scriptures According to the Masoretic Text":

> *"For the life of the flesh is in the blood; and I have given it to you upon the altar to make atonement for your souls; for it is the blood that maketh atonement* ***by reason of*** *the Life."*[9] *(Emphasis added)*

The latter part of the verse is given by Keil and Delitzch as:

"For the blood it expiates by virtue of the soul not 'the soul' itself."[10]

By this we understand that it was not the blood itself as such, but the blood as the vehicle of the soul, which possessed the virtue and value necessary for atonement and expiation. "Because the distinguishing characteristic of the blood was, that it was the soul of the being when living in the flesh; therefore it was not to be eaten in the case of any animal."[11]

Why should they not eat blood? Because God had appointed the blood for the altar as containing and representing the soul of the animal for making atonement for sin.

There is a necessity for atonement. Man is fallen and in sin, therefore, his soul or life has, as a result of that sin, been forfeited to God as a debt due to His justice. But God in His mercy has provided a way of escape for the sinner — He has appointed a substitute: the soul or life of the beast for the soul or life of the transgressor. Since the seat of life is in the blood, so that blood of the substitute beast, its very life-blood, was given to be shed in death, and presented before God upon the altar in the stead of the other and higher but guilty life which was required as the wages of sin.

After the blood of the substitute was poured before God upon the altar, the sinner's guilt was atoned (or covered). In other words, a life that was not required to be forfeited due to sin (that of the substitute) was accepted in the place of the sinner's life that was required to be forfeited due to sin; and this life, the sinner's life, was yielded back to him in peace with God and fellowship with God.

The moral and spiritual purpose of the law concerning the proper use and prohibitions concerning the use of the blood was apparently twofold. Firstly, it was intended by God to educate and illustrate for His people the reverence for life that they must have because of the place life held in the mind of God.

As in all other communications from God to man, the underlying desire of God is for man to know Him and to know Him aright. This reverence for life was to purify them from the heathen practices around them and the heathen disregard and disrespect for blood. That is just as true today as it was thousands of years ago. And it is true in the United States. The heathen practice of abortion is the ultimate disregard for life and demonstrates the depths of depravity of sinful man. The innocent blood of millions of babies is on the hands of the abortion butchers and those in authority that continue to vote to keep the murder of babies legal.

The second purpose, and the chief one, was intended to always and everywhere keep before the mind of His people the sacredness of blood as being the appointed means for expiation of sins. The blood was given by God upon the altar to make atonement for the soul of the sinner; and this by reason of the life or soul it represented.

Not only were they to abstain from the blood of animals offered up in sacrifice upon the altar, but they were to abstain from the blood of those which could not be offered up. In other words, abstain from all blood. Thus, every time they ate of the flesh of animals, they were reminded of the solemn truth taught them by their God: without shedding of blood there is no remission.

Man was never to forget this or count it lower; regardless of the circumstances. This held true even when hunting for food. After the hunt was successful, the hunter must pause and carefully drain all the blood from the victim he had killed, and with all due reverence and diligence cover that blood with the earth. This symbolic act would consistently remind the Israelite of the God originated ordinance that the blood, the life or soul, of an innocent victim must be given if there was to be forgiveness of sin.

An important question arises with respect to the atoning power in the blood, whether it was simply as blood itself, or as blood that had been shed in death. In other words, whether we are to emphasize the blood alone, or the blood in connection with the death which preceded, and in which it flowed out.

Some would separate the blood from the death going before and give significance only to the blood itself; making the blood, not the death, the core element of the sacrifice. This is taken even further by placing total emphasis on the blood as the seat of life, and not that which was placed upon the altar, thereby stating that it was not necessarily a life that had been taken, but the life was in the blood of the victim. This blood, as held by those of this persuasion, was then offered up in sacrifice generally as the payment of a sort of redemption fee or compensation for debt owed, with faith in God's pardoning mercy. This false view reduces the sacrifice of blood to merely parting with property, a dear and living creature in relation to the offeror.

But this is insupportable in view of Biblical atonement. The idea of atonement throughout the Bible is that of a covering and can never be associated with a compensatory payment, an idea alien to the Hebrew culture and language and one not found in Scripture in regard to sin. The value and significance of the blood is found in the value of the soul or life contained in and represented by the blood that was shed in sacrificial death. The two cannot fail to be regarded as in fact one. The basis plainly is found in the life-blood of the substitutionary victim offered in the place of and bearing the guilt and doom (symbolically, of course) of the offeror. This, and this alone, in the presence of a righteous God, could suffice to cover the guilt, or the person who committed it, so that fellowship could be restored and reconciliation effected.

The blood alone, without the death, was insufficient to atone. The death alone, without the blood presented in the presence of God, was insufficient to atone. The two were and are inseparable in effecting atonement for sin. God has so appointed it that way. It is one work of atonement. The blood and death are indivisible yet distinguishable.

As God, He knew the heart of the offeror and knew that an innocent life had been taken. He knew all these things to be. But He still required that after the shedding of blood, that *that* blood be presented before Him upon the altar to make atonement for the soul of the guilty sinner. The blood must be literally and physically presented before God in the prescribed manner representing the innocent life that was given up in substitution for the worshipper. Atonement was not effected by the blood itself, but was effected by the death of the acceptable substitute. However, God still required that *that* blood be presented before Him as a testimony not only to Him but to the worshipper. The worshipper knew that the blood represented the death of the innocent substitute in his behalf. And the blood was God's formal approval of the transaction.

In light of Leviticus 17:11, a lesson is herein made clear for application in the life of a believer regarding the sacredness of all that is associated with or connected to sacred things of God. Any and all things associated with God and the worship of Him, particularly those things that directly regard His revelation of Himself to man in our behalf in salvation, are to be treated with the most profound and utmost reverence. Not necessarily in the formalistic, cold and indifferent manner of most in denominational traditions. Not just on those certain occasions when such is the subject and purpose of the gathering. But during every waking moment, these things must be held in reverence and allow them to teach us of God, His love, and His provision for our reconciliation to Him.

Even though the blood of a deer killed for food could not be used in worship or offered upon the altar for atonement, yet because it was blood, representing that soul or life of the victim, it held such a close relationship with and had an essential nature like unto that blood used for the offering and thus was to be treated with like respect.

It is the fashion of our day and age — and one which is increasing in an alarming degree — to speak lightly, if not irreverently, of those things which are closely and intimately associated with and connected to the revelation of a holy God and the consequent worship due Him. Against everything of this kind, against every tendency in man to do so, against every opposing desire, the spirit of this law of prohibition and use warns us. Absolutely nothing which is associated in any way with that which is sacred is to be spoken of or treated in an irreverent manner, lest we come to think lightly of sacred things themselves.

What are some of these things?

One is His name. His name is used far too flippantly today by believers and pastors and not held in the high regard it should be. When used as punctuation or reaction to circumstances, it is disrespectful.

God has magnified His Word above even His name. Yet, the Bible is treated far too lightly and impugned in this day and time. We must render due reverence for the written Word of God and handle it carefully.

We do not worship these things. We worship God and God alone. These things are associated with His revelation and are for our learning and for us to get to know Him and thus are due proper respect and reverence. Not a formalistic application, such as the Pharisees, but in the heart of man a place and esteem that is fitting for holy things of God.

This irreverent treatment of holy things is a crying evil not only throughout the English speaking world, but, alas, is becoming more prevalent and acceptable in fundamental and evangelical circles. A warning must be exclaimed to beware this tendency.

Why?

After irreverence is accepted and practiced, far too often open denial of the Holy One of Israel and of His Son the Lord Jesus Christ, our Saviour follows closely. Heresy and apostasy lie at the doorstep.

The blood of Christ, which represented that holy life which was given on the cross of Calvary for our sin is most holy — an infinitely holy thing! And what is God's estimate of its sanctity we may perhaps learn — if we submit to the Holy Spirit of God and allow Him to lead us into all truth as we look through the symbol to that which was symbolized — from this passage of Scripture in Leviticus and the law laid down by God through Moses. That law required that all blood, because it outwardly resembled the holy blood of sacrifice, hence, the seat and vehicle of life itself, should be treated with the utmost and careful reverence due it.

And, sad to say, though safe to say, those who most need the lesson taught therein by this command and prohibition by God are exactly those who find it the hardest to appreciate it, and to whom the injunctions, lessons, symbols, and typology still seem, in their ignorant, arrogant, or unlearned ways, to be regulations that are unworthy of the dignity and majesty of Almighty God. Their outward show of high esteem for God and their overly pious concern for God's dignity betray a lack of understanding of God and reveal a soul not in communion with Him.

---

1 Principles of Biblical Hermeneutics. Hartill, J. Edwin

2 Ibid.

[3] Ibid.

[4] Hebrews 8

[5] Hebrews 9:22

[6] Fairbairn, Patrick. Typology of Scripture. (Kregel Publications; Grand Rapids, MI. 1989.

[7] Ibid.

[8] Ibid.

[9] The Holy Scriptures According to the Masoretic Text. Vol. 1, Genesis to II Kings; The Jewish Publication Society of America; (Philadelphia, PA; 1955)

[10] Keil, C. F. and Delitzch, F., Commentary on the Old Testament in Ten Volumes. William B. Eerdmans Publishing Company; (Grand Rapids, MI)

[11] Ibid.

CHAPTER NINE

BLOOD BROTHERS

"one of his brethren may redeem him:"
Leviticus 25:48

Why was it necessary for the one who was to be our Redeemer to be the God-Man? Why could He not redeem us and deliver us from sin as God? Could He not simply decree us redeemed upon certain conditions achieved?

The answers to these and many other questions regarding the fall of man, the incarnation, the subsequent death of Christ, and our redemption may be found in God's law of the goel, or Kinsman-Redeemer. This law illustrates perfectly why Christ had to come as He did to do what He did where He did when He did: born of a virgin, die in man's place, on the cross, approximately 2000 years ago.

As has already been shown previously, for fallen and sinful man there can be no approach unto God nor fellowship with God without atonement. The justice of God demands it. But the love of God determined the method of satisfaction of this demand. This method was death through the shedding of blood, an innocent substitute for a guilty sinner. Life must be offered in sacrifice in order for life to be restored by God to man who was spiritually dead and alienated from the life of God.

> *And you* hath he quickened, *who were dead in trespasses and sins; (Ephesians 2:1)*
>
> *Having the understanding darkened, being alienated from the life of God through the ignorance that is in them, because of the blindness of their heart: (Ephesians 4:18)*

In other words, the sinner must be redeemed from the guilt and penalty of sin by the paying of a price. "The wages of sin is death." Always has been. Always will be.

The law of the goel or Kinsman-Redeemer typifies the office and work of Christ.[1] This is seen in four points. First, the kinsman redemption was of persons and an inheritance.

> 25 *If thy brother be waxen poor, and hath sold away* some *of his possession, and if any of his kin come to redeem it, then shall he redeem that which his brother sold.*

> 48 *After that he is sold he may be redeemed again; one of his brethren may redeem him: (Leviticus 25:25, 48)*
>
> 4 *But when the fulness of the time was come, God sent forth his Son, made of a woman, made under the law,*
>
> 5 *To redeem them that were under the law, that we might receive the adoption of sons. (Galatians 4:4-5)*
>
> 7 *In whom we have redemption through his blood, the forgiveness of sins, according to the riches of his grace;*
>
> 11 *In whom also we have obtained an inheritance, being predestinated according to the purpose of him who worketh all things after the counsel of his own will:*
>
> 14 *Which is the earnest of our inheritance until the redemption of the purchased possession, unto the praise of his glory. (Ephesians 1:7, 11, 14)*

This point does not require much explanation and is not the focus of this study. Suffice it to say that, as persons, man was in need of being redeemed.

Second, the redeemer must be a kinsman. For this reason, Christ took upon himself our flesh and blood.

> *Forasmuch then as the children are partakers of flesh and blood, he also himself likewise took part of the same; that through death he might destroy him that had the power of death, that is, the devil; (Hebrews 2:14)*

He took upon himself our nature and not the nature of angels or any other created being.

> *For verily he took not on* him the nature of *angels; but he took on* him *the seed of Abraham. (Hebrews 2:16)*

He was born of the virgin Mary, "made of a woman" assuming our humanity, sin excepted.

> *But when the fulness of the time was come, God sent forth his Son, made of a woman, made under the law. (Galatians 4:4)*

He was fully man and fully God. That means that He was 100 % man, sin excepted, and 100 % God. He of necessity came by way of conception in the womb of Mary, a virgin, never having known a man, by the union of the egg of Mary with that which came from the Holy Ghost as He overshadowed her. The result was the Son of God.

Be very careful at this point. When it is stated that the result was the Son of God, God the Son, that in no way implies that the Son of God had His beginning at the moment of conception. The Son of God is eternal and co-equal with the Father and the Holy Ghost. That which had its beginning at conception was the body prepared for Him by the Father.

> *Wherefore when he cometh into the world, he saith, Sacrifice and offering thou wouldest not, but a body hast thou prepared me: (Hebrews 10:5)*

The body of Christ did not exist prior to the conception and incarnation in the womb of the virgin Mary.

The Lord Jesus Christ is eternally pre-existent and assumed the body prepared for Him by the Father. Thus it can be stated that the result of the conception in the womb of Mary was the Son of God. He instantaneously and simultaneously occupied the body prepared for Him at that moment.

In order to be truly a kinsman, He must be human, and human He was in all respects, yet without sin.

> *For we have not an high priest which cannot be touched with the feeling of our infirmities; but was in all points tempted like as* we are, yet *without sin. (Hebrews 4:15)*

Not only was this required to establish His legal right to the throne of David, but it was required in order for Him to fulfill that which only a kinsman could fulfill, the redemption of man from the slave market of sin and death. The physiological aspects of His conception and birth were examined earlier and establish His qualifications and right to perform the duties of the kinsman-redeemer. Oh, the wonder of God's love and plan of redemption!

The third point in the law of the goel or kinsman-redeemer is that he must be able to redeem. The price of the redemption must be fully paid before the penalty is removed and the offending party restored.

> **4** *And I thought to advertise thee, saying, Buy* it *before the inhabitants, and before the elders of my people. If thou wilt redeem* it, *redeem* it*: but if thou wilt not redeem* it, then *tell me, that I may know: for* there is *none to redeem* it *beside thee; and I* am *after thee. And he said, I will redeem* it.

> [5] *Then said Boaz, What day thou buyest the field of the hand of Naomi, thou must buy* it *also of Ruth the Moabitess, the wife of the dead, to raise up the name of the dead upon his inheritance.*
>
> [6] *And the kinsman said, I cannot redeem* it *for myself, lest I mar mine own inheritance: redeem thou my right to thyself; for I cannot redeem* it. *(Ruth 4:4-6)*
>
> *Their Redeemer* is *strong; the LORD of hosts* is *his name: he shall throughly plead their cause, that he may give rest to the land, and disquiet the inhabitants of Babylon. (Jeremiah 50:34)*
>
> [11] *I am the good shepherd: the good shepherd giveth his life for the sheep.*
>
> [18] *No man taketh it from me, but I lay it down of myself. I have power to lay it down, and I have power to take it again. This commandment have I received of my Father. (John 10:11, 18)*

Last, we see that the kinsman-redeemer must pay the just demand in full.

> [27] *Then let him count the years of the sale thereof, and restore the overplus unto the man to whom he sold it; that he may return unto his possession. (Leviticus 25:27)*
>
> [18] *Forasmuch as ye know that ye were not redeemed with corruptible*

things, as *silver and gold, from your vain conversation* received *by tradition from your fathers;*

19 *But with the precious blood of Christ, as of a lamb without blemish and without spot: (1 Peter 1:18-19)*

Christ hath redeemed us from the curse of the law, being made a curse for us: for it is written, Cursed is *every one that hangeth on a tree: (Galatians 3:13)*

These last two points of the law of the goel can be met by Jesus Christ alone. He is established as a kinsman through His virgin birth as a man, the God-Man, the Son of God. His ability to pay the price in full is established by His origin, He is God the Son. Christ, and Christ alone, is able to meet the demands of God's justice requiring atonement for the guilty sinner. Man does not even qualify to redeem himself. He is not able to pay the price. Angels cannot pay the price. No created being can pay the price. Only Jesus Christ can pay the price that is required.

The price of the atonement was the shed blood upon the altar as representing the life that was poured out. This was the method determined by God for the satisfaction of the just demands of His law. The reason for this is given in Scripture where it says that the life is in the blood.

The underlying fact that the value of the life was the measure of the value of the blood, at once gives the blood of Christ its inestimable, inconceivable, infinite, and eternal value. Therefore, it could be said by the Apostle Paul,

For it is not possible that the blood of bulls and of goats should take away sins. (Hebrews 10:4)

It is not the blood in the arteries and veins of the substitute, it is the blood placed upon the altar after the death of the substitute that is efficacious for atonement. Two statements must be made at this point and must be clearly understood before progressing any further in this study.

The first statement is, "The blood of Christ, apart from His sacrificial, vicarious, volitional death upon the cross of Calvary, could not atone for sin."

The second statement is, "His death upon the cross, apart from the blood that was shed and subsequently presented before God in fulfillment of the typology of the Old Testament system, and representing that life that was poured out in death for sinners, His death apart from that blood could not atone for sin."

His is one work. It is indivisible yet distinguishable.

The two are inseparable in their requirement and results. The blood and the death are inseparable. They must both be present. Either one without the other is insufficient to meet the demands of God's justice. This must be understood if a study of the blood of Christ is to make any sense at all.

"Salvation is God's thought." How could God acquit and justly account an ungodly man to be righteous? This problem required infinite wisdom to solve, infinite love to implement, and infinite value to accomplish. How it was accomplished has been given to us in Scripture,

> *Whom God hath set forth to be a propitiation through faith in his blood, to declare his righteousness for the remission of sins that are past, through the forbearance of God; To declare, I say, at this time his righteousness: that he might be just, and the justifier of him*

which believeth in Jesus." (Romans 3:25-26)

Faith in the propitiatory sacrifice of Christ, His death upon Calvary and His shed blood, are the means which God employs to solve the problem. And this solves it to God's complete satisfaction and pleasure; God Himself, the perfectly just and Holy One, being the judge.

Man cannot fully comprehend this solution nor perceive all its meaning and beauty; but he can learn much from the light shed upon it by God's Holy Word as he is led by the Holy Spirit of God. Where he fails to comprehend, he must apprehend by faith and patiently await until all things be made clear in that perfect Day when faith shall be sight.

That which can be learned of this transaction, the atonement for our sins, and not for ours only, but for the whole world, is much. The value of His blood, and, thus His ability to pay the full price of redemption, is found in the value and virtue of His life. Not just the life that was manifested as He walked upon this earth for thirty-three years, but His life as the Life of God and as the source and sustainer of all life.

His Sonship makes His blood of infinite and inestimable value. It is blood; it is the blood of the God-Man, God in human form, fully God and yet fully man. It is the blood of man's kinsman come to redeem, and as such is agreeable to the law in the payment of the penalty. It is the blood of the Son of God, and therefore acceptable to the Lawgiver in its value. It was, and is, the blood of humanity as created by God, yet the merit of it was and is derived from His divinity.

The clear and correct understanding of the hypostatic union is of utmost importance at this point. Christ was one person, with two natures. It was not His blood as the son of a virgin woman, but His blood as He was the Son of God which had sovereign value sufficient to atone and meet the just demands of a thrice holy God. The value of the blood of Christ in no way derives from the vastness of the sin penalty that was paid nor the greatness of the punishment whereby it was shed, but derives from the dignity of the Divine person from whom it flowed — the Son of God. And the value is a perpetual value.

There must be a distinction made between the value or virtue of the blood of Christ and the work it accomplished; namely, our redemption. The work of the blood was appointed in a certain time, but the virtue was not restrained to a certain time; rather, it was communicated to believers of all ages from the foundation of the world until the extent of the last ages of the world. The blood of Christ was applied from the foundation of the world, though it was not shed until the fullness of time. Old Testament believers had the benefit of the promise of redemption before the accomplishment of the sacrifice for redemption. The redemption man now has is upon the account of the blood of Christ already shed; the redemption they had then was upon account of the blood of Christ to be shed in time.

Had Christ not agreed with the Father in the eternal past before ever the world was and promised the shedding of His blood, the pouring out of His soul in death, all hope of reconciliation to God and redemption from the curse were lost.

His office as Mediator and Sacrifice was of a more ancient date than His incarnation and humiliation. He was the same before as after His taking upon Himself our flesh and blood, and as such was Mediator of His covenant in prospect as well as in history. The actual payment of the penalty due is not of absolute necessity before the deliverance of the captive may be effected. The promise of God was sufficient. The blood of His sacrifice as shed reaches to us today after 2000 years since it was poured out; but that same blood that was shed for us then reached unto Adam 4000 years before it was shed.

Redemption for fallen man is wrought solely by His worth as He is the Son of God. The blood shed upon Calvary, therefore, was not only the blood of Jesus Christ, "a man approved of God,"[2] fully man, but it was the blood of the Son of God, God the Son, fully God and co-equal with the Father. The blood of Jesus Christ received its value and virtue from His Sonship, that eternal relation in which He stood with the Father.

It is a misleading and somewhat inaccurate statement to say that His blood was the "very blood of God." This kind of statement leads to many false teachings concerning Christ, His incarnation, humanity, Deity, and the teachings concerning the "form of God."

A more accurate statement is that the blood of Jesus Christ is the blood of the God-Man, the Son of God, God the Son. Yes, Jesus Christ was and is God. Therefore, the former statement can be held to be true in a very limited sense. At the same time a person says that the blood of Christ was the very blood of God, a similar statement can be made that "The blood of Christ was the very blood of man" and be completely accurate, for man He was (sin excepted).

But these are confusing and open ended statements and must be avoided when proclaiming the Gospel in order to avoid false teaching or erroneous understanding of Scripture and the nature of God. A little more accuracy and attention to detail in this regard would avoid the confusion. The blood of Christ is the blood of the God-Man; and His name is the Lord Jesus Christ, and He is God the Son..

Since sin is an infinite offense against a holy and infinite God, no mere creature of whatever status within creation can satisfy the vicarious payment of the penalty given the infinite nature of the offense. The blood of Jesus was not only that of a man, but the blood of that person that was and is the Son of God; the blood of Him who was surety for us as the Son of God before He was surety for us as the Son of Man. This distinction also must be understood to grasp the theological significance of His blood.

He is the eternal preexistent One who alone could meet the righteous demands of the law. He interposed in our behalf and in our stead as the Son of God before He was the Son of Man and shed His blood. It was that blood of that person, the Son of God, who offered Himself to be our surety in eternity past, and was accepted of the Father in that relation; so that, though His humanity was a creature like as we, and was necessary to fulfill the requirements of the law and fulfill the types of the Old Testament, that assumption of humanity added no worth or value to the blood for the satisfaction of the law.

The blood was the blood of a creature and that blood — His blood — came into existence at His birth. The value of His blood derived from His deity, being the Son of God, and as such took upon Himself the seed of Abraham. He is the same person that was the brightness of God's glory and the express image of His person; the same person who upholds all things by the word of His power; who accomplished, by Himself, our redemption by the shedding of His blood. To depend upon any other thing — ANY other thing, person, works — for salvation is injurious and an offense to the blood of Christ and tramples His blood under foot, esteeming it of less worth than infinite.

Jesus Christ, the Son of God, is our Kinsman-Redeemer because of His supernatural conception and virgin birth as the Son of Man. Jesus Christ is able to redeem based upon the eternal worth and virtue of His life and blood. Not only is He a Kinsman, not only is He able to redeem, He effected our redemption by paying the cost in full — He died for us.

> *And* that *he died for all, that they which live should not henceforth live unto themselves, but unto him which died for them, and rose again. (2 Corinthians 5:15)*

Had it not been absolutely necessary in the mind of God, who can account for God inflicting such suffering, or permitting it to fall, on His dearly beloved Son, who is holy, harmless, undefiled, and separate from sinners? The death of Christ, if He were not Divine, was the consequence of His perjurious and suicidal tendencies; if not the atoning sacrifice indispensably necessary to satisfy divine justice, then a display of injustice and cruelty towards the Son on the part of the Father.

Whatever views are held by sinful man, the teaching of Scripture is abundantly clear that God could not, cannot, nor will not, consistent with His justice, forgive our sins on our mere asking or penitential efforts. This means that God will not forgive us just because we ask. He will not forgive us because of good works that we do. He cannot forgive us just because we do not do bad things or are better than our neighbors or that church member down the aisle.

God sustains the character of a righteous judge; and rather than disregard the demands of His own law, thus overthrowing His moral government, the Father is willing to apply the penalty to His own dear Son. And the Son, who holds such reverence for the will and law of His Father, patiently, willingly is led as a lamb to the slaughter so that His death may meet the demands of God's justice in forgiving and redeeming the guilty offender whom He also loved.

Christ, the Lord Jesus Christ, God the Son was willing and able to pay the price as our Kinsman-Redeemer to purchase us back, redeem us out of our state of alienation from God the Father. He was willing and able to pay whatever price demanded by the Father, the Righteous Judge, as demanded by the law and satisfactory to the justice of God. That price was more than His blood; and not blood only. For the wages, the price required, of sin is death. That price must be paid; be paid in full to the extent that it is sufficient for all. He must die.

The life of the flesh is in the blood, the Bible teaches. Such eternal weight, importance and reverence is placed upon the blood by God because of this that God decreed the manner in which all blood is to be treated. The life is in the blood. And the life that is in the blood is the life of the creature in all of its capacity, quality, quantity, vitality, value and virtue. From this we see that when Christ offered His blood to be shed in payment for sin, far more was involved, the meaning far deeper than meets the mind.

He was offering up His life in exchange for our life upon the altar, His blood must be shed in the outpouring of His soul in death; and that blood, the blood that held its virtue and value derived from the Divine Life that was therein, must be presented before God the Father, the Righteous Judge, who must be satisfied and to whom reconciliation must be accomplished; that blood presented as evidence that the payment was accomplished, the life poured out in exchange for the guilty, offending sinner. The testimony of that blood before God would be and is a perpetual testimony that redemption is finished and the believer is a purchased possession of the Son, the Kinsman-Redeemer.

Such a price was necessary because of the nature of the offense and the effect upon God of that offense. God is immutable; ever being and remaining unchanged, unchanging, and unchangeable. However, in His relationship and bearing toward man, a change occurred wrought by man. Fellowship was broken; spiritual death intervening. Man could no longer approach God, be accepted by God, be acceptable to God, nor have fellowship with God. Sin is disobedience and rebellion; a manifestation of contempt of the authority of God, robbing God of His due honor. The introduction of sin could not but awaken His holy wrath and invoke His justice. This put man in an opposite relationship with God, one of opponent, adversary, at enmity with God.

God's desire was to restore and continue in love and friendship with man, but was prevented by His justice and holiness. The love of God was unchanged towards man, unaffected by man's actions, attitude, and disposition. That bears repeating and some emphasis. The love of God towards man was unchanged even when man rejected God and sinned against God. God still loved us.

But as vast as the love of God is, it was impossible to readmit man into fellowship with Himself. God is holy and righteous. Sin cannot enter into His presence. The effects and results of man's disobedience and sin caused such an awful condition. Reconciliation must be effected and could only originate with God. God must dictate the terms according to His justice and law.

As Adam was the federal head and representative of all mankind, endowing his descendents with the sin nature and death, so Christ stands as the Head of all whom the Father gave Him.

> *For as in Adam all die. (1 Corinthians 15:22)*
>
> *My Father, which gave* them *me, is greater than all; and no* man *is able to pluck* them *out of my Father's hand. (John 10:29)*
>
> 22 *And hath put all* things *under his feet, and gave him* to be *the head over all* things *to the church,*

> 23 *Which is his body, the fulness of him that filleth all in all. (Ephesians 1:22-23)*

For our sake He undertook His work of mediation, becoming our advocate[3] in the eternal ages of the past in the Hall of God's Justice before the throne of God the Father. Divine justice, along with every other attribute of God's divine nature, concurred with the proposed arrangement set forth by the Son on behalf of guilty sinners; an arrangement which would cost the Son everything, cause great travail of His soul, yet satisfy the divine justice of God.

Furthermore, the arrangement being acceptable to the justice of God, justice along with all the attributes of divine nature, sanctioned the arrangement and imputed its results to those who would accept it on His terms of repentance toward God and faith in our Lord Jesus Christ.[4] Now the question can be answered, "Who shall lay anything to the charge of God's elect?" Justified by God. Nor can any condemn, Christ has died in their stead, the price paid.

> 33 *Who shall lay any thing to the charge of God's elect?* It is *God that justifieth.*
>
> 34 *Who* is *he that condemneth?* It is *Christ that died, yea rather, that is risen again, who is even at the right hand of God, who also maketh intercession for us. (Romans 8:33-34)*

The imputation of Adam's sin to all men is an act of justice; the imputation of the righteousness of Christ to those who believe in Him is an act of grace, and grace alone.

> *For by grace are ye saved through faith; and that not of yourselves:* it is *the gift of God: (Ephesians 2:8)*

It is right and proper for justice to require the guilt and punishment of Adam's race as sinners; but imputing the righteousness of Christ to believers rises as far above justice as the Divine nature stretches out in love. Justice cannot speak out against such an act; yea, justice stands speechless before the love and grace of God because justice must be fully satisfied and abundantly honored by it. This plan, this arrangement set forth before the foundation of the world did not originate in the justice of God, but in the love of God from the heart of God, which provided the requisite payment vicariously through the only begotten Son of God.[5] This distinction ought never to be forgotten. And it is this very act that manifests the love of God, for God is love.

> *In this was manifested the love of God toward us, because that God sent his only begotten Son into the world, that we might live through him. (1 John 4:9)*

Why was it necessary for Christ to die?

What was the nature of His death upon the cross?

Why would God devise such a plan before the creation of the universe?

Why would the Son of God propose dying even before he spoke creation into existence and stooped down to form man from the ground?

The answer to these questions is found in the one underlying attribute of God — love.

Before the creation of this universe and all that is therein, before the creation of angels and all the heavenly host, there was only God. God, in three persons, Father,

Son and Holy Ghost, inhabited eternity. God alone is eternal, without beginning and without ending. There was no Heaven wherein His glory does even now shine forth in brightness unto which man cannot approach.

> *Who only hath immortality, dwelling in the light which no man can approach unto; whom no man hath seen, nor can see: to whom* be *honour and power everlasting. Amen. (1 Timothy 6:16)*

There was no earth, nor universe full of stars and galaxies, to engage His attention. There simply was nothing and no one, but God alone; and this not for just a time or an age, but from eternity past. God was self-contained, self-sufficient, self-satisfied; in need of nothing.[6]

"God was under no constraint, no obligation, no necessity to create. That He chose to do so was purely a sovereign act on His part, caused by nothing outside Himself, determined by nothing but His own mere good pleasure; for He 'worketh all things after the counsel of His own will' (Eph. 1:11). That He did create was simply for His manifestative glory."[7] We were and are created for His good pleasure.

> *Thou art worthy, O Lord, to receive glory and honour and power: for thou hast created all things, and for thy pleasure they are and were created. (Revelation 4:11)*

"We love Him because He first loved us."[8] He did not love us first among His creation. The meaning is far more than that. The succession of events, although an inappropriate term in relation to eternity and God, starts with God before the foundation of the world. Before creation, He loved us. Before He created us, He loved us. He loved first — and then the thought of God concerning man and his salvation. He loved first — and then the creation of the universe and man. Even though He knew that we would sin and rebel against Him, He loved us and then created us already knowing and having in place the plan for our redemption.

All of this was rooted and found its origin in God and His love. Springing forth from the love of God was the redemptive plan as the way chosen by God to manifest not only Himself to a creation of His doing, but also to manifest His love as only He could do and to communicate the breadth, depth, and height of that love as described in the most well known verse of the Bible, John 3:16. "For God so loved..." He "so loved," an extent that reaches beyond the comprehension of man.

"Greater love hath no man than this"[9] than to die in another's stead; the giving up and pouring out of life in the place of and in the behalf of another who is guilty and rightly condemned to die. God, in His infinite love, grace and mercy, prepared and planned to demonstrate to man and all creation so great love by the redemptive plan; He would die in man's place to pay the penalty due for sin. God would die. That was how God chose to manifest Himself in love to all creation. It is no wonder that the angels wonder and marvel at such as this.

In order to understand more fully what this encompasses, it is necessary to understand what death is and what death is not. That is why we spent a chapter discussing death. Of course, God could not cease to exist. So if God were to die, it would not involve a cessation or termination of His existence. So it is with man, upon physical death man does not cease to exist. Were he to cease to exist when he died physically, whence the need for redemption? Man is an eternal being morally responsible to

God and will live forever somewhere. While in the physical body received at birth, man lives upon this earth. After physical death, man will then either live with God or apart from God forever.

Death does not mean termination of existence. Death is separation. Death is the absence of life. Death does not take away life; but, rather, it is the residue that is left when life is gone. In the absence of life there remains death, the state of separation from the body.

Spiritual death is the same. Spiritual death is the residue after the removal of God's spirit from man in the garden when man sinned against God and fell. Spiritual death is separation from God and alienation from the life of God[10]; the life is out, all that remains is death.

"The wages of sin is death."[11] But remember that the death penalty pronounced upon Adam and his fallen race was not simply that of physical death. In pronouncing the penalty, God said that "dying thou shalt die." Physical death is a secondary consequence of sin. Spiritual death is the penalty for sin. Separation from the body results from the curse of sin, but the separation from the life of God is the wages of sin.

In the day that Adam ate of the fruit of the tree, in that very day and at that very instant God had no other choice but to remove His spirit from the spirit of man. Fellowship with God was broken. The life of God was gone out of man. This penalty is pronounced upon all men for that all have sinned. And this penalty must be paid in full.

> *For all have sinned, and come short of the glory of God. (Romans 3:23)*
>
> *Wherefore, as by one man sin entered into the world, and death by sin; and so death passed upon all men, for that all have sinned: (Romans 5:12)*

But God who is rich in mercy loved us with so great love before ever the world began and Christ became the Lamb slain in payment of that penalty pronounced upon sinful man. The price that He must pay is death — separation from the life of God. The penalty was not cessation of existence. The penalty was not torture at the hands of the Devil in Hell for three days. The penalty was not the torture of the beatings and crucifixion suffered at the hands of the Romans and the Jews. The penalty was not His physical death.

He, the Eternal Son of God, who has been eternally co-existent with the Father, never for a moment throughout all eternity experiencing anything but the intimate fellowship with the Father; never having been apart from or separated from the Father; He must be separated from the Father in spiritual death.

This is something that was inconceivable to the angelic host who cry "Holy, Holy, Holy" around the throne. This is something that had never been possible, never occurred, and was incongruent with God's eternal state and attributes. But yet, the Son of God offered Himself to pay that penalty in love for man and in the process manifest the Father and declare Him unto man.

The redemptive plan reached its zenith upon the cross during the three hours of darkness that fell upon the earth. It was during those three hours, which from God's perspective is an eternity, that the Son of God hung suspended between Heaven and earth rejected by man and separated from the Father as the Father and the Holy Ghost had no other choice but to withdraw their presence from the Son while He became sin for us.

That which was taking place upon the cross during that three hours was of such magnitude that nature could not look upon it as the sun hid its face. During those three hours, while He was sin for us, He was separated from the Father and Spirit in spiritual death, a death like ours, to pay the penalty for sin, so that we could have restored to us His very life, Life Eternal.

He did not cease to be God the Son when the Father and Holy Spirit withdrew their presence. He remained distinctly one of the triune Godhead. He was and is God the Son. To attribute less than Deity to Him because of the departure of the Spirit is to attribute Deity to Him because of the presence of the Spirit. And this is not so. He is God, God the Son. And all this we accept by faith, not fully comprehending the transaction that occurred upon the cross.

The magnitude of what happened during those three hours is unsearchable. Man cannot begin to conceive the agony that was our Lord's in the Garden as He contemplated the "cup" that He must bear. That cup was not the cross. That cup was separation from the Father in spiritual death to redeem us. And He was the only one in all of creation and eternity that was able to be a substitute for man. Only He could meet the just demands of God's law. If He did not, men would be condemned without hope. The price to be paid was infinite. An infinite offense required an infinite penalty that could only be paid out of infinite love.

To consider that the Son of God would voluntarily allow Himself to be separated from the Father; to consider that the Father would allow His Son in whom He had such great pleasure to become sin; to consider that God would do such an unimaginable thing for a creature of His making that rebelled against Him in defiance; to consider all this is to begin to see the significance of the blood of Jesus Christ.

The life is in the blood. That life which was in the blood of Jesus Christ was both human life and the Life of God the Son. The life He shared with the Father and the Spirit must be offered up in sacrifice for payment of the sin penalty. That life, not only His physical life, but that spiritual life He enjoyed in eternal communion with the

Father and the Spirit must be offered up and poured out through the shedding of His blood.

His shed blood represented that life that He poured out in death as a substitute for sinful man. And just as the high priest could not enter the Holy of Holies without blood[12] so could our Lord not enter into the Holiest of all in Heaven without that blood that represented to God a life poured out in death for another. To not do so would be to undermine the types of the Old Testament which are pictures and shadows of things to come given to instruct us in the ways of God.

Our blood brother, one like as we, but yet infinitely greater than we, took our place to pay our price with His life poured out through His blood. This He did because He loves us. No greater love, no greater sacrifice could be imagined. And His blood, that precious blood, is right now in the presence of God in the Holy of Holies of Heaven itself testifying to His great love, the price that was paid, and signifying our redemption.

To all this can only be said, "To God be the glory, great things He hath done."

---

1 Schofield, op. cit. pg. 765.
2 Acts 2:22.
3 1 John 2:1
4 Acts 20:21
5 John 3:16
6 The Attributes of God. A. W. Pink; Reiner Publications; Swengel, PA.
7 Ibid.
8 1 John 4:19.
9 John 15:13.
10 Ephesians 4:18.
11 Romans 6:23.
12 Hebrews 9:7.

CHAPTER TEN

HOW SHOULD WE THEN LIVE?

"we should live together with him" 1 Thessalonians 5:10

The significance of the blood is found in the life of that blood, and not in the blood itself. The significance reaches far beyond the actual fluid known as blood. That life that was in the blood of our Lord Jesus was the life of the God-Man, the Son of God, God the Son. This life is Eternal Life.

> *(For the life was manifested, and we have seen* it, *and bear witness, and shew unto you that eternal life, which was with the Father, and was manifested unto us;) (1 John 1:2)*

When referring to the significance of the blood, significance is understood as something signified, something of import, meaning or bearing; the quality of conveying or implying; containing some concealed or special meaning as a sign or token; to show or make known by a sign or token. When the Holy Spirit did signify through the prophets concerning Christ, He did so through sign and typology. The type, of course, was the actual event, person, item, etc. in the prophets time. The antitype was to be found in a future time. Many of the types have their antitype in Christ. The blood of the sacrifices, as well as the sacrificial ceremonies, speak of greater things found in the antitype Christ.

The blood was appointed by God as the means of atonement for sin. But it is the means of atonement as it is the bearer of the soul, or nephesh. It is not the matter of the blood itself that atones, but the soul or life abiding therein and represented thereby. The soul of the offered victim atones for the soul of the man.

The appointed sacrifices could not but point forward to the perfect sacrifice of the Lamb slain before the foundation of the world, the Messiah. The insufficiency of the blood of irrational animals to effect a real and eternal atonement for sin was and is apparent to the conscience of man. Not one single animal ever voluntarily offered himself to take a sinner's place. The only supposition that satisfied God's righteous demands and justice is that a perfect, ever available sacrifice lay in the future, represented by the types of Old Testament sacrifices.

The specific service rendered by the blood in all sacrifices was to be an atonement for the sinner's guilt — and that service rendered upon the altar. The laying on of hands of the offeror upon the head of the substitutionary, blameless, blemishless victim ceremonially transferred the guilt to the victim. The principle involved in this transaction is carried forward into the New Testament and can be simply interpreted. Jesus Christ, as personal Saviour, becomes available in salvation of the sinner only when the sinner comes with heartfelt conviction of sin, and with mingled sorrow and confidence unloads his entire burden of sin and guilt onto Christ.[1]

The blood of the sacrifice was collected by the priest and sprinkled by him upon the altar. On the day of atonement, the blood was also sprinkled upon the mercy-seat. This sprinkling of blood was the most sacred part of the entire service, since it was that by which the life and soul of the substitutionary victim were to be considered given to God as Lord of life and death. The justice of God was symbolically satisfied and the blood of the victim upon the altar stood as testimony to the offeror and God as a pure and spotless thing, the very image of God's own holiness. In being presented and received there upon the altar, it still represented the soul or life of the offeror who was thus restored to fellowship and divine favor.

The application to Christ is obvious upon slightest reflection. He died as man's substitute and representative becoming sin for man as One who knew no sin, bearing the full weight and guilt of the sin of all mankind in His body upon the cross. He poured out His soul unto death[2] through the prescribed shedding of blood. God's righteous demands of His law and His justice were fully met when that life was poured out represented by the shedding of His blood. God was satisfied and glorified.

When that life that was laid down in ignominy and shame was again resumed in honor and triumphant over death, and the actual blood in which that life resided and which it represented was presented before the Father in Heavenly places, it spoke of the believer's acceptance in the Son to the possession of eternal life and restoration to fellowship with God for eternity.

The life that was freely poured out in death through shedding of blood was the life of the God-Man — fully man and fully God. The quality of that life derived from the divine nature. It was eternal life, a person, the Lord Jesus Christ Himself. To stop our consideration of the blood of Christ at the fluid level is to rob Him of the true glory that is His, to halt short of the true meaning and significance of that blood, to tinker with idolatry, and rob ourselves of the joy and fellowship of His suffering and the life that He imparts at salvation.

The blood of Christ was just like our blood physiologically. The blood of Christ was different than our blood theologically. The life is in the blood and it was His life that was offered. And it is His life that is imparted at salvation.

How should we then live?

Since He gave His life for us in death, as represented before God by the shed blood, so that He could give His life to us at salvation, then it behooves us to consider to what end and purpose He did so.

> 9 *For God hath not appointed us to wrath, but to obtain salvation by our Lord Jesus Christ,*
>
> 10 *Who died for us, that, whether we wake or sleep, we should live together with him.* *(1 Thessalonians 5:9-10)*

The purpose for which Christ Jesus our Lord died was that we should live together with Him. That was why the Father sent Him as seen in 1 John 4:9,

> *In this was manifested the love of God toward us, because that God sent his only begotten Son into the world, that we might live through him. (1 John 4:9)*

The Lord Jesus was sent by the Father in such a way as to manifest His love for us and for the purpose that we might live. And the life we are to live together with Him does not refer primarily to some blissful state in the sweet by and by. Oh, no. The Apostle Paul is very clear when he says that we are to live together with Him "whether we **wake** or **sleep**."

In other words, it makes no difference if our two feet are still on this earth, conducting our daily lives as usual or whether we have departed "this life" to be present with Him in Heaven. There is no difference. Whether we are alive here and now or have physically died and gone to Heaven, we are to live together with Him. We are to share His life here and now just as we will share His life then and there.

And it is exactly the very same life: here and now or there and then. It is His life, Eternal Life, Jesus Christ Himself in us. He died so that we can live together with Him. And that life of living together with Him begins immediately upon conversion. At that moment of new birth, Jesus Christ Himself, who is Eternal Life, moves into our bodies in the person of His other self, the Holy Spirit, to share His life with us. We then are to live together with Him from that moment on. Physical death is just another occurrence on our journey. It does not change the access we have to His life; it does not change the quality of that life; it does not change anything about His life that is in us which we are to share.

How should we then live?

Quite simply stated by the Apostle Paul,

> *I am crucified with Christ: nevertheless I live; yet not I, but Christ liveth in me: and the life which I now live in the flesh I live by the faith of the Son of God, who loved me, and gave himself for me. (Galatians 2:20)*

By living together with Him we find that it is Christ Himself living in us. We are crucified with Him on Calvary. He moves into our lives and lives through us. It is His life that now should motivate and energize our activity and that life that must be seen by those who observe our behavior.

In other words, when people observe our behavior or lifestyle, there should be no other explanation but God. Our reaction to circumstances, our conduct under stress and tension, our very behavior must be explicable only in terms of God in action in the man. If our actions can be explained by our breeding, our upbringing, our education, our personality, our will-power, our talent, our money, our courage, our dedication, our sacrifice, even our love for God — if our life can be explained in any of these terms (and there are many more) instead of only in terms of Christ alive and in action in the person, then although we may have the Christian life, we are not yet living it.

If what you are, if the way you live your life as a Christian can be explained in terms of you, just what do you have to offer to the person down the street? The way he lives his life can be explained in terms of him, and so far as he is concerned you just happen to be religious and he is not. There is nothing about you which leaves him guessing.

It is only when your quality of life baffles those who see you that they may be impressed truly to believe that there really is something to this Christian life. It must be very clearly obvious to the most casual as well as the most studious observer of your behavior that the kind of life that you are living is much more than highly commendable, but it is beyond their understanding.

Men, women, boys, and girls everywhere and at all times must become convinced that the Lord Jesus Christ of whom you testify and speak of so freely is Himself that which is the ingredient of your life.

And that life that He gives us at salvation is the very life of God Himself. And it is that very life that was poured out in the shedding of His blood upon the cross for you and for me. Not only no greater love, but no greater life.

Regretfully, this is not the case with many of God's people. In some cases, it is a willful refusal to live that life together with Him. This is indeed very sad. But in many cases, it is out of ignorance of just exactly what happened when they were saved and what life was imparted that allows fatigue and weariness to discourage so many good Christians.

How should we then live?

> *And the men of the city said unto Elisha, Behold, I pray thee, the situation of this city* is *pleasant, as my lord seeth: but the water* is *naught, and the ground barren. (2 Kings 2:19)*

In this passage of Scripture we have a very valuable illustration. It is of course an actual historical event with real people having experienced all that was written. But these events that have been recorded on the pages of God's Word are for our learning and admonition. Underlying these events are principles God wants us to learn. And after all is said and done, He wants us to get better acquainted with Him. That will solve the vast majority of problems we suffer today.

In this particular passage in the book of Second Kings, we have before us a very beautiful city. This city was the dream destination of vacationers and merchants alike. Those who traveled through her complimented the people of the city on their city's beauty and tranquility. It was so attractive and the scenery was such as to make all who saw it desire to move there and live.

The people of the city smiled in return. Yet, there smiles were covering an inner sorrow and grief. Every compliment and kind word about their city just made the pain that much worse. It hurt, it really hurt inside because they knew the truth of their beautiful city. "The water was naught, and the ground was barren." But it was their painful little secret with which they lived.

The phrase "the water was naught" does not mean that there was not any water. There was water, alright; but it was not good water. The word translated naught is the Hebrew word ra'. The meaning of this word gives new light to this story. Of the 663 occurrences of the word ra' in the Old Testament, it is translated naught only three times. It is translated evil over 400 times. Various other translations are: wickedness, wicked, mischief, hurt, bad, trouble, sore, affliction, ill, adversity, harm, noisome, grievous, sad. That is quite an impressive list.

As an adjective its meaning is even more impressive: bad, evil, disagreeable, malignant, unpleasant, unhappiness, misery, displeasing, bad value, worst, hurtful, vicious in disposition. I think maybe we get the point.

The word ra' is pronounced rah. This presents an interesting irony. We have just seen that there is not really very much to commend this word as a desirable descriptor. As a matter of fact, if we were to use this Hebrew word, we would want the opposite of what it describes. But in

English it is used as cheer at sporting events. Cheerleaders work very hard to get the crowd worked up to yell "rah rah rah" to their team. I can just imagine a transplanted Hebrew, newly arrived in a typical American town. He decides to attend the Friday football game down at the high school. After the hometown team makes what he thought to be a good play, the crowd suddenly erupts with "rah rah rah". It might give that Hebrew pause, not to mention confusion! But that is the nature of different languages.

Whatever else could be said about this beautiful city, one thing was for sure, the water that was there was terrible to drink. There was plenty of it. The only problem was that the water was bad, like stagnant water in a pond or swamp.

When this passage says that the ground was barren, it does mean that nothing grew. This was not what we think of as a desert, nothing but dirt and sand everywhere, no vegetation, just scorched earth. This was not the case, otherwise this city would not have been as attractive as it was.

The word translated "barren" in this verse is from the Hebrew word shakol, (pronounced shaw-kole'*)*. As used in this verse the idea of miscarriage is prominent; specifically, the miscarriage of the land: the land was non-productive. There was plenty of vines, vegetation, flowers, trees, and shrubs. The problem was that there either was no fruit or the fruit fell prematurely and was not good. Everything was green with plenty of leaves and shade, there just was not any fruit. A person could get rather discouraged if all there was to eat as a result of their efforts was leaves.

This same Hebrew word is translated a little differently but with the same meaning in Malachi.

> *And I will rebuke the devourer for your sakes, and he shall not destroy the fruits of your ground; neither shall your vine* ***cast her fruit*** *before the time in the*

field, saith the LORD of hosts. (Malachi 3:11) (Emphasis added)

Again, here the sense is a lack of productivity of fruit. There were indeed trees and vines and plants that were supposed to produce. But they did not. Every year it was the same in this city. The new plants would pop up through the ground and give the promise of a productive and fruitful year this year. But, year after year it was the same story. That was the tragedy of this city.

There was the ever present hope that this would be a better year; things would be different. Yet, deep down inside their hearts they knew. They knew what was going to happen. And it did! It always happened the same way. Just when they thought things were going to get better and there was going to be fruit, the fruit suddenly fell to the ground, premature and immature, and there rotted not able to reproduce. This is the real heartbreak of that city's story. Such a beautiful place. So deceptive. Everyone was fooled, except the inhabitants. What could this be an illustration of?

The alarming fact is that it may be a very accurate picture of you! And please do not become angry when this picture is described as a carnal Christian. We must first explore just what we mean by a carnal Christian. It is not somebody who used to go to church, but has run off with some other woman abandoning his own family. That is just one kind of carnal Christian. And this is not to suggest that you are one of those.

The carnal Christian I am referring to here may be a Sunday School teacher, Sunday School superintendent, a deacon, a pastor, missionary, or many ordinary, average, earnest and sincere Christians. They are good people; the kind of people you like to know and have over for coffee and donuts. They have the right vocabulary and can even give a genuine testimony of conversion. They are truly born again. But they are tired; desperately tired. Only God knows just how tired they are. They really are not hypocrites.

They are simply overwhelmed in their spirit with a sense of defeat, frustration, confusion, a sense of futility of effort, and especially the associated sense of barrenness. Just like the inhabitants of that city in Second Kings. When you meet these folk they have the biggest smile and mean every bit of it. Their handshake is one to be remembered. As you talk to them about the blessing they are, beneath that smile is that ever present hurt because they know what you do not know. For years their labor has been in vain as they watch the fruit cast to the ground early.

Many are the examples of men and women who have persevered with all courage out of a sense of duty and obligation, love and devotion. They just keep going like the EverReady Bunny, on and on and on endlessly. But if you look deep down inside their heart, they are very tired, almost to the point of exhaustion mentally and spiritually. Over and over, they bow before God, with all sincerity, confessing their barrenness and stagnation, their emptiness and hopelessness. They want to please God and have done everything they can to the fullest of their power to work for Him. But something is missing.

Does this describe you in some or all respects?

The men of the city in Second Kings had reached the end of their rope. Fortunately for them they did not take the standard advice of the self made philosophers and counselors of their day and ours. That is, when you get to the end of your rope, just tie a knot and hang on. That bit of advice is worldly rubbish.

What are you doing on your rope anyway?

Your rope is of your making. If you tie a knot on your rope, you are stuck there and must exert your own strength to hang on just a little longer, as they advise. Far too many Christians have bought into that bit of illogic.

What to do?

Let go.

God cannot do anything as long as you are hanging on to your rope. Let go. Then you will be in God's hands, secure, and nobody can pluck you out of His hands, not even you. In other words, let go and let God. And that does not mean a life of doing nothing.

The men of the city let go of the end of their rope and went to the man of God and spilled the beans. They told the whole story. What did the man of God do?

> 20 *And he said, Bring me a new cruse, and put salt therein. And they brought* it *to him.*
>
> 21 *And he went forth unto the spring of the waters, and cast the salt in there, and said, Thus saith the LORD, I have healed these waters; there shall not be from thence any more death or barren* land.
>
> 22 *So the waters were healed unto this day, according to the saying of Elisha which he spake. 2 Kings 2:20-22)*

Now from a human point of view, if you want to keep something from growing, you spread salt on the ground. In the Old Testament many times a conquering force would salt the ground of their foes to prevent a future harvest. But that is not the case here.

Elisha went to the source of the waters, the springs, and put the salt at the source. We know that many things in the Old Testament are types or symbols of greater and higher things or people. For example, oil is symbolic of the Holy Spirit. A lamb represents the Lamb of God, Jesus Christ. Salt represents the risen life of Christ which has been imparted to believers by the indwelling of the Holy Spirit. He gave His life for us so that He could give His life to us and communicate that life through us to all creation. "Ye are the salt of the earth."

Only the life of Christ, His life lived through you with Him as the source of life and the dynamic of that life, only His life can be pleasing to God.

> *And* ***every*** *oblation of thy meat offering shalt thou season with salt; neither shalt thou suffer the salt of the covenant of thy God to be lacking from thy meat offering: with* ***all*** *thine offerings thou shalt offer salt. (Leviticus 2:13) (Emphasis added)*
>
> *Ye also, as lively stones, are built up a spiritual house, an holy priesthood, to offer up spiritual sacrifices, acceptable to God by Jesus Christ. (1 Peter 2:5)*

Do these two verse really go together? Of course. As a redeemed sinner, bought by the blood of Christ from the bankruptcy of sin, indwelt by the Holy Spirit, we are members of a royal and holy priesthood. We are to offer up spiritual sacrifices that are acceptable to God. Only Jesus Christ can make our sacrifices acceptable to God. Without Him we can offer nothing up to God that is acceptable. Only what Christ does through our yielded humanity merits the approval of God the Father. Nothing less than that is acceptable to God and He expects nothing less.

We see in Leviticus that under no circumstance was there to be any offering to God offered without salt. Without salt the sacrifices were unacceptable to God. Period. It matters not the sincerity of the offeror, it matters not the degree of devotion to God, it matters not the sense of duty and obligation felt by the priest, nor the love of the people for God, nor the great cost of the sacrifice. If it was not offered up with salt, it was not acceptable to God.

> *And thou shalt offer them before the LORD, and the priests shall cast salt upon them, and they shall offer them up* for *a burnt offering unto the LORD. (Ezekiel 43:24)*

Salt made the offering acceptable to God. It was the salt of the covenant. The salt of the covenant is none other than the resurrection life of the Lord Jesus Christ. And that life is imparted to every believer for the purpose of being the salt of the earth. His life lived through us as we yield to Him our bodies a living sacrifice.

Is that enough?

> 6 *This Ezra went up from Babylon; and he* was *a ready scribe in the law of Moses, which the LORD God of Israel had given: and* ***the king granted him all his request, according to the hand of the LORD his God upon him.***
>
> 10 *For Ezra had prepared his heart to seek the law of the LORD, and to do* it, *and to teach in Israel statutes and judgments. (Ezra 7:6, 10) (Emphasis added)*

The desire of every Christian should be to be in such fellowship with our Lord that everything he ever needs for any circumstance is always his from the hand of God upon him. And this is only accomplished as we prepare our hearts to seek the Lord and His law, to be obedient to Him and His law, and to be available to be used by Him to teach that law to others. Because of Ezra's fellowship with God, God could use him.

And God had prepared the heart of the king.

> *And I,* even *I Artaxerxes the king, do make a decree to all the treasurers which* are *beyond the river, that* ***whatsoever*** *Ezra the priest, the scribe of the law of the God of heaven, shall require of you, it be done speedily. (Ezra 7:21) (Emphasis added)*

Ezra could ask for whatever was necessary to restore true worship in Israel. And included in the list was salt.

> *Unto an hundred talents of silver, and to an hundred measures of wheat, and to an hundred baths of wine, and to an hundred baths of oil, and* ***salt without prescribing*** **how much**. *(Ezra 7:22)* (Emphasis added)

Ezra gave the king his list itemizing his needs. He was specific in amounts until he got to salt. He said that he must have unlimited quantities of salt. Ezra must never be without salt; could not run out before, during, or after a sacrifice.

"Whatever the cost, King, I must have unlimited quantities of salt."

The reason?

God will accept nothing less. All is futile without salt.

"None of what we do, King, in worshipping our God will be acceptable to Him without salt. We must have salt without limit to please God."

Do you get the picture?

> *And God* is *able to make all grace abound toward you; that ye, always having* ***all sufficiency in all*** **things**, *may abound to every good work: (2 Corinthians 9:8)* (Emphasis added)

Elisha put the salt in the source and the waters were healed. Life was introduced into death and stagnation ended and fruitfulness and productivity resulted. It is the life of Christ in you that is sufficient for the need or the work.

And to this end our Lord Himself is the perfect example.

> *Jesus knowing that the Father had given all things into his hands, and that he was come from God, and went to God; (John 13:3)*

The Son of God knew that the Father had given all things into His hands. But this was written when Christ was on earth as man. And we must recall, that as man He was man as He as God created man to be. He is our perfect example of what it takes to be a man. And as such, He knew that all the illimitable resources of God were available to Him; to Him as man. For man He was, the God-Man. God did not withhold anything from the Son while He walked this earth as man. All was available to Him. But there was one stipulation. He must act as man.

He could not act as God while on earth as man. To do so, as we have already seen, would mean that no man could have seen Him. The God-Man was man in perfection, and as such had an unlimited call upon the resources of God. He must be available and obedient.

How does that apply to us?

All that God is is available to all that we are when all that we are is available to all that He is.

This is worth remembering. It is a principle we see in the record of God's Word concerning our Lord as He ministered on earth. And it is a principle we may apply to our lives as well. Jesus Christ was totally and unreservedly yielded to His Father and the Father's will. For that reason, He had access to all things.

Our Lord demonstrated throughout His ministry that it is not the nature of what you are doing — teaching, preaching, ministering, visiting, etc. — that determines spirituality, but it is the origin of what you are doing. Not the nature, but the origin. In other words, who is doing it?

If you are doing the work, it is hay, wood, and stubble, and works of the flesh. If, however, it is God in action through your yielded humanity, He is the origin and that makes it spiritual. Whatever it is. Which of the activities of Christ was more spiritual? Raising the dead, washing the disciples feet, or spitting on the ground?

Well of course none was more spiritual than another because Jesus Christ was always available to the Father for the Father to work through Him so that He could say that "the Father that dwelleth in me, he doeth the works."[3] As man it was our Lord's responsibility to be available, it was the Father's responsibility to do the works.

> *As the living Father hath sent me, and I live by the Father: so he that eateth me, even he shall live by me. (John 6:57)*

Once we understand the relationship between the Son and the Father which formed the basis of the life of Christ, we can then understand the basis of the relationship between us and the Son which forms the basis of our life in Him. That relationship was one of total surrender — of the Father, through the Father, and to the Father.[4] And that is the relationship we should have with the Lord — of Him, through Him, and to Him.

He shed His blood, pouring out His life in our place so that He could give that life, the very life of God Himself, Eternal Life, to us. Why? So that He could communicate that life through us. And in order to do that, we must present our bodies a living sacrifice.

The Lord Jesus Christ, our Kinsman-Redeemer, who purchased us with His blood representing that life He poured out upon the cross, has every right to claim exclusive use of our bodies, our whole being, our entire selves, so that He can give Himself to us through the eternal Spirit and all our activity as a human being upon earth will be His activity in and through us. His life imparted, His life lived, His life communicated.

In John 15 Christ says that without Him we can do nothing. I am constantly amazed at how busy we can get doing nothing. We can get very tired doing nothing. We can even dedicate our entire lives to "full time service" doing nothing.

Since we are told that all things are of Him, through Him, and to Him, the question remains, what part do we play? Where do we come in? And of course the obvious answer is that we do not. We simply yield our bodies, being, selves to Him and Christ lives through us. "For to me to live is Christ."

It is our vocation to be available, it is up to Him to do. We are to be instantly available so that when He commands we obey by total dependence upon Him and in love for Him which are the criteria of faith. And in the meantime, we shall be enjoying the illimitable resources of the life He gave us, filled by Himself, motivated by Him, sustained by Him, enjoying with Him the victory He wrought through that precious blood.

> 12 *Verily, verily, I say unto you, He that believeth on me, the works that I do shall he do also; and greater* works *than these shall he do; because I go unto my Father.*
>
> 13 *And whatsoever ye shall ask in my name, that will I do, that the Father may be glorified in the Son. (John 14:12-13)*

Our blood, His blood; His life, our life — "that the Father may be glorified in the Son."

---

[1] Typology of Scripture, Fairbairn.

[2] Isaiah 53:12.

[3] John 14:10

[4] Romans 11:36

CASE STUDIES

AN INTRODUCTION

Two case studies are included here to illustrate not only error, but also how confusion can enter into the discussion of the doctrine of Christ and His blood. There are many more examples besides these that could be mentioned. This work would become too voluminous if an attempt were made to include them all. Numerous books are available by reliable authors that expose heresy and doctrinal deviancy. These books should be consulted for further study.

Whether a debate or a sermon or a book, the issue is never a man. The issue is doctrine. What is being taught? Is it true? If not, what is the truth? The person of the preacher or teacher is almost irrelevant.

The first case study is an exposition of the heresy of the eternal humanity of Christ as taught by Jack Hyles. This examination of such a heresy is necessary to understand the adverse effect upon the doctrine of the blood implied by and resulting from such an heresy. Statements made by Jack Hyles are examined in the light of the Word of God.

The second case study is included to illustrate the extent to which the debate on the blood of Christ has gone. Any debate on any issue must be based upon truth and integrity. Truth is the focal point. The second case study examines statements on record by John MacArthur and examines them in light of Scripture. Also examined are some of the *ad hominem* attacks by his devoted critics. The context in which statements are made is very important. To take a statement out of context and twist its meaning for purpose of argument is disingenuous. It also shows a lack of integrity and weakness of one's own argument. Context is crucial. This study on MacArthur is not about the man, nor even his critics so numerous, but is simply an analysis of what was said.

CASE STUDY #1

THE HYLES HERESY

"Be not carried about with divers and strange doctrines."
Hebrews 13:9

Before taking a look into the false teaching of the eternal humanity of Christ, some groundwork must be laid concerning treatment of pastors and teachers.

When a Christian questions the teachings of preachers who refer to themselves as "God's anointed," are these Christians acting Biblically? Many preachers today claim that to question them, or any preacher, is wrong and will say, "Touch not God's anointed."

They even go so far as to say that to do so is to ensure grave consequences upon the questioner. These preachers will inform their congregations that the chastisement of God will be swift and sure if they touch "God's anointed."

These same preachers will invoke 1 Timothy 5:1 where Paul tells Timothy "Rebuke not an elder." Of course this verse is misinterpreted as is the verse on God's anointed. A quick look into these verses should clarify the issue.

The verse used as proof text for "Touch not God's anointed" in reference to preachers is Psalm 105:15,

> *Saying, Touch not mine anointed, and do my prophets no harm.*

Like so many of the statements by this type of preacher, the verse is used out of context and is improperly interpreted. Since these preachers consider themselves to be students of the Bible, to misinterpret a verse and use it out of context must be done so intentionally with questionable goals in mind. If not done intentionally, it is done in ignorance and immediately places in doubt their qualifications to "feed the flock."

As mentioned before and is worth repeating, a text out of context is pretext. That is the case with Psalm 105:15. Let us put it in context.

> 1 *O give thanks unto the LORD; call upon his name: make known his deeds among the people.*
>
> 2 *Sing unto him, sing psalms unto him: talk ye of all his wondrous works.*

3 *Glory ye in his holy name: let
the heart of them rejoice that seek the
LORD.*
4 *Seek the LORD, and his
strength: seek his face evermore.*
5 *Remember his marvellous works
that he hath done; his wonders, and the
judgments of his mouth;*
6 *O ye seed of Abraham his
servant, ye children of Jacob his chosen.*
7 *He is the LORD our God: his
judgments are in all the earth.*
8 *He hath remembered his
covenant for ever, the word which he
commanded to a thousand generations.*
9 *Which covenant he made with
Abraham, and his oath unto Isaac;*
10 *And confirmed the same unto
Jacob for a law, and to Israel for an
everlasting covenant:*
11 *Saying, Unto thee will I give the
land of Canaan, the lot of your
inheritance:*
12 *When they were but a few men
in number; yea, very few, and strangers
in it.*
13 *When they went from one
nation to another, from one kingdom to
another people;*
14 *He suffered no man to do them
wrong: yea, he reproved kings for their
sakes;*
15 *Saying, Touch not mine
anointed, and do my prophets no harm.
(Psalms 105:1-15)*

Verses one through fifteen of the 105th Psalm are a celebratory hymn composed by David and sung when the Ark of the Covenant was carried up from the house of Obed-edom. This event is recorded in 1 Chronicles chapter sixteen.

The first seven verses of the 105th Psalm are full of praise and a call to praise and glorify Jehovah. Verses 8-11 remember the covenant with the patriarchs, and verses 12-15 portray Jehovah's watchcare for the infant nation.

The subjects are the patriarchs and "ye seed of Abraham," found in verse 6. The principle is Jehovah who is quoted in verses 11 and 15. Verse 15 is part of a sentence that starts in verse 13, so it must be considered in that light.

The "they" of verse 13, the "them" of verse 14 and the "mine anointed" of verse 15 are the same people. When He says, "Touch not mine anointed" He is speaking of His people Israel; all of them. And he was addressing the peoples of the "one nation to another… one kingdom to another people" in verse 13.

It is very clear. Wherever the nation of Israel traveled, those among whom they traveled were warned by Jehovah to "Touch not." Which brings up the meaning of the word "touch."

The word "touch" translated in verse 15 comes from the Hebrew word naga (pronounced naw-gah') and denotes just what we think it does, when a thing or person physically contacts another. It can also mean to strike. In the context of Psalm 105:15 and 1 Chronicles 16:22, God forbids people to touch or do harm to His people or His prophets. Of course, this does not mean that they could not shake hands, place an arm upon a shoulder, or even brush up against them as they went about their daily lives. That category of touching was covered in the Levitical law.

The forbidden kind of touching was when contact was made to do physical harm to the people of God. It has the sense of violent physical contact.

What it has nothing to do with includes questioning whether or not a prophet (or preacher) is from God or speaks for God or is speaking the truth. The people of God were constantly exhorted to check out the prophets to see if they were true or false. And of course, that has not changed today.

The next word to consider is the word "anointed." It is used in regard to the Messiah, kings of Israel, the high priest of Israel, priests, prophets, and the patriarchs. The significance of the anointing is a separation unto God for God's service. The authority for such separation and selection was God Himself. Often, concurrent with the physical anointing with oil to signify the choice by God, the Holy Spirit came upon the anointed one.

Based upon a contorted and twisted interpretation of this Psalm offered up by these preachers, how are we to know just exactly who not to "touch?" In other words, who are God's anointed and prophets? Are we to assume that because someone says they are anointed or their followers declare them to be anointed, that we are not to "touch" them or to question their teachings?

On that basis, we would have to accept as representatives of God, God's anointed, such ilk as Kenneth Copeland, Benny Hinn, Jesse Duplantis, Kenneth Hagin, Sun Myung Moon, Mary Baker Eddy, and even the Pope. Of course, that is a ridiculous position.

God's representatives are known for their purity of doctrine as well as their purity in behavior and will pass any and every Biblical test properly applied. If they do not pass the test of doctrine and character, they are phonies and their teachings are to be disregarded as heresy. A true representative of God does not fear that his teaching is criticized if he speaks the truth. The truth is well capable of defending itself and will stand any test. A true representative has only the responsibility to declare the truth which will endure close scrutiny by Scripture.

As to the matter of "God's anointed" in modern New Testament times, we turn to the writing of John found in 1 John.

> 20 *But ye have an* ***unction*** *from the Holy One, and ye know all things.*
>
> 27 *But the* ***anointing*** *which ye have received of him abideth in you, and ye need not that any man teach you: but as the same anointing teacheth you of all things, and is truth, and is no lie, and even as it hath taught you, ye shall abide in him. (1 John 2:20, 27) (Emphasis added)*

In these verses the same Greek word chrisma is translated unction and anointing respectively. John here addresses believers. Each and every believer has been anointed by God with the Holy Spirit. Each believer is a priest unto God:

> 5 *And from Jesus Christ, who is the faithful witness, and the first begotten of the dead, and the prince of the kings of the earth. Unto him that loved us, and washed us from our sins in his own blood,*
>
> 6 *And hath made us kings and priests unto God and his Father; to him be glory and dominion for ever and ever. Amen. (Revelation 1:5-6)*

Clearly presented in the New Testament is the fact that Christ is the anointed Messiah of God; and, every believer is anointed by God as a priest unto God. If any selected individual is to be considered anointed, it stands to reason on the authority of Scripture that all believers must be considered as well. Given that fact, when God says touch not mine anointed, we rest in the fact that nothing can touch us unless He wills it and allows it. No individual believer, whether they be preacher, evangelist, teacher, or whatever, no individual believer can claim from the Bible a special anointing that invokes the protection from Psalm 105:15 as is done by some today. They are not the untouchable anointed over brother believers.

Preachers are exhorted to be extremely careful not to mislead any believer. The position of pastor or teacher brings with it much responsibility.

> *My brethren, be not many masters, knowing that we shall receive the greater condemnation. (James 3:1)*

Any pastor, preacher, or teacher worth his salt would be very grateful when sincere, mature Christians care enough and go to the effort to discuss and point out an error in teaching, a position held, or a belief, even if it amounts to nothing more than poor communications that can be corrected by a different choice of words or further explanation. The unapproachable pastor is one to be avoided. If he is unapproachable, his major sin is pride and arrogance. They may be identified with the Pharisees who told the blind man whom Christ gave back his sight, "Are you going to teach us?"

The other passage of Scripture so often taken out of context and misused is found in 1 Timothy.

> *Rebuke not an elder, but intreat him as a father; and the younger men as brethren; (1 Timothy 5:1)*

This verse will be thrown at people who question a pastor's teaching or question his behavior when his behavior appears to be wrong. The word elder is translated from the Greek word presbuteros. This word has basically a twofold meaning. The primary meaning relates to physical age: the elder of two people, advanced in life, a senior, forefathers. The secondary meaning relates to an office or rank held. For the Jews it would refer to members of the great council. For Christians it would refer to those who preside over assemblies or churches. The terms bishop, elder, and presbyter are used interchangeably.

Once again we see that context will drive meaning. In 1 Timothy 5:1, 2 the entire context is in respect of physical age as can be seen by the use of "as a father" and "the younger men as brethren." The contrast and comparison jumps off the page. This verse is referring to those who are older in years. It simply exhorts that young preachers exercise care in their oversight of those who are their elders in years, as well as those who are their senior in Christian maturity. The issue should never be, "I'm the pastor. Who does he think he is?" That is pride and arrogance, and God hates it.

The preachers that throw 1 Timothy 5:1 out in defense of their believed rebukeless exalted position forget about verses nineteen and twenty.

> 19 *Against an* ***elder*** *receive not an accusation, but before two or three witnesses.*
>
> 20 ***Them*** *that sin rebuke before all, that others also may fear. (1 Timothy 5:19-20) (Emphasis added)*

The "them" of verse twenty refers back to the elder of verse nineteen. In verse nineteen elder is in fact referring to those who hold positions within the assemblies or churches. It is referring to pastors. This is the clear presentation of the context and teaching of the Word of God.

Since the position held by these men is so important to the health of the assembly or church, when they sin they are to be rebuked before all. This rebuke occurring only after receiving the accusation from two or three witnesses. Of course, this action is the extreme. An example would be a pastor, or even an evangelist, caught in adultery. Upon satisfactory presentation by the testimony and evidence of two or three witnesses, "them that sin, rebuke before all." This is the clear teaching of the Word of God. The intent is not revenge but restoration of the offending party and the purity and protection of the Church.

But what of those who teach heresy? The same applies. Them that sin in their teaching must be approached and examined to see if there is in fact false teaching or simply a matter of poor communication. Those that persist in their false teaching are sinning. They must be rebuked before all.

The matter of miscommunication or poor communication has taken on greater import in recent years as there has been a dumbing down of preachers in language skills. There is nothing more frightening in preaching than to hear a preacher say, "That ain't good grammar, but it's good preaching." That should raise a red warning flag.

The tools of a preacher consist mostly, if not entirely, of words. The preacher must be a skilled craftsman at his trade just like a plumber, carpenter, surgeon, or engineer. One could only imagine the horror to come over the faces of a family sitting in the waiting room when they hear the surgeon proclaim, "That ain't good medicine, but it's good cutting." One wonders if the patient even survived!

Many large corporations and companies today expend large amounts of resources in teaching communications skills. They realize the importance of accurate and understandable communication. An illustration of miscommunication is the old saying, "Throw me down the stairs my hat." The message is clear enough to the speaker; he wants his hat. The recipient, however, being technically oriented and desiring to be completely accurate in fulfilling the desires of the speaker, proceeds to throw him down the stairs. It is a matter of communication.

Other examples are found everywhere. Someone steps up to the front desk of the hotel and announces, "Call me a cab." The bright young freshman college student behind the desk working his way through school, says, "OK. You are a cab."

Communication foibles are even present in preaching. However, the presence of so much poor communication skill in this country does not excuse the preacher of the Gospel from mastering the language. Can you imagine reading Spurgeon or any of the other great preachers of the past if their language skills were on the low par of some preachers today?

Miscommunications may lie at the heart of the misunderstanding and there be no sin involved. But when a preacher is unapproachable and unrepentant in a teaching that is heresy, that is sin and he is to be identified and rebuked.

For the Apostle Paul to call someone more noble is indeed a compliment and worthy of study to see what caused such praise.

> 10 *And the brethren immediately sent away Paul and Silas by night unto Berea: who coming thither went into the synagogue of the Jews.*
>
> 11 *These were more noble than those in Thessalonica, in that they received the word with all readiness of*

mind, and searched the scriptures daily, whether those things were so.

12 *Therefore many of them believed; also of honourable women which were Greeks, and of men, not a few. (Acts 17:10-12)*

The Christians at Berea searched the Scriptures daily to see if what the Apostle Paul was preaching was true. Can you imagine Paul's reaction if he were like some of the preacher brethren today. "What? Who do these people think they are? Don't they know who I am? I am the great Apostle Paul; Apostle to the Gentiles. I have seen Christ. Just who do they think they are checking me out?"

Paul did not seem to mind the fact that the Bereans checked out his preaching. Rather, he was somewhat encouraged because they searched the Scriptures and did not form their opinion based solely on a particular teacher or Apostle. What was the result of their checking him out anyway? "Many of them believed." Nobility was attributed to Christians who searched out the truth of what even the Apostle Paul preached. And rest assured there is no one today greater than the Apostle Paul. Hence, all preachers are subject to "getting checked out" by those who hear them. This should be welcomed by those who proclaim the truth. It is a good test of whether a preacher is actually walking with God and is from God.

Beware of a pastor or preacher who states that his least favorite kind of Christian is the one who hears him preach and then goes home and checks him out. Red flag flying.

Another example of an unapproachable pastor that characterizes wrong Biblical application would be a pastor who can not be approached without consequence to the one who approaches him about his behavior or preaching.

This can be illustrated by a pastor who uses language from the pulpit that is inappropriate for the general congregation. This could include using God's name in vain, even in a phrase that was popular in certain parts of the country. This practice should disturb the members of the congregation and the men on his staff. Of course, with this kind of pastor, no one on his staff would dare approach him because they know that to do so would result in being labeled "disloyal" staff members; and the consequences of being disloyal are not good. Since using God's name in vain is sin, why should this pastor not be approached in the Biblical manner?

If a member of the church asked to meet with a pastor like this to discuss some of these things, the scenario would be very much like the following. The member would explain that the pastor's practice of using that particular phrase was considered by most Christians to be using God's name in vain. This pastor's indignant response could be, "That's the way God made me." Of course, the church member would not believe what he was hearing. This kind of response by the pastor would be in keeping with other behavior that accompanies pride and arrogance, such as: lying, gossip, misappropriation of funds, and character assassinations. And this pastor would call himself God's anointed!

Another example of behavior that should cause a congregation or board of deacons concern would be when the pastor sets up a dummy corporation in the name of one of his staff members and funnels bond money through that dummy corporation for his own benefit. Why people will overlook such behavior or apparent behavior is amazing. And this pastor calls himself God's anointed!

An even worse example would be covering up child molestation accusations against a staff member and helping him to get out of town before any repercussions happen. Not only is this against the law, it is reprehensible. And then for the pastor to call himself God's anointed and exempt from criticism is absurd. Yet, deacons and church members do not and will not approach a pastor like this as required by the Bible. In not doing so, they become accomplices in his sin.

The religious system these pastors have established has several earmarks of an abusive system. These earmarks include first of all power posturing. Power posturing is where a pastor will focus on himself, his position and his authority spending a lot of time reminding others of it in person and in sermons. This is necessary because this type of pastor is not secure in whether God has put him in the ministry and is based upon a deficiency in character. His authority is a postured authority.

The second earmark of an abusive system is a preoccupation with performance. Where power is postured and authority is legislated from the pastor's office, the member's performance becomes paramount; obedience, loyalty, and submission are words frequently used. And of course, the member is to be obedient to the pastor, loyal to the pastor, submissive to the pastor above all else. Loyalty to Christ and obedience to His Word (which includes commands for pastor-people relationships) is not considered being loyal enough.

A third characteristic is the presence of unspoken rules that control behavior of the members and staff. For example, no one in the church would dare say out loud, "We must never disagree with the pastor because if you do you will never be trusted and allowed to minister in his church." Here the unspoken rule is: Do not disagree with the pastor or your loyalty will be questioned. Total loyalty to Christ is irrelevant to these people, only loyalty to the pastor counts.

These are examples of self-appointed anointed. And they will tell you "Touch not God's anointed." They discourage believers from behaving like the Berean

Christians in the Book of Acts. This demand and behavior should send up red flags of warning.

All of the above should be considered in light of the other side of the issue: criticism that is sinful, destructive, rebellious, and designed to gain control. God has put gifted men in the ministry to tend the flock of God and feed that flock. They are due respect as is commanded by God in Hebrews. These men are put in the ministry by God to the end that the Church be edified and grow. They are at best men and need the prayers of those in the flock. Discernment is crucial to determine if criticism is needful (and the definition of criticism is mostly a positive attribute) or if it is harmful and originating from sin.

The Bible remains the final authority not only for what is proclaimed but for checking out what is proclaimed and rebuking where necessary. Christians must heed the warnings and instructions of the Bible to identify and point out those who teach heresy.

That is simply what these examples are attempting to do, point out error based upon the final authority of the Word of God. Those who would argue must argue with the Bible and not with the author.

Nothing in this book is intended to be personal in nature nor to be an attack upon a person or that person's reputation. There are those who will take any criticism of positions held or doctrine taught to be criticism of themselves or those whom they follow as a personal attack. They are wrong. That is their problem and one they should get over if they are to be of any real value to the work of Christ.

Charges of disloyalty will be hurled afresh and anew. It is indeed a very sad day when loyalty to Christ and His Word is insufficient for some.

These accusations are considered by this author to be nothing but the rantings of ego-centric pastors who maintain a focus upon themselves and do not point men and women, boys and girls to Christ and Christ alone. The focus of this book is on Christ. Period.

When false doctrine is found it must be exposed. That is the clear command of Scripture. Our loyalty is to Christ and Him alone and our obedience is to Him and His Word. That being the case, no sensible pastor could or should ask for any more. What pastor would not desire to have his entire congregation exercising complete loyalty to Christ and living in obedience to His Word? Were that the case, that pastor would enjoy one of the finest churches in history.

Jack Hyles pastored the First Baptist Church of Hammond, Indiana from 1959 until his death just recently. He founded Hyles-Anderson College in 1972. Hyles authored over forty books.

This case study is not meant to be and in fact is not an attack upon Jack Hyles as a pastor, or a man. It is not a criticism of his ministry. Those who would turn this doctrinal analysis into anything other than what it is — doctrinal analysis — should just get over it. Their loyalties are misplaced and they reveal themselves for what they are. They are followers of men and not of Christ.

These are harsh words, but true. The criterion is NEVER a man. The criterion is ALWAYS the Word of God. Beware any pastor or leader who makes a man the issue rather than making Christ and His Word the issue.

Far too many young preachers have sat under that kind of teaching and their very presence in the pulpits of churches across America is a danger to the flock of God. Some have not bought into this false teaching. Some have. They have been deceived and shall continue to deceive those who follow them. This is sad. The deceit and heresy has gone so far as to teach that God the Father is a corporeal being, He possesses a body. This is blatant heresy and comes from one who sat under Hyles' teaching. How many more are there who have gone so far? One can only wonder.

There is no attempt here to find a demon behind every bush. But in these last days Christians must be circumspect and diligent, especially with regard to doctrine. The adversary is smart beyond our comprehension and very wily. The deceit is gradual. Then it grows.

Heresy can be the result of ignorance or intention. Ignorance is remedial. And the remedy is the Word of God. Exhortation in this regard is designed to recover those who have been snared by the devil. It is done so out of compassion and a desire to help.

Jack Hyles has recently gone on to be with the Lord. There will be those who say that it is not right to attack a man's teaching if he cannot respond because he is dead. That argument is hollow. If that argument were to be accepted, we could not address any of the heresies of time past and expose them for what they are, heresies. Hyles' recent death does not change the intent or the manner of this analysis. Those who wish to defend his statements may do so at their will, but must do so only and strictly from the Bible. This analysis simply presents those statements by Hyles and examines them in light of Scripture which is the final authority.

As the Word of God is the final authority, this author would exhort the reader to read this analysis with open Bible and examine for himself what the Word of God has to say.

That said, a good place to start is a passage from Acts chapter twenty:

> 28 *Take heed therefore unto yourselves, and to all the flock, over the which the Holy Ghost hath made you overseers, to feed the church of God,*

which he hath purchased with his own blood.

29 *For I know this, that after my departing shall grievous wolves enter in among you, not sparing the flock.*

30 *Also **of your own selves** shall men arise, speaking perverse things, to draw away disciples after them.*

31 *Therefore watch, and remember, that by the space of three years I ceased not to warn every one night and day with tears. (Acts 20:28-31) (Emphasis added)*

The Apostle Paul is here exhorting pastors to feed the flock over which the Holy Ghost has made them overseers. And they are to be careful what it is they are feeding the flock. The flock retains some responsibility in what it is they feed upon. The flock is exhorted to watch and to be like the Berean Christians who even checked out what Paul said by studying Scripture to see if those things were so.

Paul then warns that wolves will come in and attempt to deceive the flock with false teaching. These are easier to identify, quite often, than the next group he warns about in verse thirty. "Of your own selves shall men arise" indicates that from within the church itself some would arise speaking perverse things to draw men away unto themselves. Here the word perverse means to turn aside from the truth. This warning is most awesome. Men have arisen and shall arise from within the ranks of Fundamentalism that teach perverse things, straying from the truth. They are not historic Fundamentalists.

The subject of this book is primarily the blood of Christ. In studying His blood, it is necessary to study who He is and how He came. This involved a study of what is referred to as the kenosis and hypostatic union. In that study the virgin birth is looked at very closely. This analysis concerns statements by Hyles concerning Christ because those statement have direct impact upon the nature of the blood of Christ.

The statements Hyles made concerning Christ's humanity can be lumped together under a heading The Eternal Humanity of Christ. That teaching has never been a part of the true church from year one to the present. It has, however, been a bedrock doctrine for some cults. Simply stated, this doctrine teaches that Christ is human, always was and always will be. Here are some of Hyles' statements concerning our Lord Jesus Christ followed by an analysis:

1. "Jesus did not become human in Bethlehem; He became flesh in Bethlehem."

2. "He didn't learn how to become a man when He came to Bethlehem. He already was one."

3. "Jesus says, 'Father, you have never been human. I have always been human.'"

4. "Jesus is man. He always was man."

5. "Jesus was always man or human…; Jesus did not become man in Bethlehem; He became flesh."

6. "There has always been a member of the Godhead who was human and God."

7. "[Jesus] is the human deity now. He always has been. He always will be. He did not become human when He came to Bethlehem."

8. "That nature in which He came to us in Bethlehem — that nature, we call it human nature — He always had it and He always will have it, and always shall be divinely human and humanly divine. Before man was made, this man-type existed in the Godhead. Before this clay was ever fashioned, this humanity existed in the divinity."

9. "He always had the same human tendencies we have. He had the same human reasoning that we have."

10. "The incarnation part: God brought the original down beside the degenerate copy to show me what I was meant to be."

11. "God didn't look down one day and say that man is a sinner, I think I'll make a God-man. No, He always was the God-man. Just like we've got those fire extinguishers over there in case of fire, there was a God-man in case a God-man was ever needed. And before Bethlehem, He was the God-man."

12. "He has my nature. He always has had my nature. He didn't learn how to be a man when He came to Bethlehem, He already was one."

13. "God decided to 'make some more human beings,' a 'whole race of little Jesuses,' so He created Adam and Eve.

14. "The Father and I can't understand each other because I've never been like Him, and He's never been like me. Jehovah does not reason with our reasoning. Jesus always has reasoned with our reasoning. Jehovah will never reason with our reasoning. And Jehovah looks down and sees me weak, and sinful, and frail, and imperfect. He says, 'I think I'll kill old ______.' And Jesus says, 'Father, listen

to me for a minute, Father. You have never been human; I always have been. You never have been human in your nature; I always have been. And, Father, you never have been down there.'

" 'But did you hear what he said to those deacons?'

" 'Father, did you ever have deacons?' And the Father says, 'No, Son, you know better than that. I never had deacons.'

"And Jesus says, 'I did.' He said, 'I've been down there.' He said, 'When I died, the chairman of my board was out cussing. The treasurer was committing suicide. And all the board members forsook Me and fled.'

"What He says is, 'Father, have mercy on ______.' Thank God, there's somebody in the heavenlies who understands me.'"

"Jesus sits today at the right hand of God the Father, Jehovah God, and He says, 'Father, let me tell you what it's like.'"

"You know why I can come boldly to the throne of grace this morning? 'Cause Jesus is there softening God the Father up for me before I get there."

"God the Father and God the Son don't see Heaven alike. God the Father sees Heaven as God. God the Son sees Heaven as God sees it and as man sees it. So He can reach out and fellowship with God and reach out and fellowship with man."

In examining these statements several may be lumped together because of their similarities or because they are repetitions of the same theme. Also, reference will be made to chapters and subjects covered in the body of this book, such as the kenosis, hypostatic union, incarnation, etc. The reader is encouraged to reread those sections in connection with specific comments by Hyles.

Any one of the fourteen statements alone should have caused red flags to go up in the mind of a discerning Christian. The first question asked concerning such a statement would be to ascertain if it was a misstatement. As quite often happens to preachers and public speakers, they will say something the wrong way not giving the true thrust of their meaning. They get their words mixed up. What the audience hears is either confusing or gives the opposite meaning of that intended by the speaker.

If that is the case, and the speaker or preacher is approached about it, supposing he is approachable in the first place, he then can reflect upon what he said and either apologize for the miscommunication and confusion, or confirm that what he said is what he meant. Again, this type of miscommunication happens with some degree of regularity with fallible people. They misspeak or speak in a confusing way that causes the hearer to not understand what is meant or to understand that the speaker is taking an opposite position than originally thought. And most of the time, clarification is forthcoming from the preacher. But what if there is no clarification and the statements persist for years and are repeated? The latter is the case with Hyles.

These statements were made over several years and never retracted to this author's knowledge or the knowledge of other authors with whom contact was made. This is not a case of a misspoken thought on occasion, but a pattern of speaking that reveals a consistent doctrinal position. Taken individually the statements would cause a small stir that could easily be resolved. But the pattern is a disturbing one given the resistance to doctrinal accountability.

Now, as to the statements themselves. The first eight statements listed above are of the same general sense. They address what is called the eternal humanity of Christ. In other words, Jesus Christ was human from eternity past.

This is made clear when Hyles says, “Jesus is man. He always was man.” That is succinct, clear and direct. It is also heresy.

The eternal humanity of Christ is a doctrine of the cults and has never been espoused by the New Testament church. No Fundamentalist theologian has ever taught this. This teaching is clearly completely outside of Independent Fundamental Baptist belief and is in fact outside of all that is taught in the Word of God. Again it must be very clear that to teach the eternal humanity of Christ is heresy and, consequently, those who teach it are heretics. And heretics must be identified, their names called out and separated from the assembly.

We shall not revisit in detail the discussion of the kenosis and hypostatic union. If they are not understood at this point, they should be restudied until they are clear. It is very important that these be settled if the discussion of the blood is to have any Biblical foundation in truth and its efficacy on our behalf. Crucial to understanding the blood of Christ is a proper understanding of the Eternal Son of God before and after Bethlehem.

As proof texts for his position, Hyles' used Hebrews 13:8 and John 1:2.

> *Jesus Christ the same yesterday, and to day, and for ever. (Hebrews 13:8)*
>
> *The same was in the beginning with God. (John 1:2)*

These verses have absolutely nothing to do with the humanity of Christ. They deal with His immutability and eternality respectively. In Hebrews 13:8, the Apostle Paul is declaring that Jesus Christ is the Messiah of the Old Testament and being co-equal with Jehovah God is immutable: unchanging and unchangeable. This is in reference to His nature and essence as God. His form is not addressed nor alluded to here.

In John 1:2 “the same” does not refer to sameness, rather, it refers back to verse one and refers to the Word. “The Word was in the beginning with God.” That is so straightforward as to defy misunderstanding.

At this point it is prudent to point out that the word human does not appear in the Bible. The word man is translated from the Greek word *anthropos.* So, when Hyles refers to Jesus always being human he must be referring to Jesus always being man. This has several problems.

First, to be man not only implies but demands that there be an entity of spirit, soul, and body. That body is described in Scripture as flesh and blood. That is the way God created man. That is the only way to which man is referred to in the Bible. From this we must assume one of two things concerning Hyles’ statements that Christ was human before Bethlehem. Either He had a body like ours or He did not. In order to be man, He must have a body like unto our body. That is the order of things in God’s creation.

If Jesus Christ had a body from eternity past, consider that this implies that matter can be eternal. If He is eternal as God is, and He is, and if He had a body like ours, that body had to consist of matter. Where did that matter come from? Did He have a physical body before God spoke all that there is in the universe into existence? If Christ has a body that was eternal from eternity past, then we must assume the eternality of the matter of which that body is comprised. This leads directly into evolutionary thought concerning matter and energy.

If His body, consisting of matter, was created by God, did God create this person known as the Son of God? Absurd. The Son of God, God the Son, is uncreated Deity co-equal with the Father and the Spirit in the trinity of the Godhead.

To escape this argument by allowing that Christ was man without a body before Bethlehem is to completely redefine the term man. The definition then becomes one of cultic derivative and completely extra-Biblical. Jesus Christ was not man before Bethlehem. But He is the same before and after Bethlehem in essence and nature; just not in appearance.

Another problem with this position that Christ was man from eternity past is that by definition and default this would make Him the "first man." If there were no other men before Him, He had to be the first. That just makes sense.

However, Scripture takes a clear position on this.

> 45 *And so it is written, The **first man Adam** was made a living soul; the **last Adam** was made a quickening spirit.*
> 46 *Howbeit that was not first which is spiritual, but that which is natural; and afterward that which is spiritual.*
> 47 *The **first man** is of the earth, earthy: the **second man** is the Lord from heaven. (1 Corinthians 15:45-47) (Emphasis added)*

It is unequivocally clear from this passage that Adam was the first man. He, Adam, was the first to possess humanity and be a man as God created man to be. And that creation of man included body, soul, and spirit. It is just as clear that Jesus Christ was the Second Man. He was not the first, but the second. His humanity came after that of Adam.

In fact, the body of our Lord had to be prepared by the Father when He, the Lord of Heaven, assumed our humanity.

Wherefore when he cometh into the world, he saith, Sacrifice and offering thou wouldest not, but a body hast thou prepared me: (Hebrews 10:5)

Earlier in this book in the discussions on the kenosis and incarnation, the assumption of humanity by Christ is detailed. The statement "There has always been a member of the Godhead who was human and God" is clear heresy.

Statements number eight and thirteen above fall right in line with the apostate teachings of Copeland, Hinn, Hagin and the rest of the Faith Movement crowd. It is an attempt to bring Christ down to man's level or bring man up to His level. They preach another Christ who is not Christ indeed. They bring not that doctrine John wrote of in his epistle, and we are to separate ourselves from them for they are not of the faith.

The statement, "He always had the same human tendencies we have. He had the same human reasoning that we have" is blasphemy. Jesus Christ our Lord did not have the same human tendencies we do. We are in the flesh; redeemed, regenerated, and reconciled to God, but still in this body of flesh with its attendant sinful tendencies and lusts. His reasoning was always from the perspective of Deity before Bethlehem. After the incarnation, His reasoning was from the perspective of Deity for divine He was; yet also human, sin excepted. Our reasoning is tainted with sin. His was not nor can be. At best, Hyles' statement is sheer stupidity. At worst, it is apostasy.

The last statement given above is one that dumbfounds the reader. How can any preacher of the Gospel of Christ make such statements? The imaginary discussion related by Hyles in statement number fourteen attacks the equality of the Godhead and puts division between the Father and the Son. It questions God's omniscience. It questions God's ability to fellowship with man on God's terms. What a ludicrous thought that the Father cannot understand us. Yes, we have an advocate with the Father, Christ Jesus our Lord. But not because the Father does not understand us.

The verses describing the Father as merciful, understanding, all-wise, loving, compassionate, etc. are so numerous as to almost be beyond counting. In every book of the Bible, the grace and mercy of God the Father is manifest. His great love for us, because He in fact knew us, was manifest on Calvary. The picture seen by a reader of the Bible is opposite that portrayed by Hyles in the comments above.

A derivative of this teaching is that God the Father is a corporeal being: He has a body with blood in it. That is being taught in so-called Baptist churches today. From that teaching derives the teaching that the blood of Christ came directly from Heaven and was solely the blood of God. As pointed out in this book, that is a misleading and ambiguous statement. It opens the door to dangerous ground.

God does not nor never did have blood. God does not nor never did have a body.

> *God is a Spirit: and they that worship him must worship him in spirit and in truth. (John 4:24)*

Just how much clearer does the Bible have to make it? Teaching that the blood of Christ came only from the Father in Heaven leads to teaching that there is a body in Heaven with blood in it. To say that Christ was eternally human is to imply a presence of a body, since that is the Bible definition of man. Did that body have blood? Was that the same blood He had on earth?

These heretical teachings concerning the eternal humanity of Christ and the blood coming from a Father God with a corporeal body completely disavow the doctrine of the kinsman redeemer and make a mockery of the very system of redemption designed by God. It also lessens that redemption by actually reducing the preciousness and actual cost of our redemption.

The doctrine of the eternal humanity of Christ is another example of sloppy Bible study resulting from sloppy scholarship. It reveals a disdain for the study of the original languages, a lack of respect for good Bible education, and the result of a lack of accountability for doctrine within the New Testament Church.

CASE STUDY #2

THE MACARTHUR DOCTRINE AND DEBATE

"without shedding of blood is no remission." Hebrews 9:22

This case study is not a criticism of John MacArthur as a man, as a pastor, or of his ministry. It is simply and only an analysis of statements by him or attributed to him concerning the doctrine of the blood of Christ; and statements made by his critics. As stated earlier, the man is not the issue. A man is never the issue. What a man teaches about Christ and His Word is the issue. "Taking sides" is not what this is about. There are those who will ask which "side" we are on. That is ridiculous and childish. We are not choosing up sides on the playground. Simply put, we stand on the truth of the Word of God.

The effort in this study is to make some sense out of the debate centering on the blood of Christ and analyze statements by MacArthur and others on that subject. The analysis is in light of Scripture. Nothing in this study should or may be construed to be a defense of MacArthur nor a defense of his critics. They are not the issue. Nothing should be construed to be a defense of their teaching. This case study is an analysis of statements and how they measure up to the light of Scripture. Every effort is made to reduce these arguments and statements to the underlying truth at issue and examine them from a Biblical perspective.

I expect that there will be those who misconstrue statements in this book and take statements out of context to find something to attack. Their ministries seem to be nothing more than *ad hominem* attack ministries. It is one thing to defend the truth and earnestly contend for the faith; it is another to just keep yapping at someone's heels in order to be noticed and gain a reputation. These same men take a text out of context which is pretext for a proof text to prove their pet theories. Beware of these preachers. The whole counsel of God must be considered from the Genesis to the Revelation.

The following are some of the statements by MacArthur or attributed to him by his critics. We shall discuss these statements and look at some of the comments by his critics.

The first thirteen quotes are not mentioned by MacArthur's critics but are included here as a result of reading his commentary on Hebrews chapters 9, 10, and 11. (Where the parenthetical reference is to a page number, it refers to the Hebrews Commentary.)

1. "Only on the basis of the blood of a goat would God have fellowship with Israel, and only on the basis of the blood of Christ will God have fellowship with men." (p. 223)

2. "The primary basis on which we can draw near to God in faith is **the blood of Jesus**." (p. 260)(Emphasis MacArthur's)

The basis, indeed, of fellowship between man and God is the blood of Christ that was shed on Calvary. With this statement, no Fundamental Baptist, no true evangelical, no honest student of the Bible, no seeker after the face of God can disagree. MacArthur here makes clear that the basis of fellowship is literal blood and that blood was a goat's blood in the Old Testament and the blood of the Lamb of God in the New Testament.

3. "How does Christ minister in His heavenly sanctuary? What does He do as our eternal High Priest? He does three things, primarily. First, His service is in **His own blood**, not that of sacrificial animals." (p. 229)(Emphasis MacArthur's)

Emphasis is placed upon the blood of Christ in His service as High Priest in Heaven.

4. "God is satisfied when a man puts his faith in the shed blood of Christ." (p 235)

This is fundamental to salvation. MacArthur does not evade the issue of the necessity of the blood of Christ in the new birth but puts it at the foundation. This is in keeping with the truth of the Gospel as clearly spelled out throughout the Epistles.

5. "He was to ratify the New Covenant through His own blood, just as the Old Covenant was ratified by Moses with the blood of animals." (p. 237)

6. "He recognized that God had to be satisfied, and He offered His own blood — His own self— on our behalf." (p. 239)

Again, the necessity of the offering of His literal blood in ratifying the New Covenant and meeting God's righteous demands is recognized by MacArthur. He further states that Christ offered up His own blood and then inserts "His own self" into the sentence. This does not indicate the one as opposed to the other. It indicates the extent of the offering — His own self. That is what the shedding of blood is about, as we have seen.

7. "But in Christ's shed blood, His perfect sacrifice, **we have confidence to enter the holy place,** into God's very presence." (p. 260)(Emphasis MacArthur's)

8. "The blood of Jesus Christ, however, counts for everything, and the person who trusts in His atoning work can come with complete boldness before God, claiming all the blessings and promises in His Son." (p. 260)

9. "The blood of animals allowed only the high priest to enter the veil briefly. Jesus' blood allows everyone who believes in Him to enter the veil permanently." (p. 261)

Without the shed blood of Christ there is no entrance granted into God's very presence. To say that the blood of

Christ "counts for everything" is to put the proper value on the blood. Infinite value.

10. "But Jesus, through His shed blood, satisfied God's justice in our behalf, so that we can now claim God's mercy and grace." (p. 260)

The only way to satisfy the holy and just demands of a righteous God was the shedding of blood. This Christ did in our stead. That is fundamental to the Gospel and MacArthur here affirms that.

11. "In Christ our sins are covered in the blood and our lives are transformed." (p. 263)

12. "God is satisfied with the sprinkling of the blood of Christ, and sin is removed and our consciences are free." (p. 263)

An exception that could be taken with statement number eleven above is a technical one. This statement is preached by virtually all preachers that are still true to the Word. The technical exception I would mention is that our sins are not "covered" by the blood of Christ, THEY ARE CLEANSED. The point is clear. The New Testament nowhere claims that the blood of Christ covers our sin but repeatedly makes it perfectly clear that our sins are cleansed, washed away. There is a significant difference. If they are only covered, they are still there somewhere. Just like a dirty stain in a white shirt is not covered, but washed away by the laundry never to reappear on the shirt, so Christ has washed away our sins, cleansed throughly, so that they will be remembered against us no more. They cannot be found, it cannot be said they are "over there under that blood." The Bible is explicit. They are cleansed perfectly. They no longer exist. Maybe this is more than a technical point when we consider the power that is in the blood to accomplish a complete elimination and cleansing of our sin.

> 13. "When Jesus died, His blood removed our sins, and when we embrace Him by faith, our conscience becomes free from guilt — we are cleansed **from an evil conscience.**" (p. 263)(Emphasis MacArthur's)

MacArthur here makes the same point we just finished. Christ's blood removes our sins, not covers them. There is a difference as we have seen.

The following statements by MacArthur are quoted in numerous publications by his critics. I have grouped them under four general headings for analysis and discussion. Those headings are: Symbology; Penalty and Payment; Kenosis; and the "Blood Itself." Some of his more devoted judges and critics have spent much time and effort producing vast amounts of writings examining each and every statement. The intention here is to identify the point of doctrine at issue and analyze the statements accordingly as a group. It is not necessary to go into great depth and detail on each and every statement. That only muddies the water.

Something that needs mentioned at this point is the disingenuous and fallacious arguments made against some of MacArthur's statements. Some examples.

When a critic quotes an author for purpose of analysis and discussion, even with the intent of exposing wrong teaching, accuracy is vital to validity. One of MacArthur's most tenacious critics quotes him, "Nothing in His [that is, Christ's] human blood saves." He then proceeds to misquote and add to the statement for ill effect by saying, "MacArthur calls the Blood of the Lord Jesus Christ here merely "HUMAN BLOOD." (Underlining added). This is a gratuitous misrepresentation and destroys the integrity of the critic. MacArthur did not use the word "merely" in his statement, but it was added by the critic for effect. In doing so, the meaning is completely changed. As seen earlier in our study of the kenosis and hypostatic union, and according to the testimony of the Bible and Christ Himself, Jesus Christ was a man. That means He was human. It does not mean, nor does it imply, that He was "merely" human. To propose such a preposterous inference is disingenuous and at once brings into question the critic's integrity, purpose, and even soundness of analysis. This ought not be so. It adds nothing to the discussion and causes confusion beyond belief, especially for those believers who are not well grounded in Scripture or the English language for that matter.

Another example is for the critic to be guilty of exactly what he is accusing someone else to have done. This is very evident in the literature that is available when the subject is symbology, which will be discussed shortly. For a critic to accuse someone of using symbology, and then turn around and use it himself within only a few paragraphs is indeed not conducive to convincing someone of the soundness of the argument.

Symbology

Some introductory comments are necessary before entering into this section dealing with symbology.

It is of utmost importance that there be a firm grasp of the English language and its mechanics. Proper linguistics and Bible truth are not mutually exclusive. On the contrary; the Bible is written words translated from the original languages under the providence of God into English at a time when words had distinct meaning and grammar was correct. Along the line of linguistics, grammar and word meanings, the use of something called a metonym needs to be understood. Why? Because the Bible has many instances of metonyms.

What is a **metonym**? Many have heard of synonyms or antonyms, but not metonyms. The definition will surprise you. A metonym is defined as a word used in metonymy. That really clears it up! N'est pas?

What is metonymy?

Metonymy is a figure of speech that consists in using the name of one thing for that of something else with which it is associated (as in "spent the evening reading *Shakespeare*," "lands belonging to the *crown*," "demanded action from *City Hall*") : use of one word for another that it may be expected to suggest.

— a figure of speech that consists in substituting an associated term for the name itself, as in "the *crown* decrees" for "the *ruler* decrees." [Greek < *meta* – altered + *onyma* name]

— use of the name of one thing for that of another associated with or suggested by it (e.g., "the *White House* has decided" for "the *President* has decided")

These examples clarify the use of a metonym. When a reporter says that the "White House today said that …" he is not referring to the physical structure at 1600 Pennsylvania Avenue, Washington, D.C. actually speaking. At least we hope not. Rather, it is a metonym for, as stated in the definition, "the President said…" or "the Chief of Staff said…" or anyone said something speaking for the President in an official capacity.

When people fight city hall, we do not observe a crowd punching the brick and mortar of the building. We understand that a disagreement has developed between a fine upstanding citizen and bureaucrats who run the local government. This understanding of metonymy is common although we do not think, "They just used a metonym. How quaint!"

There is another term with which familiarity must be gained called a **synecdoche**. It is a figure of speech in which a part or individual is used for a whole or a class, or the reverse of this. E.g., *bread* for *food*, or *the army* for *a soldier*.

— a figure of speech in which a part is put for a whole or a whole for a part, an individual for a class, or a material for the thing, as a *roof* for a *house*.

A word that appears often in the debate and criticisms of the day surrounding the blood of Christ is the word *symbol*. Accusations are hurled by critics that someone uses the word symbol too many times in discussing a subject such as the blood. Well, what is a symbol?

A **symbol** is "something that stands for or suggests something else by reason of relationship, association, convention, or accidental but not intentional resemblance; especially: a visible sign of something (as a concept or an institution) that is invisible."

Well, what about the Bible? Any student of the Bible knows that the Bible uses literal language and figures of speech. Figures of speech are symbolic. That includes the metonym and the synecdoche. Some examples.

> *And in those days Peter stood up in the midst of the disciples, and said, (the number of names together were about an hundred and twenty,) (Acts 1:15)*

In this verse, the word *names* is used as a metonym for *persons*. The definition in Strong's Concordance is instructive. In part it reads, "the name is used for everything which the name covers, everything the thought or feeling of which is aroused in the mind by mentioning, hearing, remembering, the name, i.e. for one's rank, authority, interests, pleasure, command, excellences, deeds etc."

A logical and correct look at this verse reveals that there were about 120 persons present. It does not mean that there were 120 different names present; e.g. Peter, Mary, Martha, Thomas, John, etc. That would be and is an incorrect rendering and understanding of this verse.

This same use of the word names is found in Revelation 3:4.

> *Thou hast a few names even in Sardis which have not defiled their garments; and they shall walk with me in white: for they are worthy. (Revelation 3:4)*

Our Lord used figures of speech extensively in His earthly ministry. One example is found in John's gospel.

> *Then said Jesus unto them again, Verily, verily, I say unto you, I am the door of the sheep. (John 10:7)*

Of course we understand that Christ is not saying that He is a literal door. The meaning is figurative and far deeper than that. The point is that He uses a figure of speech to represent a truth concerning Himself. Another example is when He said that He is the vine and we are the branches. No one takes this to be literal. It represents and teaches a much deeper truth. Metonyms are used throughout the Word of God. To employ the figurative in no way eliminates the literal.

This is especially seen with regard to the blood. Shedding of blood, which is the effusion of life, is used in the Bible to symbolize either murder or sacrifice for sin involving the death of a substitute. Death itself is not visible; only the physical results of the absence of life, which is death, can be seen by the human eye. A symbol employed for death, especially certain kinds of death, is the shedding of blood. And this shedding of blood may or may not involve the literal emptying of the veins of blood.

In the case of murder where a perpetrator would kill a victim with a fatal blow to the head, for example, there may not be much bleeding, if any. Still, if man sheds man's blood, by man shall his blood be shed: capital punishment. For those who are advocates of capital punishment based upon the Bible and who do not accept the symbolism of shed blood in this case, they should be advocating for death by literal shedding of blood. But they do not hold such a position because it is not justifiable from the Bible, and they know it.

On the other hand, in the case of sacrifice for sin, God gave explicit instructions that *all* the blood be shed in the process. That means a literal effusion, pouring out, shedding of literal blood in death. That literal blood that was literally shed represented upon the altar the life (or soul) that was poured out in death as a substitute. It was a representation, a symbol. But do not forget nor ever disregard that BOTH are required — the blood and the death. God so ordered.

The wages of sin is death — always has been; always will be. The penalty for sin is death. It is not blood. But the shedding of blood is required to represent the effusion of that life in death that is payment for the penalty. Both are required. The death of the substitute was of no merit unless and until the blood was shed AND then presented before God as testimony to God and man that payment had been made. Both the blood and the death are required.

The converse is also true. The blood of the substitute victim was of no merit unless there was death. One work of reconciliation. One work of redemption. Two component parts of one work, the blood and the death, are indivisible yet are distinguishable.

The blood of the victim speaks of the death of the victim. Both are required.

That brings us to some statements by MacArthur that have received much criticism for use of the word symbol. The mere frequency of the use of the word symbol, or any word for that matter, is irrelevant. It proves nor disproves nothing. Let us look at these statements phrase by phrase, consider the criticisms and examine them in light of Scripture.

14. "Blood is a symbol of death, and therefore follows closely the idea of a testator's having to die in order for a will to become effective." (p. 236)

The first phrase in this quote to consider is *"Blood is a symbol of death."* This statement is not inaccurate. Blood is also used in the Bible as representing guilt. "His blood be upon his head." Of course, when blood refers to sacrificial death there must of necessity be literal blood shed. This literal blood that was literally shed is then literally placed upon the altar to represent the literal death of the literal substitute. Both the death and the blood are required; but the blood speaks in a symbolic way of the death. This does not diminish the blood. But keep in mind that blood was not the penalty that was to be paid. Death is the penalty.

The second phrase is accurate that there must be the death of a testator for a will to be effective. In this same section of his commentary, MacArthur points out that "**forgiveness** demands **blood**." (Emphasis MacArthur's.) He then goes on to say on the next page that "**without the shedding of blood there is no forgiveness**."

Quote number fourteen above taken individually and analyzed phrase by phrase appears correct. However, it must be placed in its context and combined with other statements in the section from which it was extracted. Critics have a tendency to compile fragments of quotes and then infer much that is not there. This happens with alarming frequency and regularity with some professional theological head hunters. They do not put forth the effort to study the entire quote in context and allow for the possibility of unintentionally vague or ambiguous language on the part of the object of their criticism.

One must be careful in reading his so-called critics. Determination of sound doctrine comes not from reading after men who are criticizing another. Sound doctrine comes from the study of the Word and reading after those who are rightly dividing the Word of Truth in sound exegesis.

> 15. "It is possible to become morbid about Christ's sacrificial death and preoccupied with His suffering and shedding of blood. It is especially possible to become unbiblically preoccupied with the physical aspects of His death. It was not Jesus' physical blood that saves us, but His dying on our behalf, which is symbolized by the shedding of His physical blood. If we could be saved by blood without death, the animals would have been bled, not killed, and it would have been the same with Jesus." (p. 237)

The key words to look at in the first two sentences of this quote are *preoccupied* and *unbiblically*. This statement is correct. We are to be focused upon Him and Him alone. We study and learn of His death and crucifixion. But we do not focus upon it with preoccupation. We are to be preoccupied with Him. The reason many people do not wish to be preoccupied with Christ and focus on Him is that to do so will reveal sin in the life that must be dealt with. And that is uncomfortable.

The point, however, of this quote is the use of the word *symbolized.* As we discussed above, His shed blood, His blood that was literally shed, speaks of His death. Both were required. They are indivisible yet distinguishable aspects of His one work. It is unfortunate that MacArthur uses some of the words that he does that confuses this issue. But it is clear from his commentary that he believes that both the shed blood and the death of Christ were required. The use of the word symbolized does not detract from that.

His later point in the quote above is accurate, but adds to the confusion of some critics. It is true that we cannot be saved by blood alone absent the death of the substitute. That is accurate. It holds true in the case of the Lord. The converse is true. We cannot be saved by His death alone, the shed blood is required. God so ordered it. MacArthur appears to not disagree with this overall in his commentary. But he does occasionally muddy the water with language that befuddles some .

16. "Again, however, we need to keep in mind that the blood was a symbol. If Christ's own physical blood, in itself, does not cleanse from sin, how much less did the physical blood of animals. It is not surprising, then, that the Old Covenant allowed a symbol for a symbol. A Jew who was too poor to bring even a small animal for a sacrifice was allowed to bring one-tenth of an ephah (about two quarts) of fine flour instead (Lev. 5:11). His sins were covered just as surely as those of the person who could afford to offer a lamb or goat or turtledove or pigeon (Lev. 5:6-7). This exception is clear proof that the old cleansing was symbolic. Just as the animal blood symbolized Christ's true atoning blood, so the ephah of flour symbolized and represented the animal blood. This nonblood

offering for sin was acceptable because the old sacrifice was entirely symbolic anyway." (p. 237)

17. "Yet this was the only exception. And even the exception *represented* a blood sacrifice. The basic symbol could not be changed because what is symbolized could not be changed. 'For the life of the flesh is in the blood, and I have given it to you on the altar to make atonement for your souls; for it is the blood by reason of the life that makes atonement' (Lev. 17:11). Since the penalty for sin is death, nothing but death, symbolized by shedding of blood, can atone for sin." (pp. 237-238)

These two quotes are an attempt by MacArthur to explain symbology in the sacrificial system. Our attention shall be on the last sentence: *"Since the penalty for sin is death, nothing but death, symbolized by shedding of blood, can atone for sin."* The main point of the sentence is correct: the penalty for sin is death and nothing but death can atone for sin. That is doctrinally sound. In fact, it is inarguable. At issue is the phrase, *"symbolized by shedding of blood."* This phrase does not negate the requirement for death. It also does not negate the requirement for shedding of blood. It appears from this statement that both are required, which is correct. We must not read into a phrase that which is not there. Inferences are unstable ground upon which to stand. We shall address the issue of the "blood itself" later.

18. "In the case of Christ the blood is a term referring to the violent and sacrificial character of His death." (*Grace to You* article, May 1976, p.10)

This quote is not a very good statement. It was written to an individual in a personal letter in response to a direct question on a specific subject. This sentence should not be given the same weight as statements made in his commentary. But it is an unfortunate statement. Why? Because the blood of Christ is a term referring to the blood of Christ. The shed blood speaks of His death and the nature of that death. But the shed blood is also a separate and distinct entity from that death in the economy and administration of God's justice. This quote would best have been left unsaid. It is confusing when injected into an analysis of MacArthur's teaching on the blood.

19. "The shedding of blood has nothing to do with bleeding, it simply means death, violent sacrificial death."(Ibid.)

This is another confusing statement. It is also an overstatement or oversimplification in attempting to answer the question that was posed to him in the original correspondence to which he was responding. First, shedding of blood in a purely physical and observable aspect is nothing but bleeding. But it is more than just bleeding. Shedding of blood, bleeding, in sacrifice is to be all the blood, as we saw earlier in this book. God made it perfectly clear in His instructions concerning sacrifice that all the blood was to be shed. So, shedding of blood has to do with bleeding in a special sense that all the blood is bled out. I think his point was that shedding of blood and bleeding, as in that which happens from severe wounds where blood gushes out, are not the same. But he is not clear on this point. Of course, shedding of blood does not "simply" mean death, violent sacrificial death. Shedding of blood means shedding of literal blood but it also speaks of or represents the death of the substitute in sacrifice.

Penalty and Payment

The rest of the quotes are taken from a booklet entitled "John MacArthur's HERESY on the Blood of Christ" by D. A. Waite. He quotes MacArthur from several sources including letters, articles, and audio tapes. (This author does not recommend this booklet as an analysis of MacArthur's teaching.)

20. "The phrase 'Christ died for our sin' (Romans 5:8; 1 Corinthians 15:3) expresses the truth that death was the penalty, not blood. The gospel in 1 Corinthians 15:4 hits the issue 'Christ died'. (1 Peter 2:24) is not saying we are saved by His wounds, that is a symbol also referring to His death."

Unwarranted inferences should not be drawn from this statement in isolation. If MacArthur is to be maligned for his teaching, it should be for direct statements of error rather than inferences drawn and extraneous meaning imputed to his statements. Again, this is not in defense of MacArthur. But in analyzing statements made in light of Scripture, intellectual honesty must be maintained. Inferences are dangerous ground that only serve those who feed upon controversy.

The first sentence of this quote is rather straight forward, "The phrase 'Christ died for our sin' (Romans 5:8; 1 Corinthians 15:3) expresses the truth that death was the penalty, not blood." The wages of sin is death. However, again, MacArthur interjects confusion by adding, "not blood." The penalty was death not blood, but the payment of the penalty included the shedding of blood. This position MacArthur supports elsewhere in his writings. It is disingenuous to infer that MacArthur is here pitting the one against the other. 1 Peter 2:24 in no way implies that we are saved by the wounds themselves. The stripes and wounds were received as part of the death He died. Wounds cannot save. Stripes cannot save. Only God can save. The wounds and stripes were inflicted and received during the process of His substitutionary act of dying for us. They speak of His death and all that surrounds it. The quote is correct. The verse is not saying that we are literally saved by His literal wounds.

> 21. "If we say it is the blood that saves, what are we saying? His actual blood, physically, saves us? ... we are saved by His substitutionary death for us, not by the chemicals in His blood."

The truth of the last part of this quote is so obvious it almost defies logic to argue against it. Some do. It is true that we are saved by His substitutionary death for us. That is inarguable. It is also true that we are not saved by the chemicals in His blood. To argue that we are saved by the chemicals in His blood is to reduce the act of redemption to a merely physical transaction that eliminates the overriding spiritual nature of the act. If we are saved by the chemicals in His blood, several questions arise that seem ridiculous but must be answered to defend such a position.

What were those chemicals?

Are those chemicals present in human blood?

What was the nature of those chemicals and whence their quality to save lost mankind?

And on it could go. The point is obvious after some study of the blood.

One wonders why such an outrage and attack upon MacArthur and not others who have held this view. Consider this quote from Donald Grey Barnhouse found on page 128, Volume II of his commentary on Romans:

> "Now, I do not believe for one moment that there was any cleansing

> value in the actual chemical elements of the blood that flowed from the veins of Christ. The supposed relics of that blood are, of course, a horrible hoax perpetrated upon poor unfortunate people by those who hold them in their power."

Barnhouse is here saying the same thing as MacArthur. I have not seen nor heard an equivalent outcry against Barnhouse. One need only read Barnhouse more extensively to see his love for his Savior and utmost regard for His blood.

Barnhouse concludes his commentary on Romans 3:25 thusly:

> The blood of Christ has flowed and salvation is provided and paid for. God is reconciled and now turns toward the sinner. There are not three places in the universe where sin may be; there are only two. Your sin is either upon yourself and will be judged even to the lake of fire; or your sin is on the Saviour and has been judged in the shedding of His blood — in the pouring out of His life. ...I know that I stand cleansed in His ransom, with all my sins forever paid for by the shedding of this precious blood. Will you in this moment turn away from every alluring voice that would keep you from your salvation and come to the Saviour that His blood might avail for you and cleanse you from all your sin?
>
> Behold now is the accepted time; behold now is the day of salvation. The

> day of the flowing fountain of His blood is still here. Today, beware lest the judgment of the cross take the place of the mercy of the cross. For the day of the end of mercy will come and the day of full judgment will succeed it. Woe to the man who is not hidden in the refuge of the riven side of the Lord Jesus Christ. There in that cleft rock from which the blood flowed we shall be forever safe."

Will MacArthur's devoted critics call Barnhouse an "arch heretic?" I doubt it.

22. "It was His death that was efficacious, not His blood."

This quote, standing alone, is confusing and appears to pit the blood against the death. It is unfortunate that MacArthur is unclear in this statement. Maybe the context would enlighten it somewhat. Both the death and the shed blood were required in the process of redemption. As pointed out before, they are indivisible yet distinguishable in the one work of Christ.

23. "There is nothing else that can atone for sin but blood shed — but the death of somebody."

Here MacArthur appears to confirm what was just said. He here seems to be equating the two, blood shed and death. But in doing so distinguishes between them and recognizing the inextricability of the two. It is interesting that he put blood shed first, then death. Nonetheless, he places them together as required for atonement.

Again, we are looking at these statements in isolation and considering them on their face value.

24. “…but it was the death that was the atonement. The blood was a symbol of the violence of it.”

25. “The price of ransom was to be blood — sacrificial death.”

These two statements appear to be contradictory. In the first death is the payment. In the second blood is the payment. In the first he states that the blood was a symbol of the violence of the death. It appears that the statement supports the necessity of the shed blood being present. In the second the price of the ransom is blood which he then clarifies as sacrificial death. His language is confusing when the quotes are clipped from their context. We ask the question, Does MacArthur teach that both the shed blood and the death were required by God for redemption? It appears so. The confusion enters when he attempts to define the distinctions they each have in the redemptive act.

Kenosis

Quotes twenty-six and twenty-seven are taken from the same booklet by Waite.

26. “Jesus was 100% human; he had human blood and He shed human blood. There was nothing in the chemicals of His blood that could save. Atonement was made through His death. This is the historic position.”

27. “Acts 20:28 is not referring to God. The Scripture is speaking about Christ. The word, ‘Blood,’ in this verse does not really mean ‘blood,’ It means ‘death.’ The word, ‘death,’ and the word ‘blood,’ are symbolic of each other. Christ was 100% human, therefore, he had human blood.

> Christ received His human blood from Mary, His mother."

Not a little attention must be paid to these quotes and the comments they elicited from MacArthur's critics. It is not intended to restudy in great detail the kenosis and hypostatic union at this point. That has been accomplished in earlier chapters. The kenosis and hypostatic union are, however, at issue here.

Before examining the first quote, a look at the second quote and some remarks made by some of MacArthur's critics is necessary. The subject is Acts 20:28,

> *Take heed therefore unto yourselves, and to all the flock, over the which the Holy Ghost hath made you overseers, to feed the church of God, which he hath purchased with his own blood. (Acts 20:28)*

The first point of contention over this verse appears to be of whom it speaks. MacArthur states that the verse is referring to Christ. Some critics interpret this verse to speak of God the Father. This verse is one that is used, by many, to prove the deity of Jesus Christ. This verse clearly and plainly is referring to Christ whose Church it is and who purchased it with His very own blood. Paul here affirms, with John, that the Word was God. Jesus Christ of Nazareth is God.

The critics would have us believe that God the Father has blood. If that is so, He must have a corporeal body in which that blood flows. This is absolute heresy. It is of cultic origins. God is spirit. He does not have a corporeal body in which there is blood. This verse makes no sense if we read it to mean that God the Father purchased the Church with His blood. It makes very clear sense and agrees with the rest of Scripture when it is read to mean Christ, who is God, purchased His Church with His own blood.

The historic position of Christianity and the vast majority of commentators agree on this verse. It speaks of Christ.

These critics contend that Christ's blood is divine, not human, because it is from God. This contains several problems. First, why must His blood be one or the other, divine or human? Why can it not be both? After all, He is God. As we shall see, He was divine, therefore His blood was divine, not because of the origin of His blood and body, but because of who He is, God. And since He was 100% human at one and the same time He was 100% God, it is a simple matter for the less frustrated to conclude that He (and His blood) were both human and divine. What's wrong with that? God can do that.

To assert His divinity based upon the origin of His body is demeaning and degrading to the Son of God who is eternal. He is divine from eternity because He is God. That is why He is divine, because of who He is. He took on the form of a servant for His redemptive purpose. He was human. Two natures in one person.

In explaining His divinity based upon the origin of His blood, critics assert that the origin of His body was from God: His body was not human but divine, therefore since the body has blood His blood is divine. The fallacy here is to assert that He was not human. We shall not revisit in detail the kenosis and hypostatic union. Suffice it to say that from His own mouth and by His own testimony, Jesus Christ declared that He was a man. He was human. But be careful, not "merely" human. He was human at the same time He was God.

A question for the critics to answer is, If He was not human, if His blood was not human, then what was it? The question does not address the virtue and quality of His body and blood, but its physiological nature. If not human, then what? It was not angelic, it was not spirit, it was not some form of creation unknown to this universe. To misinterpret Hebrews 10:5 and assert that Christ's body was not human because it had its source and was prepared by God Himself opens up the interpreter to some problems. If this line of reasoning is followed that when a body is prepared by God Himself that the body is therefore divine leads to the conclusion that Adam was divine and Adam's blood was divine. God Himself formed Adam from the dust of the ground. God Himself breathed into Adam's nostrils the breath of life. Adam had his source from God directly. But Adam was not divine.

The source of the body is not the source of divinity. Jesus Christ was divine because He is God. Period. And that is regardless of the source of His body. If His body were not human, if His blood were not human, He was not an acceptable substitute and He could not be the kinsman-redeemer. If He were not human, many verses of Scripture fall into confusion.

The sad part of this whole study is to see so much written based upon erroneous inferences and imputing false meanings into the writings of others. There are those who deny the humanity of Christ. We assert His humanity, sin excepted. We assert His deity based upon who He is, He is God. God has no source. The arguments of divinity from source of body is borderline infantilism. Even the newest Christian understands the basics of who God is. It does not require a string of academic degrees to understand that God is God because He is God and that Jesus Christ is God because He has always been God, co-equal with the Father and Spirit in eternity.

Matthew Poole, in his commentary on the Holy Bible, says it very simply and understandably.

> If Christ had not been man, he could have had no blood to shed: had he not been God, the blood which he shed could not have been a sufficient price of redemption. Oh the depth of the riches of the wisdom and knowledge of God, who found out such a ransom; and the breadth, and length, and depth, and height of the love of Christ, who paid this ransom for us!

MacArthur's error in quote number twenty-seven above is to say that the word blood does not really mean blood but it means death. *"The word, 'Blood,' in this verse does not really mean 'blood,' It means 'death.'"* In the original language from which our Bible was translated, the word means blood. Blood means blood. Death means death. One may speak of and represent the other in their inextricable attachment to a single work, but they are separate and distinct. He confuses the issue and misspeaks if he intends to make them interchangeable. They are not interchangeable but are inextricably united in Christ's one work; the one speaks of the other.

MacArthur rightly asserts that Christ was 100% human and one must conclude from reading the rest of His commentary on Hebrews that he also asserts that Christ was without sin. He is in agreement that Christ was 100% human, sin excepted; and Christ was 100% God. This is not a point that can be attacked by the critics with any success from Scripture.

MacArthur makes a proper conclusion that, since Christ was 100% human, sin excepted, He had human blood. However, he errs after that point. Christ did not receive His blood from Mary His mother. That is partly true as we saw in our study of embryology and genetics. He received His blood from both His mother and His Father. That will not be revisited here.

The Blood Itself

28. "Nothing in His human blood saves."

29. "There is no saving in the blood itself. We cannot say that the very blood of Jesus, His physical blood, is what atones for sin."

30. "There is nothing in the actual blood that is efficacious for sin. Did you get that? The Bible does not teach that the blood of Christ itself had any efficacy for taking away sin. Not at all."

31. "It does not mean the literal blood of Christ is efficacious."

32. "There is nothing in the chemistry of His blood to save us."

By now it should be obvious that MacArthur is trying to say something about the blood at the physiological level. It has been confusing to say the least. Also by now the reader should have learned that MacArthur errs in quote twenty-eight above.

How so?

There is something that is in His blood that can save. The life of the flesh is in the blood. And the life that was in His blood was the very life of God, eternal life, which is that life that was laid down in sacrificial death as our substitute. The right death could not have occurred without the right life being present in His blood. That is what was in His blood that could save.

With that in mind, looking at MacArthur's statements in isolation and at face value, they must be analyzed differently. One critic assaults MacArthur's position on the blood by accusing MacArthur of holding that the blood itself does not save. Are we to assume this critic is asserting that the blood itself alone does save? And what of this phrase, "blood itself?" A closer look is required.

To refer to the blood itself would seem to indicate reference to the physical aspects of the blood such as red blood cells, white blood cells, plasma, etc. In other words, the actual fluid flowing through the circulatory system of man. The blood itself absent any invisible factors. Words having the meaning they do would lead us to conclude after our study thus far that the actual fluid blood, the chemicals if you will, could not save us. There is insufficient virtue therein. There must be life. And life is apart from but residing in the blood itself. So a differentiation is necessary.

"There is no saving in the blood itself. We cannot say that the very blood of Jesus, His physical blood, is what atones for sin." The first sentence is correct if referring to the red fluid, the actual, literal, physical blood alone of Christ. Without the life of Christ in the blood, there is insufficient virtue. It is not the blood, but the quality of the life therein, eternal life. But in that blood was eternal life which was sufficient and efficacious when poured out in volitional, sacrificial, and substitutional sacrifice. It derives, furthermore, that the second sentence is technically correct. His physical blood cannot and did not atone for sin without that life that was laid down. Absent the laying down of that life, the blood could not and does not save. The point to be understood is far deeper than the superficial physicality of the blood and actuality of the death. That which must be reflected upon is who He is, what He did, how He did it, and that He did it for us. That is discussed in the chapter on how we should then live.

The rest of the quotes above are restatements of the same theme that seem to add further to the confusion. In order to understand where MacArthur is possibly coming from, they must be read in light of the physical compared to the supernatural within the physical.

The Preservation of the Blood

This subject is included here separate from the categories above because the focus is shifted from the statements by MacArthur to the doctrine itself of the preservation of the blood of Christ. MacArthur is quoted by the Sword of the Lord in January 1988 as saying,

> "The literal blood of Christ ran into the dirt and dust, and nothing in Scripture hints that it now exists in any tangible or visible form."

This author disagrees with that position. Others have written such things as:

> "It is wrong-headed… to be curious or concerned about what happened to the blood which Jesus shed."

> "What became of the blood that was shed is of minor consequence."

> "To me it is a matter that is unimportant."

MacArthur is not the issue here. Nor are any of these other men. The issue is what the Bible teaches about the blood of Jesus Christ our Lord.

Some contend that Christ took His blood to Heaven in some sort of cup or vessel to present it there before the throne of God and that it is still there in that vessel. No Scripture supports such an idea directly or by way of typology. We reject the idea of a chalice somewhere in Heaven containing the blood of Christ.

But this does not mean that we reject the presence of the blood in Heaven nor of its preservation. The Bible is instructive in this matter. The exhortation by Barnhouse that where the Bible is silent on a subject we are to be also is taken with all due regard. However, on this subject the Bible is not silent.

Opponents of the preservation of the blood argue that typology does not support it. They only accept the typology of the Old Testament sacrifices to a point and no further. They contend that to conform to the sacrificial type, the High Priest would have to kill Jesus. This argument we find disingenuous for two reasons. First, the High Priest of Israel at the time of Jesus condemned Him to death and called for His crucifixion. But secondly and most importantly of all, Christ is our High Priest and He of His own will dismissed His spirit in death in our behalf. That is fulfillment of the type.

Another aspect of typology these opponents put forth as not being fulfilled is that the High Priest would have to apply the blood to the mercy seat. Christ Himself is the mercy seat and His blood was "applied" during the sacrifice of Calvary by His allowing it to happen. His blood was on Him visibly. He, the mercy seat, was sprinkled with His own blood. This having taken place during the sacrifice. It is true that the atonement was completed when Christ cried out, "It is finished." The Scripture had been fulfilled.

Hebrews chapter nine is a good starting point for a discussion on the fulfillment of type by Christ's death and shed blood. In this passage, the writer continues his comparison of the old covenant and the new covenant and a comparison showing Christ to be far superior to the high priests who served in the flesh.

Of particular note in chapter nine is verse seven,

> *But into the second* went *the high priest alone once every year,* ***not without blood****, which he offered for himself, and* for *the errors of the people: (Hebrews 9:7)(Emphasis added.)*

The Apostle Paul, whom we believe to be the writer of Hebrews, under the inspiration of the Holy Ghost, who wrote the entire Bible, inserts this phrase here for a purpose, *"not without blood."* The high priest dare not enter into the Holy of Holies without blood under penalty of death. This requirement was unchanging and there were no exceptions. He must first enter with blood for himself, then with blood for the people. But never, never, never was he under any circumstances to enter beyond the veil without blood. God so ordered it.

The blood upon the mercy seat was the focus of the entire religious ceremony of the Hebrews. The work of atonement was not completed until God's appointed representatives of the people, the consecrated priesthood, had sprinkled the mercy seat with the blood of the substitute. The mere bringing of the substitute to the altar, the laying on of hands which represented the transference of guilt from the offerer to the substitute, and the taking of the life of the substitute by blood shedding resulting in death which was the penalty, all of these were necessary but insufficient for atonement until the presentation of the blood before God for God's approval and acceptance. There must be formal approval from Heaven. This blood, so presented and accepted by God, gave assurance to the offerer both of a satisfaction rendered for him in death and a life granted to him in the presence of God.

The blood upon the altar was not of minor consequence or little importance to the Hebrews or to their God who had ordered how atonement was accomplished. Great principles are here involved. While it is true that the blood upon the altar spoke of the required death of the substitute, it was of no less importance in the ritual. The blood without the death of the victim was without merit. The death of the victim was without merit without the blood — and that blood presented before God upon the altar as a testimony that life had been poured out in substitutionary death in response to the just and holy demands of God.

"Not without blood."

And that blood must be upon the mercy seat.

Dropping down to verse twenty-five of Hebrews nine, we read,

> *Nor yet that he should offer himself often, as the high priest entereth into the holy place every year **with blood of others**; (Hebrews 9:25) (Emphasis added.)*

Again the writer of Hebrews emphasizes that the high priest must not go into the Holy of Holies without blood. And this blood was not his own blood but the blood of substitutes. *"Every year with blood."*

How does this type and foreshadow hold in the case of Christ. Verse twelve,

> *Neither by the blood of goats and calves, but **by his own blood** he entered in once into the holy place, having*

> *obtained eternal redemption* for us. *(Hebrews 9:12) (Emphasis added.)*

Christ as High Priest entered *"by his own blood."* Those who would oppose the doctrine of preservation would change the word "by" to "through" translated from the same Greek word, *dia*. That introduces subtle changes in meaning. Frankly, none of the opponents of preservation have qualifications any where near those used by God for the translation of the original languages into the King James Version of the Bible. When God decided to preserve His Word for English speaking people, He prepared and used men of vast qualifications in the Bible languages. These were devout men who feared God. They were true scholars of the Word. It would behoove us to just go with "by" in this case rather than the opinions of lesser qualified men who would use "through."

There was a reason for His entering by His own blood. Verse twenty-three,

> It was *therefore necessary that the patterns of things in the heavens should be purified with these; but the heavenly things themselves with better sacrifices than these. (Hebrews 9:23)*

The patterns of things in the heavens were those things in the earthly Tabernacle. They were real things patterned after Heavenly things. The earthly things were purified with the blood of animals. The Heavenly things "themselves" were purified with better than the blood of animals. Keeping true to typology, blood better than the animals, blood able to do what animal blood could not do, blood that was able to meet the demands of God, that blood was presented by Christ.

> 24 *For Christ is not entered into the holy places made with hands,* which are *the figures of the true; but into heaven itself, now to appear in the presence of God for us:*
> 25 *Nor yet that he should offer himself often, as the high priest entereth into the holy place every year with blood of others;*
> 26 *For then must he often have suffered since the foundation of the world: but now once in the end of the world hath he appeared to put away sin by the sacrifice of himself. (Hebrews 9:24-26)*

Christ did not enter into the Temple in Jerusalem ("holy places made with hands") which represented the true (something true must be of necessity be; it cannot 'not be'), but into the "true" which is Heaven itself to do what the high priests did for centuries which was to appear in the presence of God for us. And this He did — appear before God for us. This He did in the reality of Heaven itself which is the pattern of those things of the old covenant. This appearance He does not do yearly, but has done it once, not entering as those high priests did with the blood of others, but with His own blood. This appearance by Christ in the presence of God, once in the end of the world, was to put away sin and that by the sacrifice of Himself, presenting His own blood before God as testimony of that Life that was poured out unto death, even the death of the cross.

> *Whom God hath set forth* to be *a propitiation through faith in his blood, to declare his righteousness for the*

remission of sins that are past, through the forbearance of God; Romans 3:25)

The same Greek word, *hilasterion*, translated as propitiation here is translated mercy seat in Hebrews 9:5,

And over it the cherubims of glory shadowing the mercyseat; of which we cannot now speak particularly. (Hebrews 9:5)

God has set forth Christ to be the mercy seat for His people through faith in His blood. Christ is Himself the mercy seat, that which propitiates. Christ Himself, as the mercy seat, has the blood upon Him as testimony before God of that which was accomplished. And He, Christ, now appears in the presence of God as our mediator. When He appeared before God after Calvary, He did so in fulfillment of the Old Testament type where the priest said nothing in the Holy of Holies, but simply placed the blood upon the mercy seat. Christ appeared before God, and we can imagine, He said nothing but simply presented Himself, the mercy seat, the blood present upon Him which "speaketh better things than that of Able." The blood of sprinkling speaks. It speaks now and in order to do so must be there now. It holds grammatically from verse twenty-four and it holds typologically from the old things being fulfilled in Christ.

Not that His blood was carried to Heaven in some glorious chalice. Oh, no. It was carried to Heaven upon the living Mercy Seat to be presented before God where it now speaks. Oh the depth, and breadth, and height, and length of the wisdom and love of God.

Why should it be otherwise? The fulfillment of typology does not require a contorting of Scripture nor logic. It is straightforward and easily understood when accepted. The blood of Christ is now present in Heaven on the mercy seat speaking better things than that of Able.

Barnhouse posits in his commentary on Romans, Volume II, pages 128-129 that the blood of Christ fell into the ground and stayed there.

> I am inclined to believe that the actual blood of Christ went to the dust of the earth like any other chemical element, and that it returned to that earth as a part of the earth. It would be the consonant answer to the statement of God to Cain that the voice of his brother's blood cried from the ground demanding justice. The actual blood of Christ could have gone back to the dust of the ground, announcing symbolically (not in the superstition of the acolyte of Jerusalem) that the righteous basis for all judgment has now been established by virtue of which God will take vengeance upon the ungodly and announcing also that one day even the earth itself shall be ransomed from the thralldom of sin's curse and the very desert and waste place shall blossom like the rose.

The author cannot agree with this completely. Yes, the blood of Christ cries out that God's just demands have been met. And one day the earth will be redeemed from the curse. Christ has paid the ransom for our sin with His own blood. The earth that now is shall be purged with fire. He did not shed His blood for the earth. He shed His blood for us.

Without compromising, let us consider that Barnhouse may be partially correct. How so?

Not all of the blood of the substitute was placed upon the mercy seat. All of the blood of the victim was shed; but, not all was presented upon the mercy seat. There were other purposes for the rest of the blood as we see in the book of Leviticus. There is no question that during the scourging and crucifixion, some of the blood of our Lord would fall to the earth. That is just the law of nature and nature's God. Gravity was not suspended for the crucifixion. If Christ wanted to take all of His blood to Heaven, that would be no problem for Him to accomplish contrary to the critics who ask, "How could He gather up all that blood scattered all over the place from the beatings to the cross?" Again, we respond, "He is God. He can do that."

In keeping with typology, it may be fitting to consider that some of the blood was poured out upon the earth as well as sprinkled upon the mercy seat, Christ Himself. These are thoughts for consideration and study, not by way of compromise, but by way of searching for the truth as given in the Word of God in both the Old and New Testaments.

The issue is not John MacArthur or his teaching. Nor is the issue his critics, devoted or otherwise. The issue, the only issue and focal point there ever should be, remains Christ our Lord. To know Him better begins in His Word. The Word of God, not the words of man, is the final authority for faith and practice. The Word of God is our portal for knowing Him better.

But wrongheaded men who have stuffed volumes of theological facts into their brains quite often reveal a relationship with Christ that is brain-deep and not life-deep. To know Him aright is to go beyond the knowledge of His omnipresence to the experience of His manifest presence. This experience of His manifest presence is not as the confused charismatics would have it done with all their noise, commotion, and vain repetitions. But this manifest presence will be in the inner man where Christ does and must dwell. His manifest presence is also evident in the life of the believer who has his focus upon Him.

Preceding this, of course, is redemption and regeneration. "Ye must be born again." And no man, woman, boy, or girl can come to the Father but by Jesus Christ and Him alone. There must be repentance toward God and faith in our Lord Jesus Christ. We are saved by grace alone through faith alone in Christ alone.

With all this both MacArthur and his critics agree. They agree that without shedding of blood there is no remission. They agree that Christ died for our sins and shed His precious blood to redeem us. This focus must be maintained for effective evangelization of the lost.

Alas! At this point the fingerpointing begins and men, women, boys and girls are not led closer to our Lord as a result. Debate and discussion about doctrine is a healthy exercise. But the end result and aim of it all is to know Christ better and to point people to the Lord. Ad hominem attack ministries out to destroy the ministry of a brother in Christ are counter-productive. They may even aid and abet the adversary.

By all means, heresy and apostasy must be identified, exposed and rejected. But it must be indeed heresy (false teaching) or outright apostasy. Attacks upon men and their teaching should not be over grammar, semantics, or differing views of the English language. Above all, disagreements and debate over doctrine must be done with integrity and not with gratuitous attacks stemming from second-hand information and hearsay. Without a doubt, if one were to dig deep enough into any preacher's teachings or writings, a misstatement or error could be found and exploited for criticism.

Just keep it simple. Start with the basics and fundamentals of the Gospel. If in agreement, then proceed to doctrine concerning Christ and His Church. Absent pride and egotism, many men would find common ground for ministry.

However, this does not imply, nor may the reader infer, compromise on the fundamentals of the faith and the truth of Scripture. If we are indeed followers of Christ and not of men, the Holy Spirit will lead us into all truth and on the way reveal to us who else is there with us. Focus must be maintained upon Christ and not men.

ATTRIBUTIONS

American Peoples Encyclopedia. Grolier.
Arnow, L. Earle, et al. Introduction to Physiological and Pathological Chemistry. St. Louis. C. V. Mosby Company, 1961.
Berkhof, Louis. Systematic Theology. Grand Rapids, MI. Eerdmans Publishing Company, 1938.
Brown, Driver, Briggs, Gesenius Lexicon.
Carter, Tom, compiled by. 2,200 Quotations from the Writings of Charles H. Spurgeon. Grand Rapids, MI. Baker Books, 1988.
Compton's Encyclopedia, comptonsv3. Web.aol.com.
Dehaan, M. R. The Chemistry of the Blood. Grand Rapids, MI. Zondervan, 1943.
Easton's Bible Dictionary. Electronic text and markup copyright 1995 by Epiphany Software.
Encyclopaedia Britannica. Benton. 1974.
Expositor's Bible, The. Edited by W. Robertson Nicoll, volume 1. Wm. B. Eerdmans Publishing Company. Grand Rapids, MI, 1940.
Fairbairn, Patrick. Typology of Scripture. Grand Rapids, MI. Kregel Publications, 1989.
Gaebelein, Frank. The Pattern of God's Truth. Chicago. Moody Press, 1954.
Greene, Oliver B. The Epistles of John. Greenville, SC. The Gospel Hour, Inc., 1966.
Guyton, Arthur C. Textbook of Medical Physiology, 3rd ed. Philadelphia. Saunders, 1966.
Hanegraaff, Hank. Christianity in Crisis. Eugene, OR. Harvest House Publishers, 1977.
Hartill, J. Edwin, D.D. Principles of Biblical Hermeneutics. Grand Rapids, MI. Zondervan, 1947.

Hodge, Charles. Systematic Theology, in three volumes. Hendrickson Publishers, Inc. edition. 1999.

Holy Scriptures According to the Masoretic Text, The. Volume 1, Genesis to II Kings. The Jewish Publication Society of America. Philadelphia, PA, 1955.

Ironside , H. A., Litt.D. Studies in The Epistle to the Hebrews and Titus. Neptune, NJ. Loizeaux Brothers, Inc., 1932.

Keil, C. F. and Delitzch, F. Commentary on the Old Testament in Ten Volumes. William B. Eerdmans Publishing Company. (Grand Rapids, MI)

Kimber, Diana Clifford, et al. Anatomy and Physiology, 14th ed. New York. MacMillan, 1961.

Lee, Robert Greene. Payday Someday and Other Sermons by Robert Greene Lee. Nashville, TN. Broadman & Holman Publishers, 1995.

Lynch, Matthew J. et al. Medical Laboratory Technology and Clinical Pathology, 2nd ed. Philadelphia. Saunders, 1967.

McConnell, D. R. A Different Gospel. Peabody, MA. Hendrickson Publishers, Inc., 1988.

Milne, Bruce. Know the Truth. Illinois. InterVarsity Press, 1982.

Morgan, G. Campbell. The Crises of the Christ. New Jersey. 1936.

Murray, Andrew. The Blood of Jesus. Springdale, PA. Whitaker House, 1993.

Murray, Andrew. The Blood of the Cross. Springdale, PA. Whitaker House, 1981.

Murray, Andrew. The Holiest of All. Springdale, PA. Whitaker House, 1996.

Phillips, John. Exploring Romans. Neptune, New Jersey. Loizeaux Brothers, Inc., 1991.

Pink, Arthur W. Exposition of the Gospel of John. Grand Rapids, MI. Zondervan Publishing House, 1945.

Pink, Arthur W. The Attributes of God. Swengel, PA. No copyright date.

Pulpit Commentary, The. Edited by H. D. M. Spence, Joseph S. Exell, volume 2, Wm. B. Eerdmans Publishing Company, Grand Rapids, MI, 1950.

Robertson, A. T. The Best of A.T. Robertson. Nashville, TN. Broadman & Holman Publishers, 1996.

Scofield, C. I. The Scofield Reference Bible. New York. Oxford University Press, 1917.

Sproul, R. C. The Holiness of God. Wheaton, IL. Tyndale Publishers, Inc., 1985.

Strong, James. The Exhaustive Concordance of the Bible. New York. Abingdon Press, 1890.

Thayer, Joseph Henry. Thayer's Greek-English Lexicon of the New Testament. Grand Rapids, MI. Associated Publishers and Authors, 1889.

The New Westminster Dictionary of the Bible. Philadelphia. Westminster Press, 1970.

Theological Wordbook of the Old Testament. Originally published by Moody Press, Chicago, Illinois. 1980.

Thomas, Maj. Ian. Chapter six is based upon a sermon by Maj. Thomas

Torrey, R. A. What the Bible Teaches. Fleming H. Revell Company, 1898.

Torrey, R. A., Dixon, A. C., et al, editors. The Fundamentals, 4 volumes. Grand Rapids, MI. Baker Books, 1933.

Torrey, R. A. Torrey's New Topical Textbook. Electronic text and markup copyright 1995 by Epiphany Software.

Towns, Elmer L. Theology for Today. Lynchburg, VA. Liberty University.

Vincent, M. R. Word Studies in the New Testament. Wilmington, DE. Associated Publishers and Authors, 1972.

Vine, W. E. Vine's Expository Dictionary of Old Testament and New Testament Words. Copyright LTD, 1940.
Walvoord, John F. Jesus Christ our Lord. Moody Press, Chicago; 1969.
Webster's Third New International Dictionary of the English Language, Unabridged. Encyclopaedia Britannica. 1976.
Wuest, Kenneth S. Wuest's Word Studies, 4 volumes. Grand Rapids, MI. Eerdmans, 1966.